The Formation of the Economic Thought of Karl Marx

Ernest Mandel

The Formation of the
Economic Thought
of Karl Marx
1843 to *Capital*

Translated by Brian Pearce

New York and London

To Gisèle,
who enabled me to write this book as a happy man

Contents

I

From the Critique of Private Property to the Critique of Capitalism

Marx and Engels did not travel the same route to arrive at the ideas they came to share. "They had in common the same philosophical starting point, namely, Hegel's dialectics, [Bruno] Bauer's 'self-consciousness,' and Feuerbach's humanism; they then made the acquaintance of British and French socialism, but whereas this became for Marx the means whereby he ordered his thoughts regarding the struggles and aspirations of his epoch, for Engels the same role was played by British industry."[1]

This difference resulted, no doubt, from differences in character and temperament—the more speculative nature of Marx's genius, the greater impetuousness of Engels'. Chance and material circumstances also played a part, however. While Marx emigrated from Germany to France, Engels was sent to England to learn the conduct of business affairs, and there came into contact with the reality of large-scale capitalist industry. It was the shock of this encounter with the contradictions of bourgeois society that was to decide the course of his thinking for the rest of his life.[2]

1. Franz Mehring, in *Aus dem literarischen Nachlass von Karl Marx und Friedrich Engels, 1841–1850*, Vol. I, p. 359.
2. "While in Manchester, it was tangibly brought home to me that the economic facts, which have so far played no role or only a contemptible one in the writing of history, are, at least in the modern world, a decisive historical force; that they form the basis for the origin of the present-day class antagonism; that these class antagonisms, in the countries where they have become fully developed, thanks to large-scale industry, hence especially in England, are in their turn the basis of the formation of political parties and of party struggles, and thus of all political history." (Frederick

If Marx developed almost unaided the entire economic "panel" of Marxist theory, it is to Engels that the credit is due for having been the first to urge Marx to take up the study of political economy and for having grasped, in a "brilliant sketch," the central importance of this science for communism.[3] This "sketch," written at the end of 1843, was the first economic work by either of the two friends; Ryazanov correctly ascribes it a "very great importance in the history of the development [of the beginnings] of Marxism." [4] It must be emphasized that it was also Engels who, though two years Marx's junior, was the first to declare himself openly a communist and to regard as necessary and inevitable a radical revolution which would abolish private property.

As early as the end of 1842, when he was only just twenty-two, Engels ended an article on the Prussian monarchy by predicting a bourgeois revolution, and began an article on Britain by announcing the approach of a social revolution.[5] At that same time, in an article published in the *Rheinische Zeitung* ("Der Kommunismus und die Augsburger Allgemeine Zeitung"), Marx was still rejecting communism, while stressing the need to study it thoroughly in order to be able to criticize it adequately.[6] Nevertheless, the two founders of scientific socialism were already attacking the problem from the same angle: by criticizing the neo-Hegelian conception of the state, by discovering the existence of social classes, and by analyzing the inhuman effects of private property and competition.

We are able in both cases to follow the trajectory of their thinking from point to point: from criticism of religion to criticism of philosophy; from criticism of philosophy to criticism of

---

Engels, *On the History of the Communist League*, in Karl Marx and Frederick Engels, *Selected Works*, Vol. III, pp. 173–190. The piece was written as an introduction to the 1885 German edition of Marx's pamphlet *Revelations About the Cologne Communist Trial*.)

3. Marx expresses this opinion of the *Outlines of a Critique of Political Economy* in his Preface to *A Contribution to the Critique of Political Economy*. (*Selected Works*, Vol. I, p. 504.)

4. Marx and Engels, *Historisch-kritische Gesamtausgabe* (*MEGA*), I, 2, pp. lxxii and lxxiii.

5. Ibid., I, 2, pp. 346 and 351.

6. Ibid., I, 1, 1, p. 263.

the state; from criticism of the state to criticism of society—that is, from criticism of politics to criticism of political economy, which led to criticism of private property.

With Marx, however, the purely theoretical aspect was to remain predominant throughout this period, and the evolution of his thought was to result in the *Introduction to the Critique of the Hegelian Philosophy of Right* (end of 1843 and beginning of 1844). With Engels it was the practical aspect, the criticism of British bourgeois society, that took the ascendancy, both in the *Outlines of a Critique of Political Economy* and in *Die Lage Englands* (*The Condition of England*), which appeared in the journal *Deutsch-Französische Jahrbücher* at the same time as Marx's well-known critique.

It is generally accepted that Marx took little interest in political economy during his university studies. The list that has come down to us of the books he studied while at Berlin university does not include a single one devoted to this subject.[7] In a letter of September 28, 1892, to Franz Mehring, Engels, discussing Marx's years at the universities of Bonn and Berlin, writes: "He knew nothing whatever about political economy. . . ."[8]

Nevertheless, Pierre Naville is right in seeking to mitigate the excessively hard-and-fast character of this view. In fact, Hegel himself had been profoundly affected in his youth by economic studies, in particular by the work of Adam Smith;[9] Marx saw

---

7. D. I. Rosenberg, *Die Entwicklung der ökonomischen Lehre von Marx und Engels in den Vierziger Jahren des 19. Jahrhunderts*, p. 35.

8. Marx and Engels, *Ausgewählte Briefe*, p. 541.

9. It was Plekhanov who first emphasized the importance of Hegel as a precursor of historical materialism, by his according to *economic development* a central place in the explanation of what is specific in each nation or civilization. The relevant articles by Plekhanov appeared in 1891 in *Die Neue Zeit* and were reprinted in *La Revue Internationale*, No. 22, April–June 1950.

In his masterly work, *Der junge Hegel*, Georg Lukacs studied in detail the economic ideas of the young Hegel. In particular, he showed the central position occupied by *labor* in Hegelian anthropology. Hegel wrote in 1803–1804: "The greater the extent to which labor is carried on with the help of machinery, the less is its value, and the longer it has to be carried on in this way." This sentence constitutes a brilliant anticipation of what Marx and Engels were to write forty years later. (Georg Lukacs, *Der junge*

the Hegelian system as a veritable philosophy of labor. "When he read the *Phenomenology of Mind*, the *Philosophy of Right*, and even the *Science of Logic*, Marx thus not only discovered Hegel but already, through him, was aware of that part of classical political economy which was assimilated and translated into philosophical terms in Hegel's work; so that Marx would not have gone about his systematic criticism of civil society and the state according to Hegel if he had not already found in the latter's writings certain elements which were still live, such as the theory of needs, the theory of appropriation, or the analysis of the division of labor." [10]

Marx had already moved from philosophy to politics, the first step in his intellectual development, when he became editor of the *Rheinische Zeitung* in 1842. His fundamental position continued to be one of struggle for a "human" state; he still took his stand on "human rights" in general, on the struggle against feudal survivals. Like Hegel, he considered that the state should be "the realization of freedom." [11] But even at this stage he had discovered a contradiction between this ideal notion of the state and the fact that the *Stände* (estates) represented in the provincial diet of the Rhineland strove to "drag the state down to the level of the idea of private interest." In other words, as soon as he tackled a current political problem—namely, the new law on theft of wood—he came up against the problem of social classes. The state, which ought to embody the "general interest," seemed to be acting merely on behalf of private property, and, in order to do this, was violating not only the logic of law but even some obvious principles of humanity. [12]

Marx had already grasped that private property, to the defense of which the state seemed to wish to devote itself exclusively, resulted from a private, monopolistic appropriation of a common

---

Hegel, pp. 421, 423, 440, etc.) Nor should it be forgotten that in Hegel's *Logic* labor is the original form of praxis. We shall return to the problem of Hegel's economic ideas in Chapter 10.

10. Pierre Naville, *De l'aliénation à la jouissance*, p. 11.

11. Paul Kaegi, *Genesis des historischen Materialismus*, p. 120.

12. *MEGA*, I, 1, 1, pp. 281–282.

asset.[13] And he perceived in a penal provision which assigned the *labor* of the thief to the owner of the wood, in order to compensate him for his losses, the chief key to his future theory of surplus value: unpaid forced labor is the source of "percentages," that is, of interest and of profit.[14]

From this first entry into the subject, a political critique then led the young Marx to the threshold of a criticism of "civil society," a criticism of political economy.[15] Before crossing this threshold, however, and immersing himself in the subject that was to be the chief preoccupation of his life as a scholar, he seemed to feel a constant need to look back, to retrace his steps, to make sure he had not missed any alternative solution, and to settle finally with all the ideologies he had just outgrown. During the two years between October 1842, when he began his articles on the *Debatten über das Holzdiebstahlgesetz* (Debates on the law against the stealing of wood), and the beginning of his studies in political economy, undertaken in Paris, the young Marx was to draw up a balance sheet of the two movements—Hegelian philosophy and utopian socialism—that he had to transcend before he could give his own ideas a definitive form. (The term "transcend" must be understood here in its Hegelian, dialectical sense, which implies that all that is valid in the positions transcended remains preserved in the new positions.)

In order to help understand how the young Marx's economic ideas evolved, it is interesting to trace the origin of his concern with social questions. Having first discovered their existence through the poverty of the Moselle vinegrowers and the debates

---

13. Ibid., pp. 274–276.
14. Ibid., pp. 289, 297.
15. Marx himself wrote on this subject: "In the years 1842–1843, as editor of the *Rheinische Zeitung*, I experienced for the first time the embarrassment of having to take part in discussions on so-called material interests. The proceedings of the Rhenish Landtag on thefts of wood and parcelling of landed property, the official polemic which Herr von Schaper, then *Oberpräsident* of the Rhine Province, opened against the *Rheinische Zeitung* on the conditions of the Moselle peasantry, and finally debates on free trade and protective tariffs provided the first occasions for occupying myself with economic questions." (Marx, Preface to *A Contribution to the Critique of Political Economy*, in *Selected Works*, Vol. I, p. 502.)

about the wood-thieves, he began to run into them at every step as he started on a detailed criticism of Hegel's philosophy. He found that "the estate of direct labor" (*der Stand der unmittelbaren Arbeit*)—that is, the mass of those who own nothing—in fact forms the precondition for the existence of bourgeois society.[16] And to this "artificially caused poverty" he counterposes enjoyment as the true aim of mankind. Writing to Ruge, the publisher of the *Deutsch-Französische Jahrbücher*, he declared that "from this conflict of the political state with itself one can everywhere deduce the truth about society." [17] Nevertheless, while proclaiming himself already an opponent of private property, which he described, in his criticism of the theory and practice of law, as the source of all injustice, he still declined to call himself a communist.

Marx's study of problems of the philosophy of the state led him to read Rousseau, Montesquieu, Machiavelli, and especially a number of historians of the French Revolution who influenced him profoundly and led him to study French socialism, offspring of the tendencies which the Revolution had set free.

His last rejection of communism is found in the above-quoted letter to Ruge, dated September 1843, and his first profession of faith as a communist is dated March 1844. Between these two dates a political evolution took place which was to be definitive for the rest of his life.[18]

What was the decisive factor in this evolution? It is hard to

16. *MEGA*, I, 1, 1, p. 498. Günther Hillmann says that Marx's first encounter with the problem of private property was also a personal encounter. As editor of the *Rheinische Zeitung*, it seems that he came into conflict with attempts by a group of shareholders to save the paper from being banned by the censors by making political concessions. ("Zum Verständnis der Texte," in *Karl Marx, Texte zu Methode und Praxis, II, Pariser Manuskripte 1844*, p. 205.)

17. *MEGA*, I, 1, 1, p. 574.

18. Kaegi, *Genesis des historischen Materialismus*, pp. 140–147. In his ingenious research to find the exact moment Marx went over to socialism, Kaegi has forgotten to draw on a source of major importance, the biographical note on Marx which Engels wrote for the *Handwörterbuch der Staatswissenschaften*, Vol. VI. There (p. 497) Engels notes that it was after his arrival in Paris that Marx became a socialist, thanks to his study of political economy, of the French socialists, and of the history of France.

isolate one element in a number of influences. But however important his reading of such writers as Moses Hess—whose influence is undeniable—or his study of the French Revolution may have been, it was the overall climate of French society under Louis-Philippe, the seething of progressive ideas, the activity of the various socialist sects, the first contact that he made in real life with the working class and the situation of the proletariat, that made it possible for the literary influences to crystallize.[19]

In his first article on the Jewish question Marx had already set himself the task of examining the relationship between political emancipation and human emancipation in general, the logical conclusion to his criticism of constitutional theories of politics. In passing, he links money with private property as the source of human alienation.[20] But at the same time he reveals labor, the worker, the proletarian, as the embodiment of that alienated mankind which has to be emancipated. And in his *Introduction to the Critique of the Hegelian Philosophy of Right* he was to make the proletariat the author of its own self-emancipation, which thereby became the emancipation of mankind as a whole.

Marx had become aware that "the relationship between industry, and the world of wealth in general, and the political world, is a major problem of the modern age." This relationship, however, though grasped and criticized theoretically, can be changed only by practice.[21] But while "the weapon of criticism cannot replace the criticism of weapons," "theory itself becomes a material force when it takes hold of the masses." [22] And these masses were the proletarian masses whose emergence made a German revolution possible. Such a revolution could not but be a radical one; it could not be confined to the political (bourgeois)

19. Auguste Cornu (*Karl Marx und Friedrich Engels: Leben und Werke*, II, *passim*) correctly stresses the social and historical setting as a factor determining Marx's development, whereas Erich Thier (*Das Menschenbild des jungen Marx*) plainly exaggerates the influence of Moses Hess.

20. *MEGA*, I, 1, 1, pp. 583–584, 603.

21. This idea undoubtedly came from Hess, whose *Philosophie der Tat* (Philosophy of Action) had appeared in October 1843 in a symposium edited by Georg Herwegh entitled *Einundzwanzig Bogen aus der Schweiz*. (See Kaegi, *Genesis des historischen Materialismus*, p. 200.)

22. *MEGA*, I, 1, 1, p. 614.

sphere. "The positive possibility of German emancipation" depended precisely upon the formation of a class "in radical chains," which in striving to cast off these chains would reject *all* social chains by abolishing private property: "When the proletariat desires the negation of private property, it is merely elevating to a general principle of society what it already involuntarily embodies in itself as the negative product of society." [23]

To be sure, this discovery of the revolutionary role of the proletariat as negator of private property was still confined within philosophical limits and was not yet freed of a certain sentimental humanism—Feuerbach's anthropological principle. Engels was to say later that Feuerbach's humanism takes as its point of departure an abstract man, outside of history, since the world (the concrete social conditions) in which this man lives is never discussed.[24] The proletariat's situation was condemned as "unjust," as based on injustice, as immoral. Following Feuerbach, Marx still declared that while the proletariat was the heart of human emancipation, philosophy was its head. He had not yet grasped that the position occupied by the proletariat in the production process was the basis of its power to emancipate. He had not yet grasped that a certain level of development of the productive forces, that the realization of certain material conditions, were indispensable if communism was to be achieved. His communism was still essentially philosophical.

Nevertheless, the link between this philosophical communism and the proletariat was now firmly established. From here to the study of the "real movement of emancipation" of the proletariat —French, British, and German socialism and communism—required only one step, which Marx took at the very beginning of his exile in Paris. The transition from philosophical to proletarian communism was made without serious difficulty.

Engels arrived at communism before Marx, as already said. But his communism, too, was at first in essence clearly philosophical. It was even a communism that addressed itself first and foremost to the enlightened bourgeoisie and to the intellectuals, as can be

---

23. Ibid., p. 620.

24. Engels, *Ludwig Feuerbach and the End of Classical German Philosophy*, in *Selected Works*, Vol. III, pp. 335–376.

seen from the many articles on the communist movement on the Continent which Engels wrote at the end of 1843 and the beginning of 1844 for the Owenite weekly *The New Moral World*. "We [i.e., the German communists] can recruit our ranks from those classes only which have enjoyed a pretty good education," he declared, and he counterposed philosophical communism to the communism of the toiling masses as embodied in Weitling's communist movement.[25]

Engels understood, however, that communism is the necessary outcome of the social conditions created by modern civilization.[26] This was why he described the *parallelism* of the communist movement in Britain, France, and Germany (including German-speaking Switzerland): "Thus, the three great civilized countries of Europe—England, France, and Germany—have all come to the conclusion that a thorough revolution in social arrangements, based on community of property, has now become an urgent and unavoidable necessity. . . . The English came to this conclusion *practically*, by the rapid increase of misery, demoralization, and pauperism in their own country; the French *politically*, by first asking for political liberty and equality, and, finding this insufficient, joining social liberty and social equality to their political claims; the Germans became communists *philosophically*, by reasoning upon first principles." [27]

It must be stressed that Marx and Engels formulated practically at the same moment the fundamental program of the proletarian social revolution, namely, the abolition of private property—Marx in his *Introduction to the Critique of the Hegelian Philosophy of Right*, Engels in his articles for *The New Moral World*—in writings dated between November 1843 and January 1844, doubtless independently of each other. It is also worth emphasizing the brilliant insight shown by the young Engels when, in a single phrase, he summed up the respective contributions to be made by the three great nations of Western Europe to the world labor movement of the nineteenth century: Britain would contribute the practical success of the first mass organi-

25. *MEGA*, I, 2, pp. 444–446, 449.
26. D. Ryazanov, in *MEGA*, I, 2, p. lxxv.
27. *The New Moral World*, November 4, 1843, in *MEGA*, I, 2, p. 435.

zations (Chartism and trade unionism); France, the revolutionary struggle for the conquest of political power (a struggle which began with the tradition laid down by the French Revolution, passed through Babeuf, Blanqui, and June 1848, and culminated in the Paris Commune, the first effective conquest of power by the proletariat); and Germany, the theoretical perfecting of the first scientific socialist program. Of course, when he wrote this last he was unaware of the decisive part he himself was to play in working out Germany's theoretical contribution to the proletarian movement through his preparatory work for, and his share in the writing of, the *Communist Manifesto*.

As we have said, it was the shock caused by his confrontation in Britain with the actual proletariat, produced by large-scale industry, with its poverty and demoralization but also its formidable collective power and organizing capacity (Engels noted with admiration that the Chartists were able to collect *a million pennies* every week[28]), its fighting spirit, and its power to lift itself spiritually and morally above its material wretchedness as soon as it organized itself, that enabled Engels to go forward from philosophical communism to proletarian communism. Ryazanov recalls appositely that Engels's meeting with the first real proletarian communists—the Germans Schapper, Bauer, and Moll, who had emigrated to London—made a tremendous impression on him; one which, indeed, he himself described in his introduction to Marx's *Revelations about the Cologne Communist Trial*.[29] And we sense the effect of this practical experience in the three works that were to mark this transition: *Outlines of a Critique of Political Economy* (end of 1843), *Die Lage Englands* (January 1844), and *The Condition of the Working Class in England* (end of 1844 and beginning of 1845).

The first of these three, the *Outlines of a Critique of Political Economy*, is, as we noted, the first strictly economic work by either of the two friends. Engels says nothing substantially new

---

28. *MEGA*, I, 2, p. 369.

29. *Selected Works*, Vol. III, pp. 174–175. This impression can be compared with that made on Marx by his association with French workers' groups, which he describes admiringly in the *Economic and Philosophic Manuscripts*.

in it. He criticizes economic liberalism—the doctrine of Adam Smith, Ricardo, and McCulloch—by confronting it with the economic and social reality of industrial Britain. This criticism was to a large extent inspired by such socialist writers as Owen, Fourier, and Proudhon, but goes beyond them in its fruitful application of Hegelian dialectics to social reality.[30] And though it is still dominated by a number of moralizing and idealistic conceptions,[31] condemning trade for causing "mutual distrust" and using "immoral means to attain an immoral end,"[32] it is nevertheless marked by some remarkable insights that were later to find echoes in Marx's work, in the *Communist Manifesto*, and even in the *Grundrisse:* for example, the idea that capitalist economy is a step forward necessary "for all these petty, local and national considerations to recede into the background, so that the struggle of our time could become a universal human struggle."[33]

The starting point of the *Outlines* is a criticism of trade—of the mercantilist doctrine and of the theory of free trade. Proceeding "from a purely human, universal basis," Engels arrives at the correct conclusion that both doctrines must be criticized together. He especially exposes the hypocrisy of the liberal antimonopolist doctrine, which pretends to be unaware that free trade is itself based upon a monopoly, namely, the monopoly of private property in the hands of a minority class of society, and also that free competition inevitably leads to monopoly.

The second part of the essay deals with value; this is the weakest part, where it is seen that Engels has neither understood nor gone deeper than Ricardo. Engels discusses value by starting with

---

30. Ryazanov, in *MEGA*, I, 2, p. lxxii.

31. Emile Bottigelli (*Genèse du socialisme scientifique*, pp. 124–125) correctly observes, however, that this moral condemnation of trade, competition, etc., is based on Feuerbach's humanistic principle, which is combined with the Hegelian philosophy of history. We thus have an attempt to integrate criticism of history, society, and the economy, which can perhaps be seen as a stage in the preparation of the *Economic and Philosophic Manuscripts* and *The German Ideology*.

32. *Outlines of a Critique of Political Economy*, Appendix to *Economic and Philosophic Manuscripts*, p. 201.

33. Ibid., p. 199.

the distinction between "abstract or real" value, on the one hand, and exchange value on the other. He then examines the two schools which reduce "abstract value" to "costs of production" and to "utility," respectively. He comes to the conclusion that the "intrinsic value" of an object "includes both factors," costs of production and utility. In a passage which, to be sure, is not very clear, he seems to cast doubt on the very existence of value.[34] He comes nearer to a correct view when he criticizes the working of the "law of competition," which operates as "a purely natural law," [35] and he deduces the appearance of overproduction crises precisely from the working of this law, that is, from competition.

The piece ends with a fierce polemic against Malthus's "law of population" [36] and a description of the disastrous consequences of large-scale industry for a substantial section of the population. This is the most impressive part; it takes up and carries further the critique of capitalism made by Fourier, and it was in turn to be extended and supported by remarkable documentation in Engels's first book, *The Condition of the Working Class in England.*

It is true that in the final part of the piece we still find some mistakes, such as the idea that the worker's wage is reduced to the means of subsistence and nothing more.[37] But the criticism of Malthus is lucid and sets forth the essential argument that remains valid to this day in the dispute with neo-Malthusianism, namely, that it is fallacious to compare the increase in population with the increase in the *natural* production of the soil; it should rather be compared with the potential increase in agricultural productivity that would result from *the effective application of modern science and technique to agriculture.* The analysis of overproduction crises as a fundamental expression of the contradictions of capitalism is striking in its conciseness and in the young writer's ability to get to the bottom of things. It leads

---

34. Ibid., pp. 204–207.

35. Ibid., pp. 214–216.

36. He calls it a "vile, infamous theory," a "revolting blasphemy against nature and mankind." (Ibid., p. 219.)

37. Ibid., p. 223.

to the exposure of a senseless and absurd situation: people dying of hunger in the midst of plenty.

Above all, in this essay Engels brings together the critique of private property, which had occupied the two future friends for two years, and the critique of capitalism, which was to be their concern for the rest of their lives, by stating that *the division between capital and labor results inevitably from private property,* and that this division leads to the division of bourgeois society into opposing classes, to the division of mankind into capitalists and workers.[38]

The immoral and inhuman consequences of capitalism, of large-scale industry—the way in which it breaks up the family and causes an increase in crime—which are noted in a few striking phrases in the *Outlines,* and which the *Communist Manifesto* was to describe in a grim, unforgettable word-picture, were analyzed more fully in a work which remains to this day the most moving depiction of the social consequences of the industrial revolution.[39] *The Condition of the Working Class in England* is not a work of historial materialism in the strict sense. It is still moral indignation rather than understanding of the social process that inspires the young social critic. But this moral indignation is already revolutionary, already linked to a boundless devotion to the class exploited and crushed by capital, the class which has created all that wealth whose enjoyment capital reserves to itself.[40] Most important, the book already leads to the realization *that the actual struggle of the proletariat is the only possible vehicle for socialism.* In this sense it marks Engels's definitive break with utopian socialism and forms at the same time an essential weapon against it.

In recent years this conception has been subjected to critical examination because of the obvious historical delay in the victory

---

38. Ibid., pp. 211, 216.

39. D. I. Rosenberg notes that in *Briefe aus dem Wuppertal* (Letters from Wuppertal), a work written when he was only nineteen, Engels was already struck by the workers' inhuman working conditions "which must deprive them of all the joy of living." (Rosenberg, *Die Entwicklung,* p. 51.)

40. *MEGA,* I, 4, pp. 24–25.

of socialism in the industrially developed countries of the West. Some of the critics—either explicitly, as with Frantz Fanon, or implicitly, as with the theoreticians of the Chinese Communist Party—strive to show that the revolutionary potential of the peoples of the Third World is greater than that of the Western proletariat. Moreover, within the peoples of the Third World they assign the chief role in the revolution to the peasantry and the revolutionary intelligentsia, and consider that in those countries the industrial proletariat is to some extent a privileged social class in relation to the landless peasants.[41]

Other critics question not the revolutionary capacity of the Western proletariat in comparison with that of the peoples of the Third World, but its revolutionary capacity as such. They regard the Western proletariat as being in practice integrated into capitalist society, especially through its atomization (in semi-automated industry), the growth in its consuming capacity, and the opportunities that exist for manipulating its ideology and its needs.[42] They do not deny that the mass of those who are obliged to sell their labor power continues to increase both in absolute numbers and relative to the total working population. They do deny that this numerical increase strengthens, either directly or indirectly, the challenge to Western capitalism or even the likelihood of seeing it overthrown by the Western proletariat.

Both types of critic tend to refer more often to the youthful writings of Marx and Engels than to the writings of their maturer years. In these youthful works, and in particular in the *Introduction to the Critique of the Hegelian Philosophy of Right*, the revolutionary role of the proletariat is essentially deduced from the *negative* characteristics of this class in bourgeois society. It is presented as the culmination of a Hegelian triad, as a veritable "negation of the negation." It is because the proletariat's chains are radical that it can get rid of them only through a radical revo-

---

41. See, for instance, Frantz Fanon, *The Wretched of the Earth*, pp. 48–50, 87, *et seq.*

42. See, for instance, Herbert Marcuse, "Les perspectives du socialisme dans la société industrielle développée," in *Revue internationale du socialisme*, 2nd year, No. 8; Paul A. Baran and Paul M. Sweezy, *Monopoly Capital*, pp. 363–364; C. Wright Mills, *The Marxists*, pp. 113–115; etc.

lution. This leads contemporary critics to conclude that since the proletariat's chains have today become a great deal less radical, the hope of a radical revolution being carried out by this class has become largely utopian.

A more critical analysis of the youthful writings of Marx and Engels—and especially of the origin of their ideas regarding social revolution—shows, however, that behind the brilliant style there was still, at that stage, a lack of empirical knowledge. A remark Engels formulated forty years later, writing about *The German Ideology*, applies equally to the famous phrase about "radical chains": "The finished portion consists of an exposition of the materialist conception of history which proves only how incomplete our knowledge of economic history still was at that time." [43] The modern proletariat is not, in fact, the social class which has borne the heaviest chains in the history of the world. That definition would better fit the Roman slaves between the 1st century BC and the 3rd century AD. History has shown that it is not enough for a class to have nothing more to lose, and not to possess private property, for it to be capable of carrying out a social revolution abolishing *all* private property. When they later made their diagnosis more precise, Marx and Engels assigned the proletariat the key role in the coming of socialism not so much because of the misery it suffers as because of the place it occupies in the production process and the capacity it thereby possesses to acquire a talent for organization and a cohesion in action which is incommensurable with that of any oppressed class in the past.

There is no reason to deny the revolutionary capacity of the landless peasantry of the countries of the Third World or to doubt the fact that these countries have brought forward the largest number of participants in the revolutionary struggle, on the world scale, during the past twenty years. Two points need to be made, however, if this fact is not to be transformed into a false picture of the overall reality. First, this peasantry, as the Marxists foresaw, is in itself unable to take power and found new states; for this it needs a leadership which, by origin, composi-

43. Engels, *Ludwig Feuerbach and the End of Classical German Philosophy*, Foreword to the 1888 edition, in *Selected Works*, Vol. III, p. 336.

tion, and inspiration, is proletarian.[44] Further, this poor peasantry alone is unable to build a socialist society in the sense that Marx understood it—that is, a society which insures a full and complete blossoming of all human potentialities. It is precisely because the infrastructure of such a society can only be the product of modern large-scale industry, brought to its highest level of development, that the socialist revolution, conceived as a worldwide process,[45] though it may *begin* in underdeveloped countries, cannot be *completed*—that is, assume its full development—until it embraces the countries that are most industrially advanced.

Furthermore, when various sociologists and economists express doubt as to the role of the proletariat as the vehicle of socialist transformation in the West, they usually make one of two mistakes: they either presuppose Marx guilty of alleging an *automatic* relationship between the degree of industrial development and the degree of class consciousness,[46] or they consider the development of this class consciousness (and, in general, of the subjective conditions needed for the overthrow of capitalism) as proceeding in a straight-line fashion.

It is obvious that when Marx and Engels reached maturity they clearly grasped the dialectical relationships between the level of development of the productive forces and that of class con-

---

44. Cf. Leon Trotsky, *Die russische Revolution 1905*, pp. 44–45. Lenin: "These fundamental economic facts explain why this force cannot manifest itself through its own efforts, and why it has failed in all its attempts to do so in the history of all revolutions. Whenever the proletariat was unable to lead this revolution, this force always followed the leadership of the bourgeoisie." (Speech to All-Russia Congress of Transport Workers, March 27, 1921, in Lenin, *Collected Works*, Vol. 32, p. 278.) See also the Second Declaration of Havana.

45. Marx: "Empirically, communism is only possible as the act of the dominant peoples 'all at once' and simultaneously, which presupposes the universal development of productive forces and the world intercourse bound up with communism." (*The German Ideology*, p. 47.)

46. Cf.: "He [Marx] seems to believe that class consciousness is a necessary psychological consequence of objective economic development, which includes the polarization of owners and workers." (C. Wright Mills, *The Marxists*, p. 114.)

sciousness.[47] What Engels wrote about the British proletariat of the nineteenth century applies, *mutatis mutandis*, to the American proletariat of the twentieth century. In order to show that the latter will prove unable to fulfill its revolutionary mission, it is not enough to describe the *present* mechanisms of integration, ideological manipulation, and so on. It is necessary to show that the factors which, in the long run, work in the opposite direction—increasing international competition, which operates to erode the American monopoly on high productivity and the superiority in wages that the American workers enjoy as a result of this monopoly—will not alter the behavior of the proletariat of the United States. It is above all necessary to show that automation, which is merely the most radical form assumed by the historical tendency of capital to substitute dead labor for living labor,[48] will in the long run be accompanied by full employment and will not lead to recessions that growing inflation will be unable to hold in check. This has not yet been shown.

As to the hope of seeing the emancipating role of the proletariat carried out by "unintegrated minorities" (radical minority groups, students, the infra-proletariat, or even elements which are plainly anti-social), this comes up against the same obstacle on which the slave revolts of ancient Rome stumbled and fell. These groups are capable, at best, of desperate outbreaks. They do not possess either *objective social power* (either to insure or to paralyze production as a whole) or the lasting ability to organize themselves collectively—two characteristics which are necessary if they are to transform present-day society.

We shall see later that Marx and Engels quickly became convinced that the objective and subjective conditions favorable to the overthrow of capitalism do not develop in a straight line, but follow a curve which is distinctly influenced by the fluctuations of the industrial cycle (both the seven-year cycle and the long-

47. Cf. the Preface written by Engels in 1892 to the English edition of *The Condition of the Working Class in England*, in *Selected Works*, Vol. III, pp. 440–451.

48. Baran and Sweezy show that between 1950 and 1962 the number of unskilled workers in the United States was reduced from 13 million to 4 million as a result of automation. (*Monopoly Capital*, p. 267.)

term cycle).[49] What is essential is not to know whether or not the working class of a particular country or group of countries is temporarily passive,[50] but to know whether the objective and subjective conditions under which it lives impel it *periodically* to take the road of a general challenge to the capitalist order.

The objective conditions for such a challenge are those that result from the very functioning of capitalism—in particular, the regulation of wages by means of the industrial reserve army, the resulting insecurity, the inadequacy of wages in relation to the needs aroused by social circumstances, the alienating nature of work, and so on. The subjective conditions are, in the last analysis, those which cause the worker to regard his situation as inferior and unsatisfactory. A mass of recent publications shows that this is true in the society called the "consumers' society" no less than in the nineteenth century.[51]

---

49. See Chapter 5.

50. Cf. Engels's Introduction to Marx, *The Class Struggles in France*, in *Selected Works*, Vol. I, pp. 186–204.

51. See, for instance, A. Andrieux and J. Lignon, *L'Ouvrier d'aujourd'hui;* Hans-Paul Bahrdt, Walter Dirks, and others, in M. Feuersenger, ed., *Gibt es noch ein Proletariat?;* etc. An amusing example from Britain was recently reported by Robin Blackburn: a sociologist had devoted a study to the attitude of the workers at the Vauxhall factory at Luton toward the management of the firm. Seventy-seven percent of those who worked in the assembly department revealed a "cooperative attitude." Hardly a month after the publication of the study there was a veritable revolt in this very plant, directed precisely against this same management. (Robin Blackburn, "The Unequal Society," in Robin Blackburn and Alexander Cockburn, eds., *The Incompatibles—Trade-Union Militancy and the Consensus*, pp. 48–51.)

2

From Condemning Capitalism to Providing a Socioeconomic Vindication of Communism

It was during his exile in Paris that Marx applied himself eagerly to the study of political economy, study which he continued during his exile in Brussels, broke off when he returned to Germany, and completed at the British Museum during his exile in London. "Reading Engels's *Outlines* had made him see that it was not enough to criticize Hegel's political philosophy in order to work out, with mere negation of the state as one's point of departure, that radical theory of society which might 'grip' the working-class masses and make them aware of the need for a social revolution that would put an end to their alienation. . . . It was therefore with the well-defined purpose of finding an answer to these questions that Marx set himself to study the 'anatomy of bourgeois society' as this was to be found in the writings of the great economists. . . ." [1] We are in a position to observe the scope and diversity of Marx's economic studies through the copious reading notes he left behind, parts of which have been published.[2] (It is not known whether *all* of Marx's reading notes have yet been found.)

---

1. Maximilien Rubel, *Karl Marx: Essai de biographie intellectuelle*, pp. 117–118.
2. See Marx's Parisian reading notes, largely published in *MEGA*, I, 3, pp. 411–583. The reading notes taken while he was in Brussels and during the course of a six-week visit to England in the summer of 1845 (see Engels's Preface to Marx's *The Poverty of Philosophy*) have not been published *in extenso*, but are summarized in *MEGA*, I, 6, pp. 597–618. The reading notes taken in London in 1850–1851 were published in the appendix to the *Grundrisse*.

His study of political economy, together with his increasingly close collaboration with Engels, which began in September 1844, was to lead Marx to clarify his ideas regarding his mentors in philosophy and some of his old friends: Hegel, Feuerbach, and the young post-Hegelians of Bruno Bauer's school. Three works resulted from this polemic, which was at one and the same time a sort of internal monologue and an attempt by two men who had just become friends to understand the way their thinking had evolved: *The Economic and Philosophic Manuscripts of 1844*, *The Holy Family*, and *The German Ideology*. It is the first of these that marks a turning point in Marx's economic thought.[3]

Written after reading a series of front-rank economists, and even consisting in part of long quotations from Adam Smith, Pecqueur, Loudon, Buret, Sismondi, James Mill, and Michel Chevalier,[4] these three economic and philosophic manuscripts constitute the first strictly economic work from the pen of the future author of *Capital*. (A critique of Hegel's philosophy forms the fourth section.) They deal, successively, with wages, profit, ground rent, alienated labor in relation to private property, private property in relation to labor and to communism, needs, production and the division of labor, and money.

The philosophical concept of alienation, which Marx had borrowed from Hegel, Schelling, and Feuerbach,[5] is given a thorough socioeconomic content for the first time in the *Economic and Philosophic Manuscripts of 1844*. This concept had ceased to have an entirely philosophical content even in the *Introduction to the Critique of Hegel's Philosophy of Right*: "Marx had taken

3. In Chapter 10 I shall examine the controversies to which the *Economic and Philosophic Manuscripts* have given rise—in particular on the subject of "alienated labor"—and the relation between the works written in Marx's youth and those described as his "mature" writings.

4. In this connection, D. I. Rosenberg stresses that the dominant idea linking all the critical commentaries contained in these notes is one borrowed from Engels's *Outline of a Critique of Political Economy*: that political economy is founded on a false premise, namely, the alleged inviolability of private property. (Rosenberg, *Die Entwicklung*, p. 87.)

5. Jürgen Habermas notes that Schelling already speaks of "the outsider to whom labor and the product of labor belong," and also that Schelling foreshadows the materialist transcending of the dialectics of labor. (*Theorie und Praxis*, pp. 154–156.)

from Feuerbach the conception of man dehumanized, or alienated, or mutilated. . . . But Marx was now using this expression in a new sense. In political connections, he identified . . . dehumanized man with man despised and despicable, and he held it to the glory of the French Revolution that it had reconstituted man, that is, had raised him to the level of a free citizen.

"In doing this, however, we find ourselves gliding into a quite new context, one in which the problems are political, or at least social. Alienated man is suddenly no longer the individual attached to a religious or speculative dream world but the member of an imperfect society who is lacking in all his human dignity. Man in a dehumanized world has now become man in a dehumanized society . . ." [6]

In the *Economic and Philosophic Manuscripts* the *secret* of this dehumanized society is unveiled. *Society is inhuman because labor in this society is alienated labor.* Marx found it all the easier to reduce society and social man to labor because Hegel had already described labor as the essential core of human praxis. When he then studied the classical economists, Marx found that they made labor the ultimate source of value. The synthesis occurred in a flash, the two ideas were combined, and we have the impression of really being present at this discovery when we examine Marx's reading notes, especially the well-known commentary on his notes on James Mill [7] in which he starts from the nature of money—the means of exchange and instrument of alienation—in order to arrive at the relationships of alienation which replace human relationships.

---

6. Paul Kaegi, *Genesis des historischen Materialismus*, pp. 194–195.

7. *MEGA*, I, 3, p. 531. Here is another passage from these notes on James Mill: "Once the existence of exchange relations is established, labor becomes labor directly devoted to subsistence [*unmittelbare Erwerbsarbeit*] . . . The more multiform production becomes, the more multiform, on the one hand, do needs appear, while, on the other, the more uniform do the actions of the producer appear, the more does his labor sink into the category of labor for subsistence, until it has only that significance and it becomes quite accidental and unimportant whether or not the producer is related to his product by direct enjoyment and personal need, and whether the activity of labor itself means, or does not mean, for him, the enjoyment of his own personality and a realization of his natural talent and spiritual aim." (Ibid., p. 539.)

At the same time, philosophical communism becomes sociological communism, that is, communism based on an analysis of the evolution of societies and of the logic of this. True, in the first of the *Economic and Philosophic Manuscripts*, Marx still declares himself a supporter of the "positive, humanistic and naturalistic criticism" of Feuerbach.[8] But this humanism, too, is now given a definite socioeconomic content: it is identified with communism, which positively transcends private property, the division of labor, and alienated labor.[9]

Instead of the contrast between the "communism of the toiling masses" and "philosophical communism" that Engels had included in his articles on communism in *The New Moral World*, Marx distinguishes in the *Economic and Philosophic Manuscripts* between "crude communism" and "communism as the positive transcendence of private property."[10] The former, born of crude envy, results only in the generalization of alienated labor, a "levelling-down proceeding from the preconceived minimum." The latter, however, signifies "the positive transcendence of all estrangement—that is to say, the return of man from religion, family, state, etc., to his *human*, i.e., *social* existence."[11] And Marx already points out that this presupposes, on the one hand, socialization of the means of production, abolition of private property, and, on the other, a high level of development of the productive forces. This idea marks a step forward when compared with all the previous communist writings of Marx and Engels, as well as with those of the Utopian Socialists. It was to be developed further in *The German Ideology*.[12]

Following the logic of a critique of private property and capi-

---

8. Marx, *Economic and Philosophic Manuscripts*, p. 64.

9. Ibid., p. 135. The experience of the weavers' revolt in Silesia, which occurred while Marx was writing the *Economic and Philosophic Manuscripts*, certainly influenced his achievement of this awareness.

10. Ibid., pp. 134–135.

11. Ibid., p. 136. (The translator of this edition prefers "estrangement" to the more commonly accepted "alienation."—*Trans*.)

12. It should be kept in mind that the Swiss economist Wilhelm Schulz had already worked out similar ideas, and that Marx used Schulz's work as a basis. (See Auguste Cornu, *Karl Marx und Friedrich Engels*, Vol. II, p. 123.)

talism and not that of a general exposition of the laws of development of the capitalist mode of production, the *Economic and Philosophic Manuscripts* begin with an analysis of the *poverty* caused by private property, rather than with an analysis of the *wealth* created by commodity production (which had been the starting point of all the classical works of political economy, and was the one which Marx was himself to adopt in *Capital*). The poverty caused by private property is wholly embodied in *wages* and in the laws of evolution of wages. Wages are analyzed on the basis of the classical theory of Adam Smith and Ricardo, influenced by Malthus. Affected by competition among the workers, wages tend to fall toward the lowest subsistence level. In contrast to Malthus and Ricardo, however, Marx pointed out that this was not the inevitable consequence of some "law of increase of population," but resulted from the separation of the workers from their means of production.[13]

At the same time, Marx is already varying this "law" of wages by distinguishing among three divergent movements of wages during the three successive phases of the economic cycle—the phase of depression, the phase of boom, and the phase in which the accumulation of capital has reached its maximum expansion.

In the first phase, wages decline under the pressure of unemployment and a section of the working class sinks into degradation and the deepest wretchedness. In the third phase, wages remain stationary at a relatively low level (Marx here quotes verbatim a thesis of Ricardo's). It is thus the second phase that is most favorable for the workers, since the demand for labor power exceeds the supply, competition among the capitalists increases, and wages can rise.

Now, what happens in a "boom" period? Expansion intensifies the accumulation and concentration of capital. The number of capitalists decreases while the number of workers rapidly increases. The use of machinery spreads, reducing the worker to an "animated machine," and the machine thereby enters into direct competition with the worker. In addition, the "boom" invariably results in overproduction, which in turn leads to unem-

---

13. *Economic and Philosophic Manuscripts*, p. 68.

ployment and falling wages.[14] As can be seen in this initial diagram of the way capitalism works, increases in wages can occur only temporarily and are doomed by the logic of the system to be ruthlessly wiped out. Marx was not to modify this diagram until ten years later.

Nevertheless, he hints at the theory of "relative impoverishment" when he declares that even in a period of high conjuncture, "the capitalist is more than compensated for the raising of wages by the reduction in the amount of labor time." [15] The wording is still obscure and clumsy, but what Marx is here expressing by intuition is that those commodities which will be bought with wages may rapidly decline in value as a result of the increase in productivity; or, what comes to the same thing, that the "counter-value" of wages can be produced in a smaller and smaller fraction of the working day. Marx quotes a passage from a book by a now-forgotten Swiss economist, Wilhelm Schulz (*Die Bewegung der Produktion*), which gives noteworthy expression to the law of "relative impoverishment." [16]

Similarly, Marx does not yet distinguish accurately between constant capital and variable capital, as he was to do in his classical economic writings, but confines himself to distinguishing, as does Adam Smith, between "fixed capital" and "circulating capital." [17] In the sphere of ground rent he follows Ricardo's theory in stressing that capital eventually incorporates landed property into itself by transforming the landowner into a capitalist.

In a striking passage in which he moves along the frontier between philosophy and political economy, Marx declared that landed property must be completely drawn into the "movement of private property," that in agriculture as well the relationship between landlord and worker must be reduced to the simple relationship of exploiter and exploited, and that all personal links between the landowner and his property must cease to exist if the struggle against private property as such is to be carried on effec-

---

14. Ibid., p. 69.
15. Ibid., p. 70.
16. Ibid., pp. 72–73.
17. Ibid., p. 85.

tively.[18] Here too, *The German Ideology* was to mark an important step forward in his reasoning, which broke away completely from its philosophical and moralizing antecedents.

The best-known part of the *Economic and Philosophic Manuscripts* is the analysis of the socioeconomic roots of alienation. Under the influence of both Engels and Moses Hess, Marx draws a parallel between alienated labor under capitalism and man alienated by religion. The more the worker works the more he creates a world of objects which are hostile to him and which crush him.[19] Contrary to what he had written previously, when he had identified alienation with private property, Marx now strives to dig deeper and finds the ultimate roots of human alienation in *alienated labor*, that is, in the division of labor and commodity production. There is a constant interaction between commodity production, division of labor, and private property which produces alienation, but it is the division of labor that is its historical starting point.[20]

Marx shows that alienation is by no means limited to the alienation of the product of labor and of the means of production, which become hostile external forces crushing the producer. He makes a particularly lucid analysis of the effects which result, under a competitive system, from the production of commodities, in the matter of the *alienation of needs*. This passage is a magnificent anticipation, for most of the tendencies which Marx discerned 120 years ago were merely embryonic in the nineteenth century and were not realized on a large scale until our own time. Here is a passage that seems like a direct commentary on Vance Packard: ". . . every person speculates on creating a *new* need in another, so as to drive him to a fresh sacrifice, to place him in a new dependence and to seduce him into a new mode of *gratification* and therefore economic ruin. . . . The increase in the quantity of objects is accompanied by an extension of the realm of the alien powers to which man is subjected, and every new product represents a new *possibility* of mutual swindling and mutual plundering. Man becomes ever poorer as man, his

18. Ibid., pp. 101–102
19. Auguste Cornu, *Karl Marx, l'homme et l'oeuvre*, pp. 332–334.
20. *Economic and Philosophic Manuscripts*, pp. 116–117, 135.

need for *money* becomes ever greater if he wants to overpower hostile being. The power of his *money* declines exactly in inverse proportion to the increase in the volume of production: that is, his neediness grows as the *power* of money increases. . . . Subjectively, this is partly manifested in that the extension of products and needs[21] falls into *contriving* and ever-*calculating* subservience to inhuman, unnatural and *imaginary* appetites. . . ."[22]

A brief discussion of the inhuman aspect of the division of labor,[23] which was echoed in a famous passage in *The German Ideology* (". . . while in communist society, where nobody has one exclusive sphere of activity but each can become accomplished in any branch he wishes, society regulates the general production and thus makes it possible for me to do one thing today and another tomorrow, to hunt in the morning, fish in the afternoon, rear cattle in the evening, criticize after dinner, just

21. In a short novel appropriately entitled *Things* (New York: Grove Press, 1968), Georges Perec has given a masterly description of present-day man, slave to a mass of more and more uncontrollable objects of consumption.

22. *Economic and Philosophic Manuscripts*, p. 147. An extreme example of these "inhuman, unnatural and imaginary" appetites engendered by capitalist production is presented by the American funeral and undertaking industry, which includes "Beautyrama beds" and mattresses installed in coffins to enable the corpses to lie more comfortably. (See Jessica Mitford, *The American Way of Death*.)

23. *Economic and Philosophic Manuscripts*, pp. 163–164. Antonioni's film *Blow Up* provides a striking illustration of how excessive specialization in the divison of labor reduces man to the status of a mere object—in this instance an object for the lens of a talented photographer. As a result of the same process of reification, the photographer himself becomes incapable of establishing normal human relationships with other people. A murder is of no importance except as a reproduction in picture form, and the personality of the murdered person becomes so lacking in significance that the film deliberately keeps us in doubt until the end as to the victim's identity. Even a game degenerates eventually into mere representation and appearance, a game of tennis without a ball, in which all the actions are simply mimed by persons who remain silent, unable to communicate with each other. This inability to communicate is a tragic aspect of alienation in capitalist society. We perceive this in the tape-recordings of "conversations" between housewives, in the streets or in shops, conversations that are nothing but parallel monologues, with no relation between them.

as I have a mind, without ever becoming hunter, fisherman, shepherd, or critic" [24]), again takes up the initial idea that it is in the division of labor that the true origin of alienated labor is to be found.

True, the *Economic and Philosophic Manuscripts* do not form a mature economic work. Marx has only a fragmentary grasp of the problem of an overall criticism of political economy. This criticism still trips over a fundamental stumbling block: Marx has not yet solved the problem of value and surplus value. He has not yet grasped what was rational in classical theory, especially Ricardo's, and his economic analyses inevitably suffer. At the same time, however, the reader remains fascinated by the confident rigor of Marx's critical spirit, the boldness of his historical perspective, and the implacable logic with which he goes to the bottom of things; we are quickly convinced that, from the moment when he wrote the *Manuscripts*, Marx had already laid one of the foundation stones of his socioeconomic theory.

The Holy Family is not concerned, strictly speaking, with economic preoccupations, and its contribution to the evolution of the economic thought of Marx and Engels was rather secondary. The two authors still clung to the eclectic conception of value which Engels had set forth in his *Outlines of a Critique of Political Economy*.[25] As in the *Outlines* Engels continues to assert that under the capitalist regime it would be utopian on the part of the workers to try to achieve a reduction in their working day.[26]

---

24. *The German Ideology*, pp. 44–45. See also pp. 466–467.

25. Here are two examples. On one page Marx writes: "Value is determined at the beginning in an apparently reasonable way by the cost of production of an object and its social usefulness. Later it turns out that value is determined quite fortuitously and that it does not need to bear any relation to cost of production or social usefulness." And on a later page of the same work, he writes: "Even Critical Criticism must be capable of grasping that the *labor time* necessarily *expended* on the production of an object is included [*sic*] in the *cost of production* of that object . . ." (*The Holy Family*, pp. 47 and 68.)

26. Cf. Franz Mehring's Introduction to *Aus dem literarischen Nachlass*, Vol. II, pp. 76–77. The passage from Engels which is criticized is on p. 109.

On the other hand, the passages in *The Holy Family* which concern Proudhon are particularly interesting in the light of the polemic which was to ensue two years later, enabling Marx to set forth for the first time a general analysis of the capitalist mode of production. It is true that in *The Holy Family* Marx declares that Proudhon "is a prisoner of the premises of the political economy" which he is combating.[27] But he hails Proudhon's critique of private property as "the first resolute, pitiless, and at the same time scientific investigation of the foundation of political economy . . . This is the great scientific progress he made, a progress which revolutionizes political economy and first makes a real science of political economy possible. Proudhon's treatise *Qu'est-ce que la propriété?* is as important for modern political economy as Sieyès' work *Qu'est-ce que le tiers état?* for modern politics." [28] A large part of *The Holy Family* is, in fact, a defense of Proudhon against the "critical" German ideologists who had read him only carelessly and had even shown themselves incapable of translating him correctly.

(In passing, Marx rises above the wrong point of view Engels held in his *Outlines* regarding the relationship between wages and profits, and notes correctly that these two forms of income stand in a "hostile" relationship to each other. The "free agreement" between worker and capitalist in determining wages hides a relationship which *compels* the worker to accept the wage he is offered.)

While the *Economic and Philosophic Manuscripts* constitute Marx's first effort to criticize the classical positions of political

---

27. *The Holy Family*, p. 60.

28. Ibid., p. 46. It is interesting to compare this opinion with the one Marx formulated twenty years later regarding the same work: "His first work, *Qu'est-ce que la propriété?* is undoubtedly his best. It is epoch-making, if not from the novelty of its content, at least by the new and audacious way of coming out with everything. Of course, 'property' had been not only criticized in various ways but also '*done away with*' in the utopian manner by the French Socialists and Communists whose works he knew. In this book Proudhon's relation to Saint-Simon and Fourier is about the same as that of Feuerbach to Hegel. . . . In a strictly scientific history of political economy the book would hardly be worth mentioning." (Karl Marx, letter of January 24, 1865, to Schweitzer, in *The Poverty of Philosophy*, pp. 194–195.)

economy in the light of the reality of bourgeois society, *The German Ideology*—the main philosophical work, which Marx and Engels completed in Brussels in 1846—bases the theory of historical materialism upon a systematic transcending of post-Hegelian German philosophy. For the first time, "Marx and Engels pass from an analysis of historico-social development which could be called 'phenomenological' to a 'genetic' analysis." [29]

There are not many passages in the book that are strictly economic in subject matter: in general, these repeat what Marx had already developed in the *Economic and Philosophic Manuscripts*, although in some cases with invaluable refinements and clarifications. Thus, for example, there is the well-known passage in which the writers note the *universal* nature of communism, the need to base it upon the *worldwide* development of productive forces and needs, since otherwise "want is merely made general, and with destitution the struggle for necessities and all the old filthy business would necessarily be reproduced . . ." [30] Thus, too, the entire development of the idea that the division of labor is the source of human alienation, about which a passage has already been quoted. Again, the decisive declaration according to which "communism is for us not . . . an *ideal* to which reality will have to adjust itself. We call communism the *real* movement which abolishes the present state of things." Again, the striking definition of the productive forces which become the forces of destruction, under the pressure of capitalist contradictions. And a first definition of historical materialism itself, in some ways even more concise, and at the same time richer, than the well-known one given in the Preface to the *Contribution to the Critique of Political Economy*.[31]

Nevertheless, three real contributions to the forward movement of Marx and Engels's economic thought can be found in *The German Ideology*. The first is a more dialectical view of capitalism and world trade, the early signs of which, though not elaborated, could already be perceived in the *Economic and Philosophic Manuscripts*. The generalization of commodity relations means not only

29. Emilio Agazzi, "La formazione della metodologia di Marx," in *Rivista storica del socialismo*, September–December 1964, p. 461.

30. *The German Ideology*, p. 46.

31. Ibid., pp. 43–47, 85, 60.

the general mutilation of the individual and the general reduction of life to buying and selling;[32] it also means the potential enrichment of men's lives because it breaks the narrow framework of their local existence, in which their desires, appetites, and possibilities are narrowly limited by ignorance of what is possible for men in other parts of the world. "The real intellectual wealth of the individual depends entirely on the wealth of his real connections." And it is only through the world market that men "acquire the capacity to enjoy this all-sided production of the whole earth . . ."[33] Marx was to return to this idea in the *Grundrisse*, where he speaks of "the great historical aspect of capital."[34]

The second contribution concerns the universal development of human *needs* which modern large-scale industry has already prepared and which communism will accomplish.[35] This is closely linked to the problem of world trade. Here Marx and Engels deepen their criticism of the relation between man and things by making it dialectically more subtle. Whereas in the *Economic and Philosophic Manuscripts* the multiplication of things was still seen as an essentially negative phenomenon, in *The German Ideology* it is emphasized that a development of all human potentialities implies the universal development of man's enjoyments. This idea was also to be developed extensively in the *Grundrisse*.

The third contribution concerns the mode of distribution of the future society: ". . . the false tenet, based upon existing circumstances, 'to each according to his capacity,' must be changed, in so far as it relates to enjoyment in its narrower sense, into the tenet, 'to each according to his need'; in other words, a different form of activity, of labor, confers no privileges in respect of possession and enjoyment."[36] This warning was to appear again in the *Critique of the Gotha Programme:* it is rarely quoted nowadays in allegedly Marxist propaganda.

There is evidently a connection between these three new elements in the economic thought of Marx and Engels. The univer-

---

32. Cf. *The Poverty of Philosophy*, p. 34.
33. *The German Ideology*, p. 49; see also pp. 75–76.
34. Marx, *Grundrisse der Kritik der politischen ökonomie*, p. 231.
35. *The German Ideology*, pp. 49–50.
36. Ibid., pp. 49–50, 84, 593, etc.

sality of needs conceived as an integral part of the universality of human development is created by world trade and large-scale industry. And the rejection of any "distribution according to work done" or "according to capacities" in communist society is based precisely upon the need of insuring this universal development of *all* men.

From *The German Ideology* onward, Marx and Engels establish clearly the links connecting the abolition of commodity production with the coming of a communist society.[37] They were not to change this opinion for the rest of their lives. Conceptions which contemplate the survival of commodity production even in communist society are altogether alien to Marxist theory.[38]

---

37. Ibid., p. 47.
38. Branko Horvat, *Toward a Theory of Planned Economy*, pp. 131–133.

3

From Rejection to Acceptance
of the Labor Theory of Value

The best way to understand something is to begin by not understanding it. This time-honored popular saying is reflected in the
attitude the young Marx adopted toward the labor theory of
value, which had been worked out by the British classical school
of political economy and which was later to be brought to perfection by Marx himself.

In the critical notes which accompany his first systematic study
of political economy,[1] Marx explicitly rejects labor as the basis of
value. In *The Poverty of Philosophy*, he no less explicitly accepts
it. A period of three years elapsed between these two works, from
the beginning of 1844 to the beginning of 1847. How did Marx's
thinking on economic questions evolve during this period? Can
one define more precisely, if not the exact moment then at
least the approximate period when Marx accepted the labor theory
of value? These are the two questions which we shall endeavor to
answer.

The starting point for this analysis is found in Marx's reading
notes taken during his exile in Paris, notes which extend over an
entire year (from the beginning of 1844 to the beginning of
1845). The common assumption that these notes are in chronological order is more than plausible and has been accepted by all
the commentators known to me.[2] Attentive study of these notes
thus enables us to observe a definite evolution in Marx's attitude
to the labor theory of value.

The economists on whom Marx comments appear in his notes

1. *MEGA*, I, 3, pp. 409–583.
2. See in particular, D. I. Rosenberg, *Die Entwicklung*, p. 95.

in the following order: Jean-Baptiste Say, Adam Smith, Ricardo (in the French edition, with critical notes by Say), James Mill, John Ramsay MacCulloch, and Pierre Boisguillebert. It was in Adam Smith's work that Marx first encountered the classical definition of value. He transcribed the following passage from *The Wealth of Nations:* "It was not by gold or by silver, but by labor, that all the wealth of the world was originally purchased; and its value, to those who possess it, and who want to exchange it for some new productions, is precisely equal to the quantity of labor which it can enable them to purchase or command." [3] But he adds no comment, reserving his criticism for another passage, in which Smith deduced the division of labor from a need for exchange, the existence of exchange depending in its turn on the previous existence of the division of labor.[4]

It is when Marx tackles Ricardo that he develops his polemic against the labor theory of value. He does this by following step by step the polemic Engels had already developed on the same subject in his *Outlines of a Critique of Political Economy.* The value of commodities is still conceived as identical with their price. It is made up of an element contributed by labor and another element supplied by the materials on which labor works. Marx approves of Proudhon's remark that rent and profit are "superadded" and thus are a factor in bringing about increases in price.[5] He agrees when Say reproaches Ricardo with leaving out the role of demand in determining value. He reduces the law of supply and demand to two phenomena of competition: competition between manufacturers, which determines supply, and competition between consumers, which determines demand. But he concludes, criticizing Say, that this latter breaks down in practice into considerations of fashion, caprice, and chance.[6] And he does not at all accept the "law of markets," which postulates an ultimate identity between supply and demand, making incomprehensible the phenomenon of periodical crises.

3. Adam Smith, *The Wealth of Nations,* Book I, pp. 30–31; quoted by Marx in *MEGA,* I, 3, p. 460.

4. *MEGA,* I, 3, p. 458.

5. Ibid., p. 501.

6. Ibid., p. 493.

Marx's fundamental complaint about the labor theory of value, however, is that political economy is obliged not to take account of competition. Yet competition is a reality. In order that its laws may have greater cohesion, political economy is thus forced to regard reality as accidental and abstraction alone as real.[7]

This objection is all the more valid in Marx's eyes because he blames political economy precisely for *concealing a relationship of exploitation*, contained in the institution of private property, behind abstract juridical considerations. If in the case of private property it is necessary to come down from abstract principles to tangible reality in order to grasp the nature of "civil society," why should the same procedure not be appropriate in the sphere of value? There also the world of abstract conceptions must be abandoned in favor of "phenomenological reality," that is, the world of prices.[8]

Marx adds to this criticism of the labor theory of value a very shrewd remark about "labor value" in Ricardo's theory. "At the beginning of this chapter the philanthropic Ricardo presents the means of subsistence as the natural price of the worker, and so equally as the sole aim of his labor, since he works in order to get wages. What then becomes of his intellectual faculties? But Ricardo seeks only [to confirm] the distinctions between different classes. This is the usual circular argument of political economy. The aim is spiritual freedom. Therefore it is necessary [to impose] spiritual slavery on the majority. Physical needs are not the only aim [of life]. They therefore become the only aim for the majority." [9]

---

7. Ibid., p. 502.

8. See also Rosenberg, *Die Entwicklung*, pp. 92–93.

9. *MEGA*, I, 3, p. 504. Joachim Bischoff, in a review of this book published in *Das Argument* in October 1969, says that it is at least "questionable" to present the development of Marx's economic thinking as proceeding from rejection to acceptance of the labor theory of value. He justifies his doubts by analyzing a mere two passages from Marx and not by analyzing Marx's manuscripts of 1844 as a whole, which put my conclusion beyond doubt. After my book appeared I received the interesting and thorough study made by Walter Tuchscheerer, a young scholar in the German Democratic Republic who died prematurely, an analysis which confirms in all respects my own analysis of this period of Marx's economic thought. (*Bevor "Das Kapi-*

In the same context, Marx later bursts out at Ricardo's declaration that only the net income (presented as the sum of profit and rent) of a country matters, and not its gross income. "In the fact that political economy denies any importance to gross income, that is, to the amount of production and consumption, leaving aside what is superfluous, and that it thereby denies any importance to life itself, its abstraction reaches the peak of infamy. Here we perceive (1) that political economy is not in the least concerned with the national interest, with man, but solely with a net income made up of profit and rent, that it regards *that* as the ultimate aim of the nation; (2) that man's life has no value in itself; (3) that more particularly the value of the working class reduces to its essential cost of production, and it is there merely to [produce] profit for the capitalists and rent for the landowners." [10]

However, as soon as he examines the criticisms of Ricardo's thesis made by Say and Sismondi, Marx takes a step forward. What these two economists deny, he says, is the cynical expression of an economic truth.[11] In order to fight against the inhuman consequences of political economy, Say and Sismondi must go beyond its limits. Humanism is, therefore, something outside the science of political economy, which is thus not a human science. Despite the vigor of polemical expression, Marx is here beginning to *defend* Ricardo against his critics, to grasp that what seems cynicism is really a frank recognition of the realities of the capitalist mode of production, which other writers seek to conceal.

When he comments on the writings of James Mill, Marx resumes his complaints against "Ricardo and his school." They leave out of the picture *reality*, which shows a disparity between costs of production and exchange value, and confine themselves to an "abstract law." These notes, however, already mark a second step

---

tal" entstand, pp. 94–96, 115, *et seq.*) The same is true for a work by a Soviet author which appeared after mine, Witali Solomonowitsch Wygodski's *Die Geschichte einer grossen Entdeckung: Über die Entstehung des Werkes "Das Kapital" von Karl Marx.*

10. *MEGA*, I, 3, p. 514.

11. Marx was to use the same expression regarding the "cynical Ricardo" in an article published in *Vorwärts* of August 7 and 10, 1844. ("Kritische Randglossen zum Artikel: 'Der König von Preussen und die Sozialreform,'" in Mehring, ed., *Aus dem literarischen Nachlass*, Vol. II, p. 45.)

forward: Marx does not entirely reject the "abstract law," but regards it as merely "a moment of the real movement." When supply and demand balance each other, it is indeed cost of production that determines price. But supply and demand balance each other only by way of exception, owing to their oscillations and disequilibrium. Political economy ought therefore to explain the real movement, which represents a dialectical unity of correspondence and noncorrespondence between cost of production and exchange value.[12]

Marx's comments on the classical economists in his Parisian reading notes determine his attitude to the labor theory of value in his writings of 1844 and 1845—specifically in the *Economic and Philosophic Manuscripts* and *The Holy Family*. Labor value and price continue to be separated from each other: the former is declared "abstract" while only the latter is "concrete." In addition, as we pointed out earlier, in *The Holy Family* the labor time that the production of a commodity has cost is regarded as "forming part" of its "cost of production"; the latter is not reduced to the former.

But by the time he had finished writing *The Holy Family*, Marx had already drawn up a plan for another work, a "Critique of politics and political economy." On February 1, 1845, he signed a contract for this book with the publisher C. W. Leske, and the *Economic and Philosophic Manuscripts of 1844* were doubtless a first draft. As early as January 20, 1845, Engels was urging him to finish his book on political economy,[13] which shows that Marx already had a book of this kind on his workbench. The manuscript seems to have been lost;[14] it still existed in 1847, since in his letter to Annenkov of December 28, 1846, Marx wrote: "I wish I could send you my book on political economy with this letter, but it has so far been impossible for me to get this work . . . printed." [15]

In order to write it, Marx left his exile in Brussels for a six-week visit to Britain with Engels, and there studied all the books on political economy he was able to find in Manchester,[16] both at his

---

12. *MEGA*, I, 3, pp. 530–531.
13. Ibid., III, 1, p. 10.
14. Rosenberg, *Die Entwicklung*, pp. 279–280.
15. *Selected Works*, Vol. I, p. 527.
16. *Aus dem literarischen Nachlass*, Vol. II, p. 332.

friend's house and in public and private libraries. It was during this second systematic confrontation with political economy that he discovered the social-revolutionary use that British socialist writers had been able to make of the labor theory of value, and of the contradictions it contains as expounded by Ricardo. Among the writers he studied in Manchester in July and August 1845 were T. R. Edmonds and William Thompson,[17] who had used Ricardo's propositions in just that way. (After August he read John Bray, another writer in the same category.) Marx was later to criticize the analysis of labor value as creating a "right of the worker to the whole product of his labor," but it is more than likely that studying these authors made him realize the reasons, belonging to the realm of apologetics, why bourgeois political economy in Britain had turned away from Ricardo.

There is no proof that Marx had yet read Thomas Hodgskin and Piercy Ravenstone, Ricardo's two best proletarian disciples. But Engels, who had studied working-class agitation in Britain in great detail in order to write his *Condition of the Working Class in England*, at least knew of the effect these writers had had on the working class and on the bourgeoisie.

Ronald L. Meek writes: "Thomas Hodgskin was a name to frighten children with in the days following the repeal of the Combination Laws in 1824. It was probably inevitable, therefore, that many of the more conservative economists should come to regard Ricardo's theory of value not only as logically incorrect but also as socially dangerous. 'That labor is the sole source of wealth,' wrote John Cazenove in 1832, 'seems to be a doctrine as dangerous as it is false, as it unhappily affords a handle to those who would represent all property as belonging to the working classes, and the share which is received by others as a robbery or fraud upon *them*.' "[18] Marx, who had begun by regarding Ricardo as "cynical," could not but be struck by this abandonment of Ricardo's theory of value—cynical in a different way—for the sake of preserving the social order. I am convinced that he returned from Manchester to Brussels with much more favorable views on the labor theory of value.

---

17. *MEGA*, I, 6, pp. 597–622.
18. Ronald L. Meek, *Studies in the Labor Theory of Value*, p. 124.

A brief remark added by Marx to his notes on reading the economist Charles Babbage, written in June or at the beginning of July 1845, on the eve of his departure for Manchester, shows that he still at that time maintained a certain neutrality toward the theory in question.[19] But *The German Ideology*, written in spring 1846, contains two definite passages which mark the acceptance of the labor theory of value. There we read, on the one hand: "He [Stirner] has not even learned from competition the fact . . . that within the framework of competition *the price of bread is determined by the costs of production and not by the whim* of the bakers." [20] And on the other hand, Marx and Engels write even more clearly: "And even as regards coin, it is determined exclusively *by the costs of production*, i.e., *labor*." [21] The conclusion seems inescapable: it was after July 1845 and before finishing *The German Ideology* in the spring of 1846 that Marx and Engels were decisively won over to the labor theory of value.

It would obviously be unjust to the two friends to suspect them of changing their stand on the Ricardian theory merely on account of the *agitational value* of this theory which Marx's visit to Manchester had revealed to him. If they were able, in the course of half a year, to advance from the eclectic conception Engels had held in his *Outlines of a Critique of Political Economy* to a more precise conception of the labor theory of value—indeed, to a conception which already starts to correct certain intrinsic weaknesses in Ricardo's theory—this was above all due to the more thorough economic studies Marx had undertaken and to his transcending analytically the contradictions he had previously thought he had discovered in the labor theory of value.

This transcendence can be easily appreciated in the following terms. What had shocked Marx when he first encountered Ricardo and the whole classical school was the apparent conflict between the effects of competition—the price fluctuations resulting from the operation of the law of supply and demand—and the comparative stability of "exchange value," determined by the amount of labor needed for production. On reflection, however, his mind,

---

19. *MEGA*, I, 6, p. 601.
20. *The German Ideology*, p. 404. (Emphasis mine.—E.M.)
21. Ibid., p. 437. (Emphasis mine—E.M.)

solidly grounded in dialectics, was bound to ask whether what was apparent was really the most direct expression of reality—and whether an "abstraction" might not contain a truth that was in the last analysis much more "concrete" than the appearance.

Market prices constantly vary. If, however, one looks no further than these fluctuations, one runs the risk of quickly dissolving all economic movements in mere chance.[22] But a moment's thought, together with the empirical study of economic reality, show that these fluctuations do not occur at random but around a definite axis. If the selling price of a product falls below its cost of production, its manufacturer is pushed out of competition. If the selling price of the same product rises too much above the cost of production, the manufacturer makes a super-profit which attracts additional competitors to this branch of production and causes a temporary overproduction which brings prices down again. The cost of production is found empirically to be the axis around which prices fluctuate.

It is interesting to refer in this connection to a critical comment which Marx was moved to make when re-reading Ricardo in 1851: "Here he admits, then, that it is not a matter of producing 'wealth' in his sense of the word but of producing 'values.' The 'natural price' imposes itself as against the *market price*, but this takes place though a struggle which is nothing like the simple equalization process described by R[icardo]. When industry began, when demand usually corresponded to supply, when competition was limited and monopoly prices were normal in all industries, landed property was constantly being ousted by industrial property. This led to enrichment on the one hand and impoverishment on the other. The struggle between the market price and the real price thus did not result in the same phenomenon, and did not take place to the same extent, as in modern society. There was a permanent excess in the market price over the real price." [23]

In my view, this comment enables us to get closer to the actual way in which Marx advanced from rejecting the labor theory of

---

22. *MEGA*, II, 3, p. 531: "The true law of political economy is *chance*, a few moments of the movement of which we scholars arbitrarily fix under the name of laws."

23. *Grundrisse*, Vol. II, p. 806.

value to accepting it—namely, by analyzing the *tendencies of the historical evolution* of the relations between supply and demand in the capitalist mode of production and their connections with Ricardo's "natural price," that is, with labor value. This analysis was to bring him to conclude that, because of the enormous increase in industrial production, this "natural price" increasingly becomes the rule, while the monopoly price that differs widely from the "natural price" increasingly becomes the exception. As soon as this is accepted, one is obliged to accept the labor theory of value, since it is then established that value is determined not by "the laws of the market," but by factors immanent in production itself.

While concurrently carrying on his economic studies (preparing for the "Critique of politics and political economy," the manuscript which has been lost) and his studies of history and philosophy (preparing for *The German Ideology*), Marx formulated, at about the same period, his theory of historical materialism, which is essentially a socioeconomic determinism.[24] The history of mankind should always be studied in connection with the history of industry and exchange. Mankind starts to differentiate itself from the animal kingdom by *producing* its means of life. What men are depends in the last analysis on the material conditions of their productive activity, and this presupposes social relations among them. The level of development of the productive forces is reflected most obviously in the development of the division of labor.[25]

In other words, the conclusion of their historical and philosophical studies had brought Marx and Engels to exactly the starting point of the classical labor theory of value, which Marx was to reformulate in a quite special way: (abstract) labor is the essence of exchange value, because in a society founded on the division of labor it is the only connecting web that makes possible comparison and commensurability between the products of the

---

24. Paul Kaegi (*Genesis des historischen Materialismus*, pp. 311–327) examines in great detail the origins of the theory of economic determinism and that of ideology, which in his view are the two essential elements of the theory of historical materialism.

25. *The German Ideology*, p. 32.

labor of individuals who are separated from each other. There is a striking parallel between the way in which Marx went back from fluctuating "market prices" to a rediscovery of exchange value and the way in which an economist of our own day, Piero Sraffa, has evolved from marginalism to a theory which ultimately reduces all the "inputs" of production to "dated quantities of labor." [26] Marx and Sraffa proceeded in the same way, *by leaving aside minor, short-term fluctuations*, which are just what marginalism starts from.

When he wrote *The Poverty of Philosophy*, Marx was already a "Ricardian," to the extent that he quotes Ricardo immediately after formulating the determination of the value of a commodity by the amount of labor needed for its production. He quotes the weakest part of Ricardo's theory, that dealing with the determination of the "value" or the "natural price" of "labor" by the costs of "maintenance" of working men.[27]

But at the same time, Marx is already separating himself from Ricardo on an essential point. Writing to Annenkov on December 28, 1846, he speaks of "the error of the bourgeois economists, who regard these economic categories as eternal and not as historical laws which are only laws for a particular historical development, for a definite development of the productive forces." [28] Working out his theory of historical materialism had at one and the same time enabled him to grasp the "rational kernel" of the labor theory of value and its *historically limited character*. This conception of the historically limited character of economic laws became a no less integral part of Marxist economic theory than the labor theory of value.[29]

In Marx's view this historically limited and precise character applies to all the "economic categories"; he sees in them, in the last analysis, only a *certain social relationship*. This is clear as re-

26. Piero Sraffa, *Production of Commodities by Means of Commodities*, pp. v–vi, 34–40, 93–95, etc.

27. *The Poverty of Philosophy*, p. 50.

28. *Selected Works*, Vol. I, p. 522.

29. Professor Emile James sees in this a lasting and valid contribution to economic science. (See Emile James, *Histoire sommaire de la pensée économique*, pp. 168, 177.)

gards the category "exchange value" as early as *The German Ideology* and *The Poverty of Philosophy*. In his later writings Marx constantly returns to this same principle.[30] It is therefore impossible to agree with the attempt recently made by Milentije Popović to proclaim commodity relations valid for all human history, right down to the total disappearance of living labor, and along with them the phenomenon of abstract labor, which Marx sees as the ultimate secret of exchange value.[31]

Marx himself stated his opinion on this question very clearly. He categorically refused to identify the need for an accounting in terms of labor time (which applies to every human society, except perhaps the most advanced stage of communist society) with the *indirect* expression of this accounting in the form of exchange value.[32] And he explicitly declared that when private ownership of the means of production has been replaced by that of the associated producers, commodity production will cease, giving place to direct accounting in hours of labor.[33]

One may think Marx was right or one may try to show that he

30. ". . . articles of utility become commodities, only because they are products of the labor of private individuals or groups of individuals who carry on their work independently of each other." (*Capital*, Vol. I, pp. 72–73.)

31. Milentije Popović, "For the Re-Evaluation of Marx's Teachings on Production and Relations of Production," in *Socialist Thought and Practice* (Yugoslavia), July–September 1965.

32. Cf. Marx's letter to Kugelmann of July 11, 1868: "The form in which this proportional division of labor asserts itself, in a state of society where the interconnection of social labor is manifested in the *private exchange* of the individual products of labor, is precisely the *exchange value* of these products." (*Selected Works*, Vol. II, p. 419.) Cf. also *Capital*, Vol. I, p. 79 (the famous passage on the fetistic nature of value), where Marx declares explicitly that labor time will be the criterion of distribution of products in a socialist society, in contrast to distribution through exchange based on private labor and private property.

33. "Within the cooperative society based on common ownership of the means of production, the producers do not exchange their products; just as little does the labor employed on the products appear here *as the value* of these products, as a material quality possessed by them, since now, in contrast to capitalist society, individual labor no longer exists in an indirect fashion but directly as a component part of the total labor." (*Critique of the Gotha Programme*, in *Selected Works*, Vol. III, p. 17.)

was wrong, but one ought not to ascribe to him the paternity of conceptions that were contrary to his own. One ought not to assert that for Marx all living social labor must necessarily take the form of abstract labor creating value[34] and that socialism will mean not the abolition of commodity production but its "humanization." These ideas of Popović's are opposed to Marx's entire teaching.[35]

---

34. Milentije Popović ("For the Re-Evaluation of Marx's Teachings on Production," p. 79): "Men 'produce their life' by working and producing commodities, use values. By producing they embody, build into commodities their labor, with concrete labor they produce—create—a definite useful object (use value), with abstract labor they produce value." Here and in the rest of his article Popović suggests that for Marx "production relations" and "production of material life" always imply production of exchange value, independent of social conditions and social relations. "In this sense we can say that in society [*sic*] men 'produce their life' not only because they produce useful objects, but also because at the same time they produce values" (p. 83). "Furthermore, relations in production are independent of people's will inasmuch as they are established 'behind the backs of the producers,' outside the conscious activity of producers *or associated producers* . . ." (p. 93; emphasis mine —E.M.). "However, as a result of this the very nature of labor in the abstract—the creator of value—is being changed, and thereby also the nature of living labor. Labor, this creator of value, is no longer a mere [!] consumption of the physical strength of the producers. . . . In this way labor itself, as the creator of value, assumes for man an ever fuller human meaning, in short, it becomes humanized" (p. 104). This is not the place to analyze these propositions, which seem to me highly dubious. But it is plainly false to attribute them to Marx.

"For, proceeding from the fact that the relations [?] of the price of production are objectively given in our conditions of self-management, one arrives at the conclusion that market prices, too, are objectively [*sic*] given in our socioeconomic conditions" (p. 110).

35. Here is a particularly clear-cut passage in Marx, relating to Proudhon but also applicable to Milentije Popović: "The determination of value by labor time—the formula M. Proudhon gives us as the regenerating formula of the future—is therefore merely the scientific expression of the economic relations of present-day society . . ." (*The Poverty of Philosophy*, p. 69.)

4

A First General Analysis
of the Capitalist
Mode of Production

Between the end of 1846 and the beginning of 1848 (in other words, mainly during 1847), Marx and Engels wrote four works which contain a first critical analysis in general terms of the capitalist mode of production. Their study of the great economists of the eighteenth and nineteenth centuries had by now provided them with the picture of the way capitalist economy functions that had been lacking in their earlier writings. In Marx's *Poverty of Philosophy*, in Engels's *Principles of Communism*, in Marx's *Wage Labor and Capital*, and in the *Communist Manifesto* which they wrote together, we no longer find a mere partial view of bourgeois society, concerned chiefly or even exclusively with the misery of the proletariat. Instead we have an impressive picture in which the laws that gave rise to capitalism are examined, its historical merits are analyzed (in particular that of having made possible the abolition of all class divisions, thanks to a marvelous growth in the productive forces), and in which the labor movement and the communist movement are provided with the foundation of an analysis conceived as strictly scientific, the foundation of historical materialism. The views developed in these four works are practically identical, at least as far as economic questions are concerned, and they can therefore be discussed together.

It is not our task to analyze the relations between Marx and Proudhon, on which much has been written. It seems clear that these relations went through three stages: First, there was Marx's sincere admiration for the French socialist, a self-taught worker who was already famous, whose bold style was bound to attract

Marx (he tells us himself of entire nights they spent in discussion together), and from whom he had borrowed in 1843 and 1844 his relentless critique of private property. Then there was profound disappointment that Proudhon had not been able to follow in Marx's footsteps in achieving a serious critical mastery of classical political economy, and that he had instead let himself be drawn into the insipid and sterile utopia of the "labor bazaars" (see Engels's letters of September 16 and 18, 1846)[1] a disappointment that was mingled with genuine indignation when confronted with the confusions and mistakes that were so plentiful in Proudhon's *Philosophy of Poverty*.[2] Finally, twenty years later, there was a calmer judgment, but one that maintains, broadly speaking, Marx's scientifically correct criticism of Proudhon's erroneous propositions.

The Poverty of Philosophy is the prototype of that sort of implacable polemical writing which has often inspired the pens of Marx's followers, though not always with adequate results. In the history of Marxism it constitutes "the first concrete and comprehensive account of the materialist interpretation of history, which hitherto in his writing has been referred to only in passing, sketchily and allusively." [3] It is also "the first economic work that Marx always regarded as an integral part of his mature scientific writing." [4] From the standpoint of the evolution of Marx's economic ideas, it is the first work that offers an overall view of the origins, development, contradictions, and future collapse of the capitalist system, marking in this sense a substantial advance upon the *Economic and Philosophic Manuscripts*. It is significant that what emerges from Marx's criticism of Proudhon's economic conceptions is that he continues along the lines laid down by all the critical work he had so far undertaken, starting with his critique of Hegel's philosophy of right: fighting against the mystification

---

1. *MEGA*, III, 1, pp. 34–35 and 41–42.

2. See in particular *The Poverty of Philosophy*, pp. 32–34, where Marx shows that Proudhon is wrong in asserting, as an absolute fact, that there is a connection between the intensity of a physical need and the growth in the productivity of labor in the production of commodities aimed at satisfying this need.

3. Otto Ruehle, *Karl Marx: His Life and Work*, p. 110.

4. Pierre Naville, *De l'aliénation à la jouissance*, p. 291.

that consists in setting up immutable categories, through abstractions, the result of which is that the given state of things is proclaimed eternal and all its fundamental wretchedness is thus preserved.[5]

Wage Labor and Capital takes up and expands the same ideas, especially as regards the determination of wages. This series of articles, published in the *Neue Rheinische Zeitung* in 1849, is merely a compilation of lectures Marx gave in 1847 to the Brussels workers' association (see Marx's letter to Engels, June 3, 1864).[6]

An unpublished manuscript entitled "Arbeitslohn" (The Wages of Labor) has been found in an exercise book marked "Brussels 1847." It contains developments of Marx's ideas which go further than the text of *Wage Labor and Capital*. It was doubtless the outline of a lecture (or lectures) intended to develop those already given,[7] and also contains Marx's reading notes on the works of about a dozen economists.

It was in *Wage Labor and Capital* that Marx hinted for the first time at the essence of his theory of surplus value, though without using the term or expressing himself precisely. Capital "maintain[s] and multipl[ies] itself . . . by means of its *exchange for direct, living labor power.* . . . The worker receives means of subsistence in exchange for his labor power, but the capitalist receives in exchange for his means of subsistence labor, the productive activity of the worker, the creative power whereby the worker not only replaces what he consumes but *gives to the accumulated labor a greater value than it previously possessed.*" [8]

As for the *Principles of Communism* and the *Communist Manifesto*, these are two outlines for a Communist "profession of faith," the first being written by Engels between October 23 and 27, 1847, for the Paris section of the "League of the Just," and the second begun by Marx and Engels together on the day after the League congress held in November 1847 in London, and completed in January 1848. Both works take up the ideas con-

5. Emilio Agazzi, "La formazione della metodologia di Marx," p. 481.

6. *Der Briefwechsel zwischen Friedrich Engels und Karl Marx, 1844–1883*, A. Bebel and Eduard Bernstein, eds., Vol. II, p. 166.

7. "Arbeitslohn," in *Kleine ökonomische Schriften*, pp. 223–249.

8. Marx, *Wage Labor and Capital*, in *Selected Works*, Vol. I, p. 161.

tained in the two previous works and give them a more succinct
—and now classic—form.

The origin of the capitalist mode of production is traced in
terms that were to undergo no fundamental change, even in
Capital. One of its preconditions is the primitive accumulation
of capital, which was facilitated by the discovery of America
and the importing into Europe of the precious metals of the New
World. This caused a general fall in wages and feudal ground
rent and a considerable increase in profits. At the same time, the
development of overseas and colonial trade enlarged the available markets and increased the production of commodities. A
great number of commodities changed from being luxury products to being articles of more current consumption.

On the other hand, the decline in feudal ground rent compelled
the nobles to dismiss a substantial portion of their retinues. A
mass of vagrants and beggars appeared in the sixteenth and seventeenth centuries for whom the manufactories were to provide
work.[9] These manufactories were not set up by master craftsmen but by merchants, who at first gathered together under one
roof a certain number of producers and instruments of production, saving expense only through exercising better supervision
and insuring better protection of the capitalists from losses
through theft. Later, the division of labor led to an increase in
productivity within the manufactories, until the use of steam
power and the Industrial Revolution gave rise to the large-scale
modern factory.[10]

The mode of production thus engendered represented, above
all, *new social relations of production*.[11] "To be a capitalist, is
to have not only a purely personal, but a social *status* in production. Capital is a collective product, and only by the united action
of many members, nay, in the last resort, only by the united action of all members of society, can it be set in motion." [12]

9. Cf. a remark of Hegel's, written at Jena in 1805: "The factories and
manufactures base their existence precisely upon the poverty of a class of
men." (Quoted in Georg Lukacs, *Der junge Hegel*, p. 423.)

10. *The Poverty of Philosophy*, pp. 137–141; *Communist Manifesto*, in
Selected Works, Vol. I, pp. 110–112.

11. *The Poverty of Philosophy*, p. 135.

12. *Communist Manifesto*, in *Selected Works*, Vol. I, p. 121.

The birth of the capitalist mode of production implies a wonderful advance of the productive forces which could not have taken place without it.[13] Marx and Engels grasped the profoundly revolutionary nature of this mode of production far more precisely and clearly than the other economists of their age, even though these were mostly apologists for capital.[14] They sang a veritable hymn of praise to the glory of capitalism in their *Communist Manifesto,* which nevertheless sounded its knell: "The bourgeoisie cannot exist without constantly revolutionizing the instruments of production, and thereby the relations of production, and with them the whole relations of society. . . . Constant revolutionizing of production, uninterrupted disturbance of all social conditions, everlasting uncertainty and agitation distinguish the bourgeois epoch from all earlier ones. . . . The need of a constantly expanding market for its products chases the bourgeoisie over the whole surface of the globe. It must get a footing everywhere, settle everywhere, establish connections everywhere.

"The bourgeoisie has through its exploitation of the world market given a cosmopolitan character to production and consumption in every country. To the great chagrin of Reactionists, it has drawn from under the feet of industry the national ground on which it stood. . . . The bourgeoisie, by the rapid improvement of all instruments of production, by the immensely facilitated means of communication, draws all, even the most barbarian, nations into civilization. The cheap prices of its commodities are the heavy artillery with which it batters down all Chinese walls, with which it forces the barbarians' intensely obstinate hatred of foreigners to capitulate. It compels all nations, on pain of extinction, to adopt the bourgeois mode of production; it compels them to introduce what it calls civilization into their midst, i.e., to become bourgeois themselves. . . ."[15]

13. *The Poverty of Philosophy,* p. 100.

14. Marx even sees in this "the positive aspect of the wages system," in his "Arbeitslohn" manuscript; in *Kleine ökonomische Schriften,* p. 248.

15. On the civilizing role of capital, see also Engels's *Principles of Communism,* in *Selected Works,* Vol. I, p. 85. In the *Grundrisse* (pp. 311–313) Marx again takes up this idea of the civilizing role played by the capitalist

"The bourgeoisie has subjected the country to the rule of the towns. It has created enormous cities, has greatly increased the urban population as compared with the rural, and has thus rescued a considerable part of the population from the idiocy of rural life. . . . The bourgeoisie keeps more and more doing away with the scattered state of the population, of the means of production, and of property. It has agglomerated population, centralized means of production, and has concentrated property in a few hands. . . . *The bourgeoisie, during its class rule of scarce one hundred years, has created more massive and more colossal productive forces than have all preceding generations together.* Subjection of Nature's forces to man, machinery, application of chemistry to industry and agriculture, steam-navigation, railways, electric telegraphs, clearing of whole continents for cultivation, canalization of rivers, whole populations conjured out of the ground—what earlier century had even a presentiment that such productive forces slumbered in the lap of social labor?" [16]

But this poetic description of the achievements of the capitalist mode of production serves only to underline still more strikingly the contradictions which it at the same time engenders. For capital cannot increase without at the same time developing the proletariat. The concentration of social wealth in the hands of one social class implies a concentration of misery in the condition of another social class.[17] In order to account for this, one must start by analyzing the fundamental element of this wealth, the commodity.

The value of a commodity is determined by the labor time necessary for its production.[18] Now, capital has transformed la-

mode of production, the first mode of production since the origin of human society that was to show a tendency to spread over the entire world, or rather, to embrace the entire world in its domain.

16. *Communist Manifesto*, in *Selected Works*, Vol. I, pp. 111–113. (Emphasis mine—E.M.)

17. *Principles of Communism*, in *Selected Works*, Vol. I, p. 89.

18. In their writings of 1846–1848, Marx and Engels do not yet distinguish between *socially necessary* labor time and labor time *tout court*. Nor do they distinguish between labor power and labor, speaking of the "sale of labor," the "price of labor," and so on, a formula that Marx was to correct toward the end of the 1850's, especially in the *Grundrisse* and the *Theories of*

bor itself into a commodity, since the proletarians possess nothing but the labor power that they have to sell in order to obtain the means of subsistence, which are all in the hands of the capitalists. This labor power will thus itself be treated as a commodity and, like any other commodity, its value (in 1847 Marx still constantly uses Ricardo's term, "natural price") will be determined by the amount of labor needed for its production—in order to produce the means of subsistence "indispensable to the constant maintenance of labor, that is, to keep the worker alive and in a condition to propagate his race." [19]

This wage is essentially kept at this *minimum* level through *competition among the workers*. While retaining Ricardo's conclusions about wages, Marx and Engels go far beyond them in their analysis. They make the level of wages depend on the *rhythm of capital accumulation*.[20] And they amend the rigid conclusions of Ricardian theory by pointing out that wages do not remain stable but fluctuate, and that the "subsistence minimum"—the price of the means of subsistence necessary for the reproduction of labor power—results from a *temporary raising* of wages above this minimum during periods of high conjuncture and their *temporary fall* below this minimum during periods of crisis and large-scale unemployment.[21]

Nevertheless, although Marx and Engels accept that wages may rise above subsistence level during periods of high conjuncture and that it is only thanks to this circumstance that the workers are able to participate even to a small extent in the progress of civilization, they discover a tendency for this wage minimum, this price of labor-power, to *decline*, and this in ab-

---

Surplus Value. Engels draws attention to this correction in the prefaces he wrote thirty years later for *The Poverty of Philosophy* (1884) and *Wage Labor and Capital* (1887).

19. *The Poverty of Philosophy*, p. 51. See also *Principles of Communism*, in *Selected Works*, Vol. I, pp. 83 and 86; "Arbeitslohn," in *Kleine ökonomische Schriften*, p. 223; *Wage Labor and Capital*, in *Selected Works*, Vol. I, p. 158; *Communist Manifesto*, in *Selected Works*, Vol. I, p. 114.

20. "Arbeitslohn," in *Kleine ökonomische Schriften*, pp. 231–232.

21. Ibid., p. 235. See also *Principles of Communism*, in *Selected Works*, Vol. I, p. 87; "On the Question of Free Trade," Appendix to *The Poverty of Philosophy*, p. 220.

solute terms: "Thus, as means are constantly being found for the maintenance of labor on cheaper and more wretched food, the minimum of wages is constantly sinking." [22] This same idea is illustrated in *The Poverty of Philosophy* by the example of cotton replacing flax, potatoes replacing bread, and spirits replacing wine.[23] Later, Marx was frequently to cite the role played in this connection by the introduction of tea into the diet of the British working class.

In short, Marx and Engels still believed in a general law of *long-term decline in wages*—a position they were later to correct—and Marx defined this law, in the "Arbeitslohn" manuscript and in *Wage Labor and Capital*, by the following features: the minimum wage in different countries is different, but it tends to equalize at the lowest level. When wages fall and then recover (in the phase of high conjuncture following that of depression), they never reach the level previously lost. Competition among the workers increases constantly and tends to lower the minimum wage; taxes and the deceptions practiced by tradesmen work in the same direction. In short, "in the course of time, the workers' wages decline in a twofold sense: first relatively, in comparison with the development of wealth generally; and second, in the absolute sense, the sense that the amount of goods the worker receives in exchange becomes smaller and smaller." [24]

At the same time, taking up an idea that the economist John Barton had been the first to formulate,[25] Marx worked out a law of *capital accumulation* which was destined to play a particularly fruitful role in his subsequent work: "It is then a general law that necessarily follows from the nature of the relations between capital and labor, that during the growth of the productive forces the part of productive capital which is transformed into machinery and raw materials, that is, capital as such, grows proportion-

---

22. "On the Question of Free Trade," in *The Poverty of Philosophy*, p. 221.

23. *The Poverty of Philosophy*, pp. 62–63.

24. "Arbeitslohn," in *Kleine ökonomische Schriften*, pp. 233–234. It is this passage that enables one to speak of the young Marx as maintaining a theory of impoverishment both absolute and relative. We shall see later what became of this theory while Marx was preparing *Capital*.

25. Marx, *Theories of Surplus Value*, Part II, pp. 576, *et seq.*

ately faster than the part [of capital] which is devoted to wages; in other words, the workers are obliged to make do with an ever smaller share of productive capital as a whole. The competition among the workers becomes thereby all the more acute." [26]

What we have here is nothing less than *a first sketch of the law of the increase in the organic composition of capital,* from which follows the law of the tendency of the average rate of profit to fall, one of the fundamental laws of development of the capitalist mode of production which Marx was to discover a few years later. Let us note in passing that the concluding phrase of the quotation just given contains an error in reasoning. The fact that wages (variable capital) constitute an "ever smaller" fraction of productive capital as a whole does not necessarily imply that the share of this mass of wages that comes *to each worker* declines in absolute value. That actually depends on a whole series of independent variables: the rhythm of increase of productive capital as a whole compared with the rhythm of increase of the organic composition of capital (if, for example, total productive capital increases by 20 percent every year, while the relative share of variable capital is reduced by 10 percent each year, then the variable capital increases in absolute value); the rhythm of absolute growth of variable capital, compared with the rhythm of growth of the wage-earning labor force (if variable capital increases in absolute terms by 10 percent each year, while the size of the wage-earning labor force increases by 5 percent only, the average share received by each wage earner may actually increase); the rhythm of progress of the rate of surplus value, compared with that of productive capital; etc.

The fact that the evolution of capitalism implies a simultaneous concentration of wealth and misery at the two poles of society is already felt by Marx and Engels to be one of the causes of the periodic crises of overproduction: "Society suddenly finds itself put back into a state of momentary barbarism; it appears as if a famine, a universal war of devastation had cut off the supply of every means of subsistence; industry and commerce seem to be destroyed; and why? Because there is too much civilization,

---

26. "Arbeitslohn," in *Kleine ökonomische Schriften*, p. 242.

too much means of subsistence, too much industry, too much commerce." [27]

"The employer cannot employ the workers because he cannot sell his products. He cannot sell his products because he has no customers. He has no customers because the workers have only their labor to exchange and that is just what they cannot exchange [at that moment]." [28]

Furthermore, Marx and Engels present both the periodic crises of overproduction and the cyclical course generally taken by capitalist production as the result of the anarchy of production and free competition: "This true proportion between supply and demand . . . was possible only at a time when the means of production were limited, when the movement of exchange took place within very restricted bounds.[29] With the birth of large-scale industry this true proportion had to come to an end, and production is inevitably compelled to pass in continuous succession through vicissitudes of prosperity, depression, crisis, stagnation, renewed prosperity, and so on." [30]

Similarly in the *Principles of Communism:* "Free competition, the essential result of large-scale industry, soon assumed thanks to the facility of production an extremely intense nature; a great number of capitalists applied themselves to industry, and very soon more was produced than could be utilized. The result was

---

27. *Communist Manifesto,* in *Selected Works,* Vol. I, p. 114.

28. "Arbeitslohn," in *Kleine ökonomische Schriften,* p. 232.

29. This is what Proudhon did not understand when he dreamed of re-establishing competition after the abolition of capitalism. "Competition and association support each other," he wrote in his *Philosophy of Poverty* (1867 edition, Vol. I, p. 208). Marx warned him that if he wished to re-establish the reign of competition in a socialist society, he would risk reproducing the whole train of misery and anarchy which individual exchange and competition bring about in capitalist society. If progress without anarchy is wanted, then "in order to preserve the productive forces, you must abandon individual exchange." (*The Poverty of Philosophy,* p. 68.)

Daniel Guérin, although he tries to rehabilitate Proudhon as "the father of self-management" (i.e., of management of each factory by its workers), is obliged to give general endorsement to this Marxist criticism. (See Daniel Guérin, *Anarchism,* p. 54.)

30. *The Poverty of Philosophy,* p. 68.

that manufactured goods could not be sold, and a so-called trade crisis ensued." [31]

It should be observed that Marx does not note, except in passing, the consequences of capitalist competition as far as the equalization of the rate of profit is concerned. [32]

The crises of overproduction show that capitalist property relations and production relations have in their turn become fetters on the development of the productive forces. The capitalists strive to escape from these crises by reducing the value of, or even destroying a mass of, productive forces, and by seeking fresh markets. By doing this, however, they only pave the way for still more serious crises in the future. [33]

From that moment onward the weapons that the bourgeoisie has forged to fight against feudalism turn against it. Capital has created a social class within bourgeois society—the proletariat—which is revolutionary, if only because its conditions of existence become more and more unbearable. [34] Now, this proletariat, concentrated in large enterprises where it begins by tearing itself apart in mutual competition among all its members, becomes conscious of the need to organize in order to defend its wages. Thus, a working-class combination pursues the twofold aim of abolishing competition among workers in order to wage an even more difficult competition with the capitalists. In this class struggle the proletariat forms a class "for itself." [35]

Its struggle to defend its wages soon becomes transformed into a political struggle aimed at abolishing the wage system and creating a new society based on collective ownership of the means of production and free association of all the producers. This society can come about only at a high level of development of the productive forces, and it will see a fresh advance in their development which will make it possible to satisfy all the needs of the producers and insure the all-round development of every individual. [36]

---

31. *Principles of Communism*, in *Selected Works*, Vol. I, pp. 86–87.
32. *The Poverty of Philosophy*, p. 167.
33. *Communist Manifesto*, in *Selected Works*, Vol. I, p. 114.
34. *Principles of Communism*, in *Selected Works*, Vol. I, p. 87.
35. *The Poverty of Philosophy*, pp. 172–173.
36. *Principles of Communism*, in *Selected Works*, Vol. I, p. 94.

We have seen that the four works analyzed in this chapter constitute a first general critique of the capitalist mode of production, a first concrete application of the general method of historical materialism to a particular society, bourgeois society. The synthesis of sociology and economic science that Marx endeavored to accomplish derives its enormous superiority from the fact that it is based on a synthesis of the logical (dialectical) method with the historical method.[37] No other theory has so far achieved a synthesis which comes anywhere near the practical success of the Marxist method.

Recently the American sociologist Talcott Parsons has tried to effect a comparable synthesis. Within the framework of a highly formalized sociology and a general theory of action, he treats the economy as a special feature of a "social system" specialized in increasing the "adaptability" of the wider system.[38] This attempt at a synthesis can be considered a failure for three fundamental reasons: its largely unhistorical character, its inability to grasp the basically contradictory nature of every "social system" (and of all reality), and its rather clearly apologetic tendency in relation to the reality of present-day capitalism (monopoly capitalism, which has closely integrated the state with itself, or neo-capitalism).

Talcott Parsons alleges, to be sure, that his analysis applies to "any society" and "any" social system.[39] But this ambitious claim does not stand up to historical criticism. When Parsons says that the state of demand and conditions of production change continuously, in all societies, except in "highly traditional" primitive economies,[40] he overturns the teaching of economic history. In fact, these "continuous" changes in demand and conditions of production are only the product of generalized commodity economies—which fill only a very small part of the total history to date of *homo sapiens*. Parsons discovers the origin of "capital"

---

37. See, in this connection, Otto Morf, *Das Verhältnis von Wirtschaftstheorie und Wirtschaftsgeschichte bei Karl Marx;* and Peter Bollhagen, *Soziologie und Geschichte.*

38. Talcott Parsons and Neil J. Smelser, *Economy and Society: A Study in the Integration of Economic and Social Theory,* pp. 6–7, 21, *et seq.*

39. Ibid., p. 83.

40. Ibid., p. 42.

(defined, in the usual way of apologetics, as the totality of society's "fluid" resources: as if a primitive village's stock of seed, or the flocks of a nomadic tribe living at the stage of gentile communism, were "capital"!; as if capital were not a *social relation!*) in the links between the economy and the political collectivity, through generalization of the role played by credit in the epoch of the decline of monopoly capitalism. How then is one to explain the "normal" accumulation of capital in large-scale industry at the dawn of Britain's age of *laissez-faire*, when the role played by credit was clearly secondary, and when, moreover, credit was largely private?

The unhistorical nature of Talcott Parsons's functionalist schema is obvious when one notes that most of his definitions in the economic field are only generalizations (made hardly even a little abstract) of the essential features of a *capitalist* economy, and even of a capitalist economy in a particular phase of its development. Thus, his definition of the economy as striving to attain the "goal" of maximizing production within the framework of the system of institutionalized values[41] (as if there had not been a series of modes of production whose "institutionalized values" implied precisely *deliberate refusal* to "maximize production"!). Or his definition of the "contract" as the central economic institution (as if the contract were not the offspring of *commodity* production).[42]

His inability to grasp the contradictory character of "social systems," and *a fortiori* of "economic systems," is the most important of the three weaknesses of Talcott Parsons's schema. By eliminating *conflicts between social groups* from the foundation of his analysis; by considering the "systems" as tending to "integration," to "lessening of tensions"; by concealing the fact that the dominant "values" of a system do not at all correspond to the interests of all its members but only to those of the dominant minority, Parsons renders himself incapable of explaining either the driving force of historical evolution, which passes from one social and economic system to another (the periodical conflict between the level of development of the productive forces and

41. Ibid., p. 22.
42. Ibid., pp. 104, *et seq.*

the relations of production), or the concrete form that historical evolution takes (the struggle between antagonistic classes and social forces). Whereas the Marxist system enables us to explain historical phenomena as different as the origin of the Asiatic mode of production, the decline of the Roman Empire, the rise of the cities in the Middle Ages, the coming of large-scale industry, the wiping-out of free competition, the outburst of Fascism and its defeat, we would search in vain in Talcott Parsons's formulae for the elements needed in order to understand these varying phenomena. The few remarks about pre-capitalist social contradictions that can be found in *Economy and Society* reveal a lack of understanding which is sometimes almost grotesque.[43]

Talcott Parsons's fundamental thesis comes to grief through his incomprehension of social conflicts and their economic roots. Every "economic system," when it reaches a certain point of development, does not increase but, on the contrary, greatly reduces the adaptability of its "larger social system." The evolution of the Roman Empire after the second and third centuries A.D., or the evolution of China in the eighteenth and nineteenth centuries, provide striking examples in disproof of Parsons's schema.

As for the apologetic character of Talcott Parsons's theory, this is shown especially in the way he deals with the institutional framework of capitalist society. Labor makes the decision—within the workers' "households"!—to offer its "performance" to the "organizations," in exchange for and in consideration of "remuneration" and other "satisfactions." This decision is taken primarily(!) on the basis of a "general socialized motivation." [44] And so on. The fact of a social class with neither resources of its own nor access to means of subsistence, one which thereby suffers

---

43. See the way in which the authors deal with slavery. The slaves are bought and sold on the market "independent of their performance." (Ibid., p. 12.) But as they are human, the slaveowners have always shown some consideration for their family life (p. 137). A short talk with a specialist in the economic history of ancient Rome, or a brief analysis of the economic slave system of the extermination camps run by the S.S., would have saved the authors from writing such enormities.

44. Ibid., pp. 114–115, 121–122. See a lucid analysis of Parsons's tendency to legitimize conformity in Henri Lefebvre, *Position: contre les technocrates*, pp. 144–145.

an economic constraint precedent to any "socialized motivation," any "acceptance of the fact of labor"—the only other solution being death from starvation!—has no place in Parsons's "institutional" analysis. Similarly, one looks in vain for the slightest explanation of the fact that feudal ground rent obviously represents a product of labor not paid for by the nobility, which the latter appropriates, or the slightest attempt to disprove the analogy which can be perceived between the social surplus product in pre-capitalist times and the surplus value produced under the capitalist mode of production.

5

The Problem of
Periodic Crises

Between the *Communist Manifesto* (1848) and final publication of the *Neue Rheinische Zeitung—Politisch-ökonomische Revue* (1850), in which Marx and Engels set out in detail their views on the cyclical course of capitalist production and the crises of overproduction that from time to time shake this mode of production, a period of hardly two years elapsed. But what years these were! The revolution of February 1848 in France; the revolution of March 1848 in Berlin; the return of Marx and Engels to Germany; the first publication of a daily paper, the *Neue Rheinische Zeitung*, in Cologne, edited by the two friends; the first proletarian insurrection in June 1848 in Paris; the first ban on the *Neue Rheinische Zeitung*; the outbreak and defeat of the revolutions in Italy and Hungary; the outbreak and defeat of the revolution in Vienna (where Marx had spent two months preparing the Viennese workers for what was going to happen);[1] the triumph of the counter-revolution in Berlin; the dissolution of the German national assembly; the final banning of the *Neue Rheinische Zeitung*; Marx's expulsion from Germany; Engels's participation in the military campaign waged by the petty-bourgeois democrats in South Germany against the counter-revolutionary forces; the renewed exile of the two friends, this time in England.

After forging and perfecting the communist doctrine as the doctrine of proletarian revolution, the two young thinkers now found themselves plunged into the thick of revolutionary action

---

1. Franz Mehring, *Karl Marx: The Story of His Life*, p. 178.

itself, criticizing the hesitations, the weaknesses, the lack of logic and of courage shown by the petty-bourgeois democrats, and striving to inspire the proletarians with the utmost vigor and boldness, as for the first time they faced their class enemies in open struggle across half of Europe.[2] Like all revolutionaries, Marx and Engels believed passionately in the revolution. Like all revolutionaries, they tended to shout: "So the revolution seems dead? Long live the revolution, which will soon rise again from its own ashes!" But they were men whose minds were too rigorous, too scientific, too inclined to subject all thinking, including their own, to ruthless criticism, for them to remain victims of illusion.

In March 1850 Marx could still write, in an address sent by the Central Council to the Communist League in Germany, that a fresh revolutionary outbreak must be expected in the near future, either as a result of a new upsurge of the revolution in France or else of a war of the "Holy Alliance," waged by reaction as a whole against this revolutionary France.[3] But seven months later, on November 1, 1850, in the "Review of Events Between May and October 1850" published in the May–October 1850 issue of the *Neue Rheinische Zeitung—Politisch-ökonomische Revue*, Marx and Engels wrote: "In the face of this general prosperity, in which the productive forces are developing as exuberantly as is possible within the framework of bourgeois relations, it is not possible to talk of a real revolution. Such a revolution is possible only in periods in which these two factors—namely, modern

2. In a fascinating study, Roman Rosdolsky has shown that Engels's mistaken notion regarding the "peoples without a history" (*geschichtslose Völker*, meaning the small Slavic nationalities), which shows itself throughout the *Neue Rheinische Zeitung* and in many articles written in the 1850's as a result of the role played by the Czechs, Croats, Ruthenes, etc., during the revolution of 1848, was ultimately due to his failure to understand the socioeconomic roots of this role—that is, his failure to understand the problems of the class struggle between the Czech, Slovak, Croat, and Ruthene peasants, on the one hand, and the Polish and Hungarian landowners on the other. ("Friedrich Engels und das Problem der 'geschichtslosen Völker,'" in *Archiv für Sozialgeschichte*, Vol. 4, pp. 87–282.)

3. Marx, "*Ansprache der Zentralbehörde an den Bund*," in *Enthüllungen über den Kommunistenprozess zu Köln* (*Revelations About the Cologne Communist Trial*), p. 128.

productive forces and bourgeois forms of production—come into contradiction with each other. . . . A new revolution is possible only as the result of a new crisis. It is as inevitable as is the latter." [4]

A more profound study of the cyclical course of capitalist production had brought them to this conclusion, which remains valid, at least for the entire upward phase of international capitalism. This study covered in particular the crisis of 1847 and the phase of prosperity that followed (the results of which were recorded above all in the *Neue Rheinische Zeitung*, which from a daily paper became, in 1849, a quarterly review), and the crisis of 1857, which was analyzed in the correspondence between Marx and Engels and in the articles they wrote for the *New York Daily Tribune*.

Even before this—notably in *The Condition of the Working Class in England*, by Engels, in Marx's *Poverty of Philosophy*, and in the *Communist Manifesto*—Marx and Engels had dealt briefly with the problem of periodic crises. In the early reading notes and in the *Economic and Philosophic Manuscripts of 1844*, we see Marx reproaching Ricardo and J.-B. Say for their failure to understand the contradiction between capital's tendency to develop the productive forces without any limit, and the strict limits imposed by capital itself on consumption by the working masses. Even then he distinguished, correctly, between *physical demand* and *effective demand*.[5]

In *The German Ideology* Marx and Engels return to this same distinction, briefly analyzing the reasons why it is possible for currency crises to occur, and pointing out that an overproduction crisis is not caused by physical overproduction but by disturbances in exchange value.[6]

In addition, besides studying the economic cycle, Marx had applied himself to making a more detailed study of the connections between direct economic interests and political tendencies. This study, *The Class Struggles in France, 1848–1850*, also ap-

---

4. Marx and Engels, "Revue—Mai bis Oktober," in *Neue Rheinische Zeitung—Politisch-ökonomische Revue*, May–October 1850, pp. 317–318.

5. *MEGA*, I, 3, pp. 576–577.

6. *The German Ideology*, pp. 434–435, 570.

peared in the *Neue Rheinische Zeitung*. Its importance for the
history of the formation of Marx's economic thought lies in the
fact that it was here that he first explicitly formulated the idea
of collective appropriation of the means of production.[7]

This study led Marx to concern himself with phenomena to
which he had not previously paid much attention. The evolution
of the political attitude of the French peasantry could not be
understood except in relation to the burden mortgages and taxes
represented for them. The different sections of the bourgeoisie
opposed and fought each other because of the predominant form
assumed by the capital of each section respectively: landed property, banks, industrial or commercial property. Economic study
therefore had to abandon abstractions and generalities frequently
in order to become minutely detailed.[8] The almost day-by-day
fluctuations of stock exchange prices, the details of the government's financial policy, were integrated into the analysis. It seems
plain that this increased familiarity with problems of credit and
currency phenomena prepared the two friends for a better understanding of the "industrial cycle."

Marx and Engels had not yet, however, undertaken a systematic study of this cyclical course taken by capitalist production,
of the succession of phases of economic recovery, high conjuncture, prosperity, "boom" (economic overheating), crash, crisis,
and depression. But they did publish periodically in the *Neue
Rheinische Zeitung* a survey of current political and economic
events which increasingly became a real study of the economic
situation. In the second issue of this review—there were only
five issues: January, February, March, April, and May–October,
1850—Marx and Engels stressed the fact that the outbreak of the
revolution of February 1848 in France had had a beneficial effect
on the economic situation in Great Britain, which had been suf-
fering from a depression since 1845. "A mass of commodities de-
pressing the overseas markets had meanwhile gradually found

---

7. Engels, Introduction to *The Class Struggles in France, 1848–1850*, in
Selected Works, Vol. I, p. 188.

8. See in particular the analysis of fiscal measures and of the attitude of
the Bank on the day after the revolution of February 1848, in *The Class
Struggles in France*, in *Selected Works*, Vol. I, pp. 216–218.

outlets. The February revolution had furthermore removed from just these very markets the competition of Continental industry, while British industry did not lose any more by the disturbance of the Continental market, since it would have lost this anyway as a result of the subsequent development of the crisis." [9] As a result, British industry was able to get through the crisis more quickly than had been expected, and in 1849 entered a phase of prosperity which, according to the industrialists, exceeded any previous one.

In their review of the economic situation, Marx and Engels emphasized above all the importance of the "great overseas markets" for the economic situation of Great Britain (and of European industry generally). After mentioning in this connection the impact of the European revolutions on international trade, they bring out the decisive historical importance—"a fact even more important than the February revolution"—of the discovery of gold in California. The passage that follows reveals extraordinary prophetic vision, since Marx and Engels here foresee the digging of the Panama Canal, the shifting of the center of world trade to the Pacific Ocean (which even today is only a tendency), the industrial and commercial superiority of the United States over Europe (which was not to become a fact until more than half a century later), and even the Chinese Revolution! [10]

Whereas in the April issue Marx and Engels were inclined to forecast a new crisis of overproduction,[11] they became more cautious in the May–October issue, in which their "review" is actually a detailed analysis of the entire economic situation of the capitalist world between 1836 and 1850. This analysis already shows both a deeper knowledge of the facts and a general conception of the cycle which recognizes the strategic role played by certain factors.

Thus, the writers emphasize the fact that in Great Britain the

9. Marx and Engels, "Revue," in *Neue Rheinische Zeitung—Politisch-ökonomische Revue*, February 1850, p. 119.

10. Ibid., pp. 120–121. The Chinese "Tai-ping" revolution actually broke out on January 11, 1851, less than a year after Marx and Engels had predicted it.

11. Marx and Engels, "Revue," in *Neue Rheinische Zeitung—Politisch-ökonomische Revue*, April 1850, pp. 213–215.

superabundant investment of capital in railway building gave the impetus to the prosperity of 1843–1845; the expansion of steam navigation toward the Pacific coast of the United States, toward the Pacific Ocean, toward Australia, worked in the same direction. This wave of investments led to the setting up of a number of new enterprises, which in turn led to overproduction. But since prosperity was accompanied by more and more un- bridled speculation, it was speculation rather than overproduction that *seemed* to be the cause of the crisis. Marx and Engels correct a superficial impression and emphasize the fact that the crisis is always in the last analysis a crisis of overproduction.[12]

The international crisis of 1847, which began with the railways, spread later to the sphere of money and trade, where it was ag- gravated by the results of the failure of the potato harvest in Ireland, England, France, the Netherlands, and Belgium in 1845 and 1846, which in turn caused a considerable rise in the price of corn. Marx and Engels thus ascribe marked importance to the interaction between industry and agriculture in the mechanism of the capitalist production cycle.

They ascribe equally marked importance to purely monetary phenomena and to the key role these played in the beginning of the crisis. An initial panic in April 1847, caused by the Bank of England suddenly increasing the bank rate and by the publica- tion of the Bank's weekly balance-sheet which showed that its gold reserves had fallen to £2,500,000, did not mean the collapse of the big banking and commercial houses. This was to come about in August 1847, as a result of the bankruptcy of a series of firms specializing in trade in wheat and colonial produce, fol- lowed by a series of spectacular bankruptcies of banks and brok- ers in October of the same year.

Once more, Marx and Engels stress the role played by real overproduction in the mechanism of the crisis: excessive expan- sion of railway building, on the one hand, excessive imports (and exports) of a number of colonial products, on the other. They emphasize the same mechanism when they analyze the prosperity of 1848–1850 in British industry, which was marked much less

---

12. Marx and Engels, "Revue—Mai bis Oktober," in ibid., May–October 1850, p. 304.

by speculation than by a real expansion of production, especially of the cotton textile industry and its exports, in particular to the countries of the Far East (the authors speak of the Dutch East Indies market, "open" to British trade) and to the Pacific Ocean (affected by the feverish development of California).

Marx and Engels expressed the opinion that the irregular fluctuations of the price of cotton made the British bourgeoisie more and more dissatisfied with their dependence on the cultivation of cotton in the southern United States. They believed that Britain would try to develop cotton growing elsewhere (which was what in fact happened, especially in India and Egypt), and that this competition by free workers would deal a mortal blow to the slavery of the Negroes in the southern United States (a forecast which also proved correct).[13]

They likewise stressed Britain's role as moving force in the unfolding of the cycle in the capitalist world as a whole. It is in Britain that the cyclic movement starts, it is there that the original movement occurs. On the continent of Europe the successive phases of the cycle, which capitalist production goes through afresh each time, appear only as secondary phenomena.[14] Britain is the chief market for all the countries of the Continent, and the ups and downs of the British economic situation cause (with an inevitable delay, of course) corresponding fluctuations in the exports, and thus in the economic situation, of these Continental countries. The situation in the overseas countries—to which British industry exports much more than do the industries of the Continental countries—affects Britain long before it affects the countries of the Continent.

This analysis, which is very subtle and surpasses anything that the academic science of the age had been able to grasp, nevertheless suffers from several shortcomings. The distinction between monetary crises, which are merely reflections of overproduction crises, and "autonomous" monetary crises, which may appear even in periods of prosperity, especially in the sphere of the "automatic mechanisms" governed by the gold standard, is not adequately established. The *duration of the cycle* is grasped in a

---

13. Ibid., pp. 311–312.
14. Ibid., p. 317.

purely empirical way, unrelated to the period of reproduction of fixed capital.

These two inadequacies were on several occasions to cause Marx and Engels to forecast incorrectly the outbreak of a new crisis: in 1852,[15] 1853,[16] and 1855.[17] It was only in 1857 that a crisis eventually broke out, the average duration of the cycle under classical capitalism proving to be not six or seven years, as the two friends had first believed,[18] but seven to ten years, as Marx was to explain at length later on in the *Grundrisse* and in *Capital*.

These two factors played a determining role in the mistakes in economic forecasting made by Marx and Engels in the years 1852 to 1855. An analogy with the duration of the previous cycle (1843–1847) led them to predict, in the *Neue Rheinische Zeitung*, a new crisis for 1852. Monetary questions were principally responsible for the mistaken diagnosis offered in the articles sent to the *New York Daily Tribune*.

Throughout this period, the discovery and feverish exploitation of the gold mines of California and Australia severely upset the working of the money market. As Ryazanov points out in his commentary on the articles of 1852,[19] Marx later on corrected— in the third volume of *Capital* [20]—the impression he had had at this time that the accumulation of gold in the Bank of England

---

15. Ibid., p. 312. See also Marx's letter to Engels of August 19, 1852. (In *Briefwechsel*, Vol. I, p. 334.)

16. "Pauperism and Free Trade: The Approaching Commercial Crisis," article sent on October 15, 1852, to the *New York Daily Tribune* and published November 1.

17. Series of articles published under the title: "The Commercial Crisis in Britain," in the *Neue Oder-Zeitung* of January 11 to 22, 1855, and in the *New York Daily Tribune* of January 26, 1855.

18. "As a matter of principle in political economy, the figures of a single year must never be taken as the basis for formulating general laws. One must always take the average period of from six to seven years—a period of time during which modern industry passes through the various phases of prosperity, overproduction, stagnation, crisis, and completes its inevitable cycle." ("On the Question of Free Trade," Appendix to *The Poverty of Philosophy*, p. 214.)

19. D. Ryazanov, in *Gesammelte Schriften*, Vol. I, p. 453.

20. Marx, *Capital*, III, 2, pp. 501–502.

could only result from fluctuations in the balance of trade, closely linked with the economic situation in Britain and internationally. This accumulation might also result from a sudden increase in the production of gold, and its shipment to Britain, which could exercise an autonomous influence on the economic situation. Here we touch on one of the aspects of the *twofold nature of gold:* it is both the universal equivalent of all commodities (a function which it seems to fulfill independently of its intrinsic value) and itself a commodity, a metal produced by human labor, the value of which varies with the development of productivity in the gold-mining industry. A few years later, when Marx wrote the first chapters of *A Contribution to a Critique of Political Economy*, he was to draw attention to this contradictory phenomenon.

In 1852 Marx was still arguing by mere analogy: since the history of crises teaches us that the accumulation of an excess of capital in the banks whips up speculation to a frenzy, and that this "overheating" of the economic situation is quickly followed by crisis,[21] the excess of capital existing in 1852 must necessarily signal a crisis in the near future. A few months later, in January 1853, he was already led to correct this impression.[22] But despite this mistaken forecast, the analysis of the economic situation in 1852 contains valid elements, particularly the following pertinent observation which has retained its validity down to our own time: "There never was a single period of prosperity but they [the bourgeois optimists] profited by the occasion to prove that *this time* the medal was without reverse, that the inexorable fate was *this time* subdued. And on the day when the crisis broke out, they held themselves harmless by chastising trade and industry with moral commonplace-preaching against want of foresight and caution." [23]

As for the "crisis" of 1854–1855, Marx's mistake was more excusable because it did not result simply from reasoning by analogy or from abstract deductions. There really was a crisis of overproduction in the cotton textile industry, caused especially by a decline in exports to Australia (where there had been ex-

21. *Gesammelte Schriften*, Vol. I, p. 33.
22. Ibid., pp. 65–71.
23. Ibid., p. 34.

cessive speculation during the two previous years, following the gold "boom"). There were also serious fluctuations in the money market, caused by a sharp fall in the supply of American and Australian gold. A large number of failures of overseas firms brought about the failure of some important British firms. Nevertheless, as D. Ryazanov points out in his commentary on Marx's articles of January 1855,[24] all this did not amount to a *general* crisis but only to a *partial* crisis, during which the *autonomous* role of the monetary factor was again revealed.

In his articles of January 1855 Marx stresses the colossal importance of the American and Australian markets for the expansion of Britain's industrial production and exports. These exports more than doubled between 1842 and 1853 and out of the £100,-000,000-worth of goods exported in 1853, 40 percent went to these two countries (£25,000,000 to the United States; £15,000,-000 to Australia). Now, out of the £45,000,000-worth of British goods exported in 1842, Australia had absorbed less than £1,000,-000 and the United States only £3,500,000 (that is, the two countries taken together had accounted for 10 percent of British exports). Thus *up to 80 percent* of the *increase* in British exports, which amounted to more than £50,000,000 during this decade, was absorbed by these two "new" overseas markets. Since by 1855 this "boom" in exports seemed to have stopped, would not prosperity as a whole be struck a mortal blow? As we see, this time Marx's mistaken forecast had more substantial foundations than the one he had made in 1853.

What the author of *Capital* had underestimated was the stimulating effect of the Crimean War on the economic situation. The experience of history here provides an example of what Rosa Luxemburg was later to call the function that state orders could play as a "replacement market" in relation to external markets.[25] Supplies for the army and the development of war industries largely made up for the setback in exports to Australia. Marx acknowledged this later: in Volume III of *Capital* he classes the years 1854 and 1855 as years of prosperity.

24. Ibid., p. 500.
25. Rosa Luxemburg, *The Accumulation of Capital*, pp. 463–466.

But the following year the analysis of the "overheating," which had first been made by Engels (in a letter to Marx dated April 14, 1856), then by Marx (in a letter to Engels dated September 28, 1856), proved correct.[26] A "magnificent crash" (Engels to Marx, October 29, 1857)[27] followed and opened wide the floodgates of crisis. This time the two friends were equipped with the knowledge and possessed the empirical data they needed in order to follow the development of the crisis step by step. The crisis of 1857–1858 was, moreover, more general in its scope than previous ones: it extended over a wider geographical area and affected all branches of industry.

It was while studying the crisis of 1857–1858 that Marx discovered for the first time the relationship between the duration of the cycle and the renewal period of fixed capital. He put a question about this to Engels in his letter of March 2, 1858, and his friend replied at length two days later.[28] Thus the circle was closed, and Marx and Engels corrected to a ten-year period the mistaken supposition of a six-year cycle they had put forward seven years earlier.

Only China seemed to Marx to provide a possible additional market during the cycle that would succeed the crisis of 1857–1858,[29] and he correctly foresaw that it would not be easy to break down the resistance that Chinese agriculture, archaic and fragmented, would offer to penetration by big capital.[30] But these eight years of study of conjunctural problems had given Marx the conceptual tools with which, in *Capital*, he was to offer if not a complete theory of the capitalist cycle—he did not have the time to write that—at least the main materials with which to build such a theory.

These materials provided important inspiration to those economists of the twentieth century who, beginning with Tugan-Baranovsky—himself a "legal Marxist"—developed various theo-

---

26. *Briefwechsel*, Vol. II, pp. 105–106, 127.

27. Ibid., p. 200.

28. Ibid., pp. 252–254, 255–256.

29. Ibid., pp. 292–293.

30. See his article "Trade with China," published in the *New York Daily Tribune* of December 3, 1859.

ries of what are called periodic crises.[31] Alvin Hansen declares that "Professor Aftalion, like Cassel and Spiethoff, owes a good deal to Marx and to ideas derived from Marx by others. . . . His [Marx's] writings are full of suggestions that have influenced much non-Marxist thinking about cycles, despite the fact that more orthodox writers have not always acknowledged or even realized the extent of their indebtedness to Marx."[32]

This remark applies particularly to those who, like the writers referred to, have built their theories of crises on the duration of the cycle of renewal of fixed capital, or, in other words, on investment activity (accumulation of capital) as the chief moving force behind the crisis. But it applies also to those who have seen the chief cause of the cyclic crises in the underconsumption of the masses. In fact, both of these ideas are found in Marx's work, for the simple reason that, for him, the cause of crisis lies *at one and the same time* in capitalist competition—the irregular nature of capitalist investment—and in the lag that must inevitably occur between the effective demand of the masses and the overall production capacity of society.[33]

31. Michael Tugan-Baranovsky, *Studien zur Theorie und Geschichte der Handelskrisen in England*. This book was critically analyzed by Rosa Luxemburg in *The Accumulation of Capital*, pp. 311–323.

32. In Alvin H. Hansen and Richard V. Clemence, *Readings in Business Cycles and National Income*, p. 129. Cf. also Wassily Leontief, "The Significance of Marxian Economics for Present-Day Economic Theory," in *American Economic Review*, March 1938, p. 3.

33. I have examined this question in more detail in my *Marxist Economic Theory*, Vol. I, Chapter 11.

6

Perfecting the Theory of Value, the Theory of Surplus Value, and the Theory of Money

The crisis of 1857 had reduced Marx's already very meager resources as the *New York Daily Tribune* cut down his contributions to two articles a week. But the crisis had none the less stimulated his enthusiasm and pleasure in work, to the extent that he wrote to Engels on December 18, 1857: "I am [now] doing an enormous amount of work, usually going on until four in the morning." [1] This work focused on two things: a detailed recording of the "facts and events" of the crisis; and a working out of the "fundamental features" of economic analysis.[2] The latter part of these studies was to give birth to *A Contribution to the Critique of Political Economy*, the *Grundrisse*, and the *Theories of Surplus Value*, which together were the works that were directly preparatory to the writing of *Capital*.

For a long time Marx had been cherishing the hope of writing a systematic critique of bourgeois political economy, along with an exposition of his own ideas in the economic sphere. He had referred to this hope in 1851, when he wrote to Engels on April 2 that in five weeks he would have "finished with the whole of the economic shit" in the British Museum library and would then go on to "work out the economy at home." [3] But the need, from

---

1. *Briefwechsel*, Vol. II, p. 219.
2. Cf. Marx's letter to Lassalle of December 21, 1857: "The present commercial crisis has induced me to devote myself now to close study of the fundamental features of the economy, and also to preparing something about this present crisis." (Ferdinand Lassalle, *Nachgelassene Briefe und Schriften*, Gustav Mayer, ed., Vol. III, p. 111.)
3. *Selected Correspondence*, p. 36.

1852 onward, to do journalistic work in order to support himself, together with family difficulties and poor health, delayed his carrying-out this plan for four years. He began writing the *Grundrisse* in September 1857.[4] Maximilien Rubel notes that between August 1852 and the end of 1856 Marx was obliged to abandon his economic studies.[5]

The fact that Lassalle was able to find a publisher who would bring out Marx's economic work in installments stimulated him to finish writing it, but even so he did not have the first installment (*A Contribution to the Critique of Political Economy*) ready until January 21, 1859, and when he told Engels of this, he could not help but sigh: "I don't suppose anyone has ever written about 'money' and suffered such a lack of it himself." [6]

It was between these two dates, December 18, 1857, and January 21, 1859, or more precisely between November 1857 and the end of June 1858, that Marx probably made his most substantial contributions to the development of economic science. He reported them to Engels on March 29, 1858, in a letter which also contained the news that the publisher Duncker had agreed to publish his economic manuscript. He outlined his ideas in a letter of April 2, and summed them up on July 22, 1859: he would attempt to show the specifically social, and not absolute, nature of the capitalist mode of production by starting from its simplest phenomenon, the commodity.[7]

A Contribution to the Critique of Political Economy is best known for its Preface, which summarizes the theory of historical materialism in the author's own words; it is not our task to dwell on it. The work itself has had less impact, from the time it was published until today, owing to its abstract nature. Engels had already complained of this when Marx sketched the main outline for him.[8] All the same, the book does contain most of Marx's specific contributions to the development of economic theory,

---

4. Preface by the Marx-Engels-Lenin Institute to the *Grundrisse*, p. ix.

5. Maximilien Rubel, *Karl Marx: Essai de biographie intellectuelle*, p. 297.

6. Franz Mehring, *Karl Marx: The Story of His Life*, p. 257.

7. *Briefwechsel*, Vol. II, pp. 265–269 and 341. The April 2 letter is in *Selected Correspondence*, pp. 105–109.

8. *Briefwechsel*, pp. 269–270.

which he went on to develop in greater detail in the *Grundrisse*, a work which itself remained unknown to the public until after the Second World War. The *Contribution* was above all an improvement upon the labor theory of value as worked out by the representatives of the classical school: William Petty, Adam Smith, and Ricardo. At the same time, however, it was an improvement on the economic theories that Marx himself had worked out before his new exile in England.

In *Wage Labor and Capital*, as in all Marx's previous writings, the distinction between "labor" and "labor power" had not yet been established. Because of this, Marx had been unable to make a scientific analysis of surplus value, which follows precisely from the discovery of *a specific use value of labor power*. Neither *The Poverty of Philosophy*, nor the *Communist Manifesto*, nor *Wage Labor and Capital* contain the idea of surplus value. Similarly, in these works Marx had not yet conclusively revealed the secret of the *exchange value* of commodities. Though he had been convinced of the labor theory of value from the time of his exile in Brussels, he had not yet learned to distinguish between exchange value and prices of production, or between the latter and market prices.

Thus, in *The Poverty of Philosophy* Marx does not distinguish between exchange value and prices: the latter are nowhere to be found in his analysis. In *Wage Labor and Capital*, the term "exchange value" disappears in its turn, to be replaced by "prices." But what economists[9] had hitherto regarded as an inadmissible contradiction is now understood as an eminently dialectical reality: "It is solely in the course of these fluctuations [of prices] that prices are determined by the cost of production. *The total movement of this disorder is its order*." [10]

It was in his *Contribution to the Critique of Political Economy* that Marx was to bring his theory of value to completion, together with the labor theory of value in general, by formulating his

---

9. Including Marx himself, in his reading notes and in the *Economic and Philosophic Manuscripts*.

10. *Wage Labor and Capital*, in *Selected Works*, Vol. I, p. 157. (My emphasis.—E.M.)

theory of abstract labor, creator of exchange value.[11] He distinguishes between the two forms of labor, "concrete labor," which creates use values, and "abstract labor" (that is, a part of social labor time totally available in a society of private commodity producers who are separated from each other by the social division of labor), which produces exchange values. The two forms of value—use value and exchange value—are based on these two forms of labor. Marx sees this analysis of commodities as the culmination over a century and a half of the evolution of classical political economy.[12] And after developing his own analysis in detail, he endeavors to show the concrete historical course by which economic science has arrived at a correct conception of the nature of exchange value, giving his due to each of the great economic thinkers of the eighteenth and the beginning of the nineteenth centuries but not failing either to emphasize the shortcomings of each analysis. The small sub-chapter of the *Contribution to the Critique of Political Economy* entitled "Notes on the History of the Theory of Commodities" is thus a summary of a work devoted to "theories of value," and serves as preface to *Theories of Surplus Value*.[13]

The two pages which summarize the criticisms usually advanced against Ricardo's theory of value[14] constitute at the same time a summary of Marx's own contributions to the development

11. In the Preface, Marx describes the dialectical method which had enabled him to discover the category of abstract labor. (*Selected Works*, Vol. I, pp. 502–506.) Naville emphasizes, with justification, that this category can already be found in other authors' works, notably in those of Hegel and Adam Smith. (See *De l'aliénation à la jouissance*, p. 399.) Marx himself mentions that Benjamin Franklin had gone a long way toward discovering the category of abstract labor. (See *A Contribution to the Critique of Political Economy*, p. 62.) Rosdolsky points out that in Ricardo's writings the *specific* character of abstract labor as creator of value—distinct from that of concrete labor as producer of use values—is not analyzed. (See Roman Rosdolsky, "Ein neomarxistisches Lehrbuch der politischen Ökonomie," in *Kyklos*, No. 4, 1963, p. 642.)

12. *A Contribution to the Critique of Political Economy*, p. 56.

13. I do not propose in this study to discuss the *Theories of Surplus Value*, which is regarded as the fourth volume of *Capital* even though it was written before the first volume.

14. *A Contribution to the Critique of Political Economy*, pp. 71–72.

of economic theory. He himself calls them the theory of wage labor (the complement of the theory of surplus value); the theory of capital; the theory of competition; and the theory of ground rent; and he sets out convincing answers to these four criticisms.

If labor is the essence of exchange value, what then is the exchange value of labor? Is it not arguing in a circle to make exchange value the measure of exchange value? This objection is expressed in the following problem: given that labor time is the yardstick of exchange value, how are wages determined? [15] How does exchange take place between capital and labor, on the objective basis of an equal exchange?

Marx answers: "If a day's labor was required in order to keep a worker alive for a day, capital could not exist, for the day's labor would be exchanged for its own product, and capital would not be able to function as capital and consequently could not survive. . . . If, however, a mere half-day's labor is enough to keep a worker alive during a whole day's labor, then surplus value results automatically. . . ." [16]

It is not exchange that creates surplus value, but rather a process thanks to which the capitalist obtains *without exchange*, without equivalent, free of charge, some of the labor time crystallized in value. And this process is nothing other than the enjoyment by the capitalist of the *use value of labor power*, which has the quality of being able to produce value much in excess of the equivalent of its own exchange value, its own cost of upkeep, once given a certain level of productivity of labor, without which the capitalist mode of production would be inconceivable.

Thus it is the subtle distinction between the exchange value and the use value of labor power that becomes the basis of the Marxist theory of surplus value, the chief contribution made by Marx to the development of economic science. [17]

---

15. Ibid., p. 71.

16. *Grundrisse*, p. 230.

17. Marx himself considered his analysis of *surplus value in general*, over and above the specific forms it assumes as profit, interest, ground rent, etc., to be his principal achievement. (See his letter to Engels of August 24, 1867, in *Briefwechsel*, Vol. III, p. 395).

"A *use value* for capital, labor has only *exchange value* for the worker, the [only] exchange value at his disposal. . . . The use value of a thing is as such of no concern to the person who sells it, but only to the person who buys it. The property possessed by saltpeter of being usable to make gunpowder does not determine the price of saltpeter; this price depends on the cost of production of the saltpeter itself, the amount of labor crystallized in it. In the circulation that use values enter into as prices, their exchange value does not result from this circulation, though it is realized in this; it has already been pre-determined, and is merely realized in exchange against money. Similarly with the labor[18] that the worker sells to the capitalist as a *use value*—for the worker it is an exchange value which he wants to realize, but which is already *pre-determined* before the act of exchange takes place. . . . The exchange value of labor . . . is thus also predetermined. . . . It does not depend on the use value of labor. For the worker, it has no use value except in so far as it *constitutes an exchange value*, and not in so far as it *produces* exchange values. For capital, however, it has exchange value only in so far as it has use value. . . . It is clear . . . that the worker cannot enrich himself through this exchange, in so far as he . . . alienates his capacity for labor as a creative power. . . . He alienates his labor as a power capable of producing wealth, and it is capital that appropriates that power. The separation between labor and ownership of the product of labor, between labor and wealth, is

---

18. This passage may seem to justify Pierre Naville's observation that in the *Grundrisse* Marx does not yet distinguish between "labor" and "labor power." (*De l'aliénation à la jouissance*, p. 432.) In fact, though there are some passages in the *Grundrisse*—as in *Theories of Surplus Value*—in which this distinction is indeed not made, there are a large number of other passages where Marx distinguishes quite definitely between labor and "capacity for labor" (*Arbeitsvermögen*), which is synonymous with "labor power." See, in particular, the *Grundrisse*, pp. 200 *et seq.*, 491, 497, 502–503, 565–566, etc. The passage on p. 566 is especially characteristic. Marx speaks of the exchanging of "capacity for labor," of the use value of this "capacity for labor" which is what makes it possible for capital to function as such: "Because capital has effected the exchange of the capacity for labor on a basis of equivalence, it has effected the exchange of [i.e., obtained] . . . labor time without paying any equivalent."

thus already implied in this act of exchange itself." [19]

If the exchange value of a product is equal to the labor contained in it, measured by the labor time, how can the exchange value of a day's labor be different from the product of this day's labor, how can the product of a day's labor be greater than the wages received by the worker for this day's labor? This objection, says Marx, finds expression in the following problem: How can production based on an exchange value determined by pure labor time lead to the exchange value of labor power being less than the exchange value of the products of this same labor power?

The difficulty is resolved through an analysis of *how capital obtains surplus value*. That is to say, it too comes down to the problem of determining the value of labor power in a society in which labor power has become a commodity through the creation of a social class separated from its means of labor, which in turn presupposes the concentration of these means of production as the private property of another social class.

It is this juxtaposition of two social classes, one of which is obliged to sell its labor power to the other, *that transforms labor power into a commodity, and the means of production into capital*. And this transformation is sufficient to explain both the exchange value of this labor power and the necessary difference between the value produced by labor power and its own value, the difference that constitutes surplus value. Without the existence of this difference, the owner of capital would have no interest in buying labor power, nor would the latter be salable.

Theoretically, the problem thus comes down to the distinction between the *exchange value* of labor power (wages, the value of all the commodities needed for the reconstitution of labor power) and its *use value* (which consists in providing its buyer with unpaid labor, beyond the point at which it has produced the equivalent of its own exchange value, the cost of its own upkeep). *Historically*, the problem comes down to an analysis of how the modern proletariat was formed, the creation of an industrial reserve army, the separation of the craftsmen and peasants from their means of labor, the transformation of all the land

19. *Grundrisse*, pp. 213–214.

into private property (abolition of common lands, etc.)—that is, to the creation of a social class obliged by its destitution and insecurity to agree to sell its labor power "at the market price" determined by the law of value.[20]

In order that money may become capital and labor may become wage labor—labor that produces capital—there are needed: "(1) On the one hand, the existence of the capacity for living labor, as something existing in a purely *subjective* sense, separated from the factors of its objective reality, that is, separated both from the *conditions* of living labor and from the *means of existence*, the means of life (food), the means of maintaining the capacity for living labor . . . ; (2) value, or crystallized labor, must, on the other hand, consist in an accumulation of sufficient quantities of use values to create the material conditions not merely for the production of the products or values needed to reproduce or maintain the capacity for living labor, but also to absorb the surplus labor . . . ; (3) a relationship of free exchange—circulation of money—between the two sides, relations between the two poles based on exchange values and not on a relationship of domination and enslavement, that is, a production that does not directly provide means of life for the producers but has to go through the intermediary of exchange . . . So long as the two sides exchange their labor only as *crystallized labor*, the relation between them (with which we are concerned) cannot exist, and it is equally impossible if the capacity for living labor is itself owned as property by the other side . . ." [21]

It is this analysis of the *historically determined* character of

---

20. In his Preface to the *Grundrisse*—published by Kautsky in 1903 in *Die Neue Zeit*—Marx points out that the idea of "abstract labor" could be developed only after modern industry had reached a level of development at which a labor force made up of "factory workers" could actually be easily transferred from one branch of industry to another: "Indifference to the particular form of labor corresponds to a form of society in which individuals can easily pass from one job to another and in which any particular form of labor is accidental so far as they are concerned, and therefore a matter of indifference. . . . This situation is at its most advanced in the life of the most advanced of bourgeois societies, the United States." (*Grundrisse*, p. 25.)

21. *Grundrisse*, pp. 367–368.

surplus value, capital, and wage labor, distinct from all previous forms of class exploitation, that gives the *Grundrisse* its significance in the process of the working out of Marxist economic theory.

If, though, the exchange value of commodities is determined by the labor time they contain, how can this definition be reconciled with the empirically observed fact that the market prices of these same commodities are determined by "the law of supply and demand"? This objection, says Marx, comes down to this: How can market prices be formed that differ from the exchange values of commodities, or, still better, *how is it that the law of value can be realized in practice only through its own negation?*

This problem is solved in the theory of competition of capitals, which Marx developed thoroughly when he wrote the *Grundrisse* by working out the theory of the equalization of the rate of profit and the formation of prices of production, on the basis of competition between capitals. The famous "contradiction" which so many critics have thought they found between Volume I and Volume III of *Capital* is nothing but a vulgar echo of this old objection to Ricardo's theory, counterposing market prices to exchange value.[22] The publication of the *Grundrisse* has deprived this objection of the last trace of validity, since it shows that Marx had already worked out the "solution" given in Volume III of *Capital* before even writing Volume I.[23]

Finally, there is the fourth and last fundamental objection, which Marx himself calls "the apparently most striking objection," advanced against Ricardo's theory: If exchange value is nothing but the labor time contained in commodities, how is it possible for commodities which do not contain any labor time nevertheless to possess exchange value? Or, more simply, where

22. One of the best known of these criticisms regarding this "contradiction" between Volume I and Volume II of *Capital* was made as far back as 1896 by Eugen von Böhm-Bawerk in *Karl Marx and the Close of His System*, pp. 30 *et seq.* It has been repeated many times since—for instance, by Vilfredo Pareto in Vol. II of *Les Systèmes socialistes* (pp. 254–255, 258–259).

23. In his letter to Lassalle of March 11, 1859, Marx had stressed the contradiction between Ricardo's theory of value and his theory of profit. (Marx and Engels, *Briefe über "Das Kapital,"* p. 87.) Marx's theory of the equalization of the rate of profit enables a similar contradiction to be avoided.

does the exchange value of the simple forces of nature come from?[24] The reply to this objection was furnished by Marx's theory of ground rent. (It should be mentioned in passing that for Marx the solution of the problem of the equalization of the rate of profit and that of the problem of ground rent[25] were simultaneous and practically identical, as he shows in his letter to Engels of June 18, 1862.[26])

But hardly had the manuscript of the *Contribution to the Critique of Political Economy* been sent off to the publisher than an urgent immediate task diverted Marx from writing out a "fair copy" of all the economic discoveries he had made during 1858. This was the need to reply to the calumnies that Karl Vogt had spread against him in his pamphlet *Mein Prozess gegen die Allgemeine Zeitung.* One of these, accusing Marx of getting money by writing "hundreds of blackmailing letters" to Germans he had allegedly tried earlier to involve in revolutionary activity, produced such an echo among the liberal bourgeoisie in Germany that it became essential to issue a reply.[27] Marx therefore wrote his pamphlet *Herr Vogt,* and this kept him busy all through 1860. Though he wrote to Engels on February 3, 1860, that he was continuing his work on *Capital* and hoped (once again!) to finish it "in six weeks,"[28] we find no further reference

---

24. *A Contribution to the Critique of Political Economy,* pp. 72-73.

25. Marx worked out his theory of ground rent in the form of a critique of the theories of Rodbertus and Ricardo. He discovered that, contrary to what Ricardo supposed, there is not only a *differential* rent (a super-profit obtained by capital invested in pieces of land which are more fertile than those that bring in the average profit), but also an *absolute* rent, which arises from the fact that the organic composition of the capital invested in agriculture is lower than that of the capital invested in industry; that the capital invested in agriculture therefore obtains a surplus value which does not participate in the equalization of the rate of profit, because property in land prevents the free entry of capital into this sector, and all the capital invested in agriculture thus brings in a super-profit (as compared with the average profit obtained in the other branches of the economy), a super-profit which is appropriated by the landowners.

26. *Briefwechsel,* Vol. III, pp. 77–82.

27. Mehring, *Karl Marx: The Story of His Life,* pp. 288–293.

28. *Briefwechsel,* Vol. II, p. 377.

to his work on economic subjects in his correspondence with his best friend before the letter of June 18, 1862, already mentioned.

Before proceeding to make a more thorough analysis of the *Grundrisse,* a work that was decisive in the formation of Marxist economic theory, we must first draw attention to a final fundamental discovery made by Marx in the period between the autumn of 1857 and the beginning of 1859: the perfecting of the theory of money, achieved through a systematic critique of Ricardo's theory of money. It is mainly embodied in the second, and longest, chapter of the *Contribution to the Critique of Political Economy.*

Marx's completion of the theory of money was simply a logical application of the labor theory of value to money. If the exchange value of all commodities represents nothing but amounts of socially necessary labor, measurable in labor time, then it is obvious that a currency based on precious metals is not merely an intermediary, a mere means of circulation, as Ricardo basically supposed.[29] Gold is itself a commodity and consequently possesses its own exchange value, which is determined by the material conditions under which it is produced.[30]

It follows that the quantity theory of money developed by Montesquieu and Hume, and taken up again by Ricardo,[31] which makes the rise and fall of prices depend on an increase or reduction in the amount of currency in circulation, cannot be valid where the currencies concerned are based on precious metals. These currencies, having intrinsic value, cannot modify *by their own movements* the fluctuations in the prices of other commodities. The latter must be regarded as the *primary* movements, and the rise or fall in the amount of currency in circulation as the *derived* movement: "Hence, prices are not high or low because there is more or less money in circulation, but on the contrary, there is more or less money in circulation because prices are high or low." [32] A general fall in prices causes an ebb of the mass of

29. *Theories of Surplus Value,* Part II, p. 501.
30. *A Contribution to the Critique of Political Economy,* p. 77.
31. Marx himself relies on this theory in his *Poverty of Philosophy,* pp. 87–89.
32. *A Contribution to the Critique of Political Economy,* p. 136.

currency into hoarding, while a general rise in prices brings supplementary masses of precious metal into circulation.

It was above all his study of Thomas Tooke's great work on the history of prices that provided Marx with his material for the critique of Ricardo's theory of money. This was why Marx considered that the discovery of the law of the determination of the amount of money in circulation by the fluctuations of prices constituted "perhaps the only merit" of the post-Ricardian school of political economy.[33]

However, Marx distinguishes clearly between the laws that govern the circulation of metallic currency and those that govern the circulation of paper money, which he calls "currency tokens." "While with a given exchange value of commodities, the quantity of gold in circulation depends on its own value, the value of paper depends on its own quantity in circulation."[34] Here too we face a logical application of the labor theory of value. Paper money, the banknote, is merely an intermediary, a "token," of a mass of gold which has its own value. And if this value is spread over ten times as many banknotes, then obviously each note will represent only one-tenth the amount of gold it is nominally supposed to represent, and consequently prices as expressed in this paper money will increase tenfold in order to preserve equivalence with a certain amount of gold.

In an economy in which the use of money is general, however, money is not merely the *universal means of circulation* of all commodities; it is also the *universal means of payment*. The more the capitalist mode of production develops, the more credit expands and the more the function of money as means of payment increases in importance as compared with its function as means of circulation.[35] Marx emphasizes that *representative money* develops precisely on the basis of this function of money as means of payment, and he deduces from this a general law of the volume of money needed for the two functions—means of circulation and means of payment—to be fulfilled, given the rapidity of the circulation of money in fulfillment of these two functions. This

---

33. Ibid.
34. Ibid., p. 160.
35. Ibid., p. 193.

analysis of the roles played by money concludes with a study of the role of the precious metals as international means of payment.

It is interesting to examine some of the objections that have been raised in recent decades against the labor theory of value as perfected by Marx.[36] In this connection I will deal with the observations of Frank H. Knight, Joseph Schumpeter, Oskar Lange, and Joan Robinson.

According to Knight,[37] a labor theory of value would be justified only if labor were a rigid and non-transferable "factor of production." But the mobility of "labor," associated with the mobility of "other agencies of production," leads to a situation in which various combinations of these "agencies" are possible, and this entails determining their value by their "marginal productivity."

The only trouble is that the value of machines—their cost of production—is perfectly well known.[38] It is wholly independent of the number or value of the commodities these machines can produce. No industrialist, when he buys a piece of equipment, calculates the "surplus of value" that it will bring him. What he calculates is the saving that it will enable him to make in his costs of production (or, if you like, in his net cost per unit). And if one were to question industrialists, nine times out of ten they would say spontaneously that what interests them is "saving labor" (in the United States, machines have long been described as "labor-saving devices").

Every industrialist likewise knows that machines that just lie in the factory without moving do not produce a particle of value; for them to serve in production they have to be set in motion by living labor.[39] It is the latter, and the latter alone, that incor-

36. I have examined the traditional criticisms of the labor theory of value in my *Marxist Economic Theory*, Vol. II, Chap. 18.

37. Frank H. Knight, "Value and Price," in *Encyclopedia of the Social Sciences*, Vol. 15, pp. 218–219.

38. In order to simplify the argument I leave aside the "land factor." This, however, can easily be inserted into the argument without affecting it.

39. How then can we explain the fact that "automatic factories" make a profit, which must come from surplus value? As long as these factories are

porates new value into the commodity; as to the value of the machines and other "agencies," that is merely conserved by living labor, which transfers the equivalent value (wholly or in part) into the commodities it produces. This is also known to industrialists and statisticians, since they speak of an "added value" which is shared between the capitalists and the workers, and which is added to the "conserved value" (raw materials and machinery). The secret of this "added value" must therefore be found in labor alone. And Marx discovered this when he formulated his law of surplus value.

Schumpeter's argument against the labor theory of value and in favor of the theory known as that of "factors of production" is of the same sort. He reproaches supporters of the labor theory of value with being inspired by "ethical philosophies and political doctrines" that have nothing to do with economic reality as such. "In other words, they failed to see that all that matters for this purpose is the simple fact that, in order to produce, a firm needs not only labor but all the things that are included in land and capital as well, and that this is all that is implied in setting up the three factors [of production]." [40]

To be sure, if one wishes to come down to this level of commonplace it should be added that in order to produce a "firm" needs not only labor, land, buildings, machinery, raw materials, and money, but also an organized society, police protection, a state system that includes means of communication, an infrastructure, etc., and many other things as well. Why arbitrarily isolate "three factors of production"? Why not talk of five "factors of production": labor, land, machinery, reserves of liquid money, and state organization, and then discover five "incomes" corresponding to these "factors": wages, ground rent, profit, interest, and taxes?

the exception and not the rule, they make profit without any surplus value being produced within their walls; they merely appropriate some of the surplus value produced by the workers in other enterprises, through the working of competition between capitals. As soon as the phenomenon of complete automation becomes general in all enterprises, profits and surplus value must necessarily wither away. There is indeed no room for a "market economy" under the conditions of obvious plenty created by universal automation.

40. Joseph Schumpeter, *History of Economic Analysis*, pp. 558–559.

The capitalists and their ideologues raise a weighty objection to this: no "real contribution" is made by the state or by organized society to the new value created within the enterprise; they merely provide "external savings," an indispensable general framework. But then one is equally justified in asking whether "land" or "machinery" (not to speak of "liquid money") make any "real contribution" to the creation of new value within the enterprise, because it is recognized by implication that not everything that is a "factor indispensable for production" is thereby *ipso facto* a "source of new value." And we are thus brought back to the problem of the ultimate origin of the value "added" in production, which can only come from living labor.[41]

A more serious and more sophisticated objection is advanced by Oskar Lange in one of his early writings.[42] Lange's argument can be summarized thus: Though Marxist theory has been able to predict correctly the laws of capitalist development, it has not proved able to supply an adequate theory of prices (and especially of monopoly prices), or an adequate theory of the optimum use of resources in a socialist society, or, above all, a theory of crises, because it is fundamentally a "static theory of general economic equilibrium." [43] Moreover, the labor theory of value is incapable of explaining the nature of wages and the survival of profit, which are supposed to be determined by the technical progress inherent in the capitalist system. But this "dynamic" element is not so much a result of the internal logic of the labor theory of value as of the institutional framework of capitalism revealed by Marx. And it is his analysis of this institutional framework, rather than the labor theory of value, that is the source of Marxism's superiority as a tool of analysis for discovering the laws of capitalist development.

It seems to me that Lange's very starting point is mistaken. The labor theory of value cannot be considered a "static theory of

41. It is significant that when economists want to measure real economic progress they are forced to fall back on the progress of the *productivity of living labor* (see Jean Fourastié, *Le Grand Espoir du XXe Siècle*, pp. 7–31) and not on some "productivity of capital" or "productivity of land," whose coefficients of increase they cannot calculate as indices of economic progress.

42. Oskar Lange, "Marxian Economics and Modern Economic Theory," in *Review of Economic Studies*, June 1935, pp. 189–201.

43. *Ibid.*, p. 194.

general economic equilibrium." [44] The labor theory of value, as corrected and perfected by Marx, is indissolubly linked with the theory of surplus value. The two theories taken together, far from constituting a "static theory," form by definition a dynamic theory. They are in fact a synthesis of two opposites, a conception of equal exchange linked with a conception of unequal exchange. It is above all the exchange between labor and capital that possesses this *dual quality*.

Consequently, the "Marxist model" is by nature dynamic, since it leads to the conclusion that the production of new value, the increase in value, economic expansion, economic growth are inherent in the capitalist mode of production. This same Marxist model is not a "theory of general equilibrium" but, again, a synthesis of two opposites, a demonstration of the fact that the permanent (and apparent) disequilibrium of capitalist economic life is based on a more profound equilibrium, which in its turn gives rise to necessary and inevitable disturbances of this equilibrium (periodic crises, tendency of the average rate of profit to fall, concentration of capital, intensification of class struggle) that end by undermining the system.

Lange's idea that the dynamic element (economic evolution) results from the institutional framework rather than from the internal logic of the labor theory of value is also based on a mistake. According to Lange, the element of "technical progress" is necessary if we are to understand why wages do not "threaten to annihilate the employers' profits"; [45] capitalist profit could not go on existing except in a setting of technical progress. Lange forgets that, even without technical progress, wages *cannot* abolish profits because the capitalists *stop hiring workers* long before this point is reached. They prefer in this situation to shut down

---

44. One of the reasons why misunderstandings of this kind occur is a failure to understand the nature of the reproduction diagrams contained in Volume II of *Capital*. These diagrams are not intended to explain the "static equilibrium" of the capitalist mode of production but, on the contrary, to show how this mode of production is able to continue *despite* the constant interruption of its equilibrium and the periodic interruption of expanded reproduction.

45. Lange, "Marxian Economics and Modern Economic Theory," pp. 198–199.

their factories and thereby also re-establish an industrial reserve army—even without "technical progress." This is indeed what happens in all the more or less "prefabricated" recessions of neo-capitalism. The capitalists can wait, whereas the workers cannot because they possess neither the means of production nor the means of subsistence.

Besides, it is not only the competition between capital and labor but also the competition among capitalists that explains technical progress, according to the Marxist model. Both forms of competition result from the twofold necessity of accumulating capital and realizing surplus value under economic conditions in which the quantity of labor *socially* necessary to produce a commodity manifests itself only *a posteriori*, and is *unknown a priori*. It is these two reasons, which relate to the fundamental character of the capitalist mode of production—that is, of a system of generalized commodity economy—that are the ultimate root of the "dynamic" element in Marxist economic theory. They both follow from the very nature of the labor theory of value.

I will mention in conclusion the criticism of the labor theory of value which Joan Robinson formulated soon after the Second World War.[46] In her view, Marx, like Ricardo, was mistaken in seeking an intrinsic value of commodities "analogous to weight or color." And Marx, like Smith, sought "a measure of value which would be invariable," which he found in labor. The labor theory of value constructed on these theoretical foundations was useless, and Marx could have explained all the laws of development he discovered in much less complicated terms without resorting to the labor theory of value.

As Roman Rosdolsky has shown in detail,[47] these arguments reflect an astonishing failure to grasp Marx's ideas, although he expounded them clearly enough. Marx explicitly denied that the

---

46. Joan Robinson, *An Essay on Marxian Economics;* and "The Labor Theory of Value: A Discussion," in *Science and Society*, 1954. (The phrase about "weight or color" actually appears on p. 147 of her *Collected Economic Papers.*)

47. Roman Rosdolsky, "Joan Robinsons Marx-Kritik," in *Arbeit und Wirtschaft*, June–July 1959. (This article originally appeared in English in *The New Socialist*, New Delhi, February 1959.)

exchange value of commodities was an "intrinsic quality" of commodities in the *physical* sense; on the contrary, he showed that the common "quality" that makes commodities commensurable is not physical but *social* in nature. What Joan Robinson has not grasped is the difference between concrete labor, which creates use values and the physical properties of products, and abstract labor, which creates exchange value. Nor did Marx set out to discover an "invariable measure of value." On the contrary, he showed that the measure of exchange value must itself be a commodity, that it must itself be variable. It is just because exchange value presupposes a common quality in all commodities—the fact that they are all produced by abstract labor, by a fraction of the total labor potential at society's disposal—that it is at once social and variable, and not physical and immutable!

What all these critiques have in common is their inability to grasp the *level of abstraction* to which Marx ascended in order to discover the socioeconomic problems underlying the problem of exchange value. The question Marx tries to answer is this: Given the fact that the capitalist mode of production works through "natural," "automatic" laws, independent of man's will, how is it that thousands of millions of exchange operations, generally undertaken blindly, do not constantly produce crises and stoppages of economic activity, but on the contrary proceed within the framework of a continuity, necessarily interrupted from time to time by discontinuity? What force insures this continuity? What force is it that allots labor and capital among the different branches of industry?

When Marx declared that exchange value is constituted by abstract human labor, he was not "choosing a theory" in order to try to "demonstrate the exploitation of the working class under capitalism." [48] He was providing an answer to this question. When Marx's critics put forward their objections to his theory, they do not merely fail to set up a coherent theory in place of his; generally speaking, they fail to understand what the problem is.

Roman Rosdolsky thus opposes with good reason Joan Robinson's statement that the labor theory of value created by Marx

------

48. As Lange mistakenly implies in "Marxian Economics and Modern Economic Theory," p. 195.

would apply fully and completely only in socialist society.[49] When individual labor is directly recognized as social labor—and this is one of the fundamental features of a socialist society!—it is obviously absurd to take the roundabout route through the market in order to "rediscover" the social quality of this labor. That is why there is no room for commodity production, and *a fortiori* for "commodity value" or the "law of value," in a socialist society.

It is amazing that a writer like Maurice Godelier, who knows Marx's works well and has tried to go deeply into the study of Marxist method and doctrine, could have written: "If the capitalist system is based on a particular structure of appropriation of the surplus product, it is possible to construct ideally, through a different hypothesis regarding the structure of appropriation, the functioning of a socialist economy. We arrive at a model which is different, but which is also based on the theory of value. The theory of value thus enables us to construct a model of socialist development . . ." [50]

This is totally incompatible with Marx's conception of the theory of value. For Marx the economy of labor time, which is general in all societies, is not identical with an economy governed by the law of value; the latter is merely a particular form of the former.[51] The theory of value applies only to a society in which individual owners exchange products of labor and in which, because of this, the latter take the form of commodities (in which the amount of labor socially necessary to produce the commodities is not established *a priori* by the associated producers, but only *a posteriori* by the laws of the market). To state that the theory of value remains valid under socialism is to misinterpret the very nature of commodities, and that is what Godelier has in fact done.[52]

---

49. Rosdolsky, "Joan Robinsons Marx-Kritik," pp. 182–183.

50. Maurice Godelier, *Rationalité et irrationalité en économie,* p. 148.

51. See the quotation from the *Grundrisse,* p. 86.

52. See his definition of the commodity (in *Rationalité et irrationalité en économie,* pp. 212–213): "For Marx a commodity is an object [!] characterized by two properties: (a) it is useful, and thereby the commodity has a use value . . . (b) it is exchanged in a certain proportion with goods having a different utility. It has an exchange value, and it has this exchange value only

Just as he starts from an incomplete definition of the commodity, so also he gives an unacceptable definition of capitalism: "We have shown that the theory of capital does not really begin until the formation of surplus value has been explained. But this does not directly and by itself explain the capitalist production relationship. What is specific to capitalism is the appropriation of this surplus value by the individual who owns the means of production, that is, private appropriation of the surplus product . . ." [53] This bears a distressing resemblance to the wretched caricature that the apologists of Stalinism have made of Marxism.

For Marx, capitalism is not at all defined merely by the private appropriation of surplus value; Engels even imagines a situation in which the state appropriates surplus value on behalf of the bourgeoisie as a whole, without this meaning that capitalism has been abolished. [54] The Marxist theory of capital defines capitalism by the transformation of the means of production into capital and labor power into a commodity, that is, by the generalization of commodity production. A "socialism" in which the means of production continue to be commodities (that is, can be bought and sold on the market, which implies decentralized investment decisions, which in turn implies the possibility of periodic crises of overproduction and unemployment) and in which labor power

---

because in the first place it has a use value for other people." Cf. what Marx himself points out in the famous passage in Chapter I of *Capital*, Volume I, on the fetishism of commodities: "What is true only for this particular form of production, commodity production, namely, that the specifically social character of different kinds of *private labor carried on independently*, consists in the equality of every kind of that labor, by virtue of its being human labor, and that this specifically social character assumes an objective form, the value form of the products of labor—this fact appears, to the man mentally imprisoned in the relationships of commodity production, to be . . . definitive." (Emphasis mine.—E.M. See *Capital*, Vol. I, p. 74.) (Since, however, the translation does not bring out the main point clearly enough, I have retranslated this passage, using the German original and the French edition which was revised by Marx in 1872–1875—*Trans.*) These words might have been written for the benefit of those who wish to preserve the "commodity form" and the "value" of the products of labor under socialism.

53. Godelier, *Rationalité et irrationalité en économie*, pp. 147–148.

54. Cf. Engels, *Herr Eugen Dühring's Revolution in Science* (*Anti-Dühring*), pp. 303–304.

continues to be a commodity, would merely be state capitalism, even if private ownership of the means of production were suppressed. Capitalist production relations, of which private appropriation of surplus value is only one aspect, and which are defined, among other things, by hierarchical relations in the places where work is carried on and by the inability of the mass of the producers to dispose of the products of their labor (which implies the alienated nature of this labor) would continue to exist 100 percent.

What is true is that commodity production, which existed before capitalist production, also partially survives it and lasts during the entire transitional phase between capitalism and socialism. It lasts, however, *as a survival from capitalism*, as slag from the former society which has not yet been completely transcended, in conflict with the planned character of socialized economy. The process of building a socialist society is precisely a process of the withering away of commodity production. To try to formulate a model of socialist economy on the basis of the theory of value is as absurd as trying to formulate a model of socialist "right" based upon bourgeois "right," to employ Marx's well-known phrase from the *Critique of the Gotha Programme*.

7

The *Grundrisse,*
or the Dialectics of
Labor Time and Free Time

The *Grundrisse der Kritik der politischen Ökonomie* (Outlines of the Critique of Political Economy), which together with the *Contribution to the Critique of Political Economy* marks the highest point reached by Marx's economic work before *Capital,* constitute a huge collection of economic analyses. Conceived as preparatory studies for *Capital,* or, more precisely, as a development of the analysis of capitalism in all its aspects from which Marx's master work was to emerge, the *Grundrisse* contain both the materials used by Marx in all his subsequent economic writing and also a great many elements which were not destined to serve as ferment for subsequent works.

There are probably two reasons for this distinction. In the first place, we know that Marx was unable to complete his work of general analysis of all the elements of the capitalist mode of production. In his original plan, which dates from when he wrote the *Grundrisse,* the analysis of capital was to be followed by an analysis of landed property, wage labor, the state, external trade, and the world market. Only one-sixth of all that was planned was actually accomplished, and even then, Volume IV of *Capital* (*Theories of Surplus Value*) did not get beyond the first section. Specialists can discuss indefinitely why in 1866 Marx gave up this original plan in favor of a treatment of capital alone, in four parts: the production process of capital; the circulation process of capital; the unity of these processes, or capital and profit; and a critical history of economic theories.[1] It remains nonetheless true that there are in the *Grundrisse* a number of observations of the highest importance regarding landed property, wage labor, external trade, and the world market which are not to be found in any of the four volumes of *Capital*. These are so many seeds that were not given the opportunity to flower, but their richness nevertheless forms a source of constant stimulation to the thinking of present and future Marxists.

In the second place, the method of exposition used in the *Grundrisse* is more "abstract," more deductive, than that of *Capital*, and while there is much less illustrative material, there are, on the other hand, a great number of digressions, especially relating to history, or opening windows on the future, that were eliminated in the final version of *Capital* but which are sometimes extremely rich, real additions to Marxist theory on social and economic questions. Roman Rosdolsky, one of the leading authorities on Marx, mentions in this connection that the publication of the *Grundrisse* was "a veritable revelation" which "admitted us, so to speak, into Marx's economic laboratory, revealing all the ingenuities, all the winding paths of his methodology." [2]

1. The first writer to study this problem seriously was Henryk Grossmann ("Die Änderung des Aufbauplans des Marxschen Kapital, und ihre Ursachen," in *Archiv für die Geschichte des Sozialismus*). He ascribed the change in the plan for *Capital* to Marx's decision to deal with surplus value as a whole, independently of the forms in which it appears (profit, rent, interest, etc.). It is true that Marx himself, in a letter to Engels of August 15, 1863, speaks of having satisfied the "necessity" for everything to be "completely changed." (*Briefwechsel*, Vol. III, p. 143.) However, Marx had already fully developed the category of surplus value, as distinct from the specific forms in which it appears, in the *Grundrisse*. In his article "Das 'Kapital in Allgemeinen' und die 'vielen Kapitalien'" (*Kyklos*, No. 2, 1953), Roman Rosdolsky distinguishes thirteen variants of the plan for *Capital* outlined by Marx between September 1857 and April 1868.

2. Roman Rosdolsky, "Ein neomarxistisches Lehrbuch der politischen Ökonomie," in *Kyklos*, No. 4, 1963, p. 651. Rosdolsky, who died in 1967, has since had published a book on the *Grundrisse* entitled *Zur Entstehungsgeschichte des Marxschen "Kapital."*

In his otherwise excellent book, *Die Geschichte einer grossen Entdeckung*, W. S. Wygodski asserts (p. 81) that in the *Grundrisse* Marx had not yet developed his theory of the equalization of the rate of profit through competition between capitals. Although it is true that Marx had not yet coined

I have already mentioned the essential contributions to the development of Marxist theory that are to be found in the *Grundrisse:* the perfecting of the theories of value, of surplus value, and of money. To these should be added the perfecting of the tools of analysis which Marx had inherited from the classical school of political economy. Thus it was in the *Grundrisse* that there first appeared: the precise distinction between constant capital (the value of which is conserved by labor power) and variable capital (the value of which is increased) (p. 289); the presentation of the value of a commodity as the sum of three elements, namely, constant capital, variable capital, and surplus value $(c + v + s)$ (see especially pp. 219–343); the growth of the annual mass of surplus value by the shortening of the circulation cycle of capital (pp. 417–418); the division of surplus value into absolute surplus value and relative surplus value (pp. 311–312), and this even in the form of the distinction between absolute and relative surplus labor (pp. 264–265); the entire theory of the equalization of the rate of profit (pp. 217–362); etc.

In fact, the only elements of Marx's economic theory not found in mature form in the *Grundrisse* are the theory of the tendency of the average rate of profit to fall (though Marx already knew about this, and analyzes it, in a rather laborious way, on pp. 283–289), together with the problem of reproduction.[3]

It is above all the parts of the *Grundrisse* that were not used for *Capital* that deserve special study, and here it is imperative to refer to a passage in Marx's letter to Engels of January 14, 1858, written in the midst of the writing of the *Grundrisse*, in which the founder of scientific socialism declares: "In the *method* of treatment the fact that by mere accident I have again glanced through Hegel's *Logic* has been of great service to me—Freili-

the term "price of production," it is not true that the theory of the equalization of the rate of profit cannot be found in the *Grundrisse*. It is mentioned explicitly and is related to the competition of capital invested in different branches, with different rates of surplus value and different initial rates of profit, on pp. 338–339 and pp. 549–550. In this last passage Marx uses the wording "general price," which is identical with the wording used later, "price of production."

3. Marx first solved the problem of reproduction in a letter to Engels dated July 6, 1863. (*Selected Correspondence*, pp. 153–156.)

grath found some volumes of Hegel which originally belonged to Bakunin and sent them to me as a present." [4] It seems undeniable that the extraordinary richness of Marx's analysis and the exposition of a number of "dialectical pairs" such as "commodity and money," "use value and exchange value," "capital and wage labor," "labor time and leisure," "labor and wealth," in which the *Grundrisse* abound, was if not directly caused then at least stimulated by the author's second encounter with his old mentor.

One is impelled to compare this experience of Marx's with Lenin's second encounter with Hegel (September–December 1914, and 1915), which was closely followed by the richest period of Lenin's theoretical thinking, leading to the production of *Imperialism: The Highest Stage of Capitalism* and *State and Revolution*. As Marx himself declared, and as Lenin emphasized on many occasions, it was indeed the application of the dialectical method of investigation to economic problems, begun by Marx, that enabled him to make his chief economic discoveries. It was thanks to this method that he set economic phenomena in a total context (the mode of production, the relations of production) driven by its own internal contradictions. It was thanks to this method too that he was able to grasp clearly the historically determined character, limited only to a particular period of human history, of the phenomena of commodity economy and of the "categories" that are the *reflection* of this economy. [5]

It is hard to decide which are the more valuable, these brilliant passages of analysis, which possess a prophetic power of genius, or the historical passages, which substantially complement the historical parts of *Capital*.

As has already been mentioned, Marx distinguishes in the *Grundrisse* between the general category of "surplus value" and the particular forms in which it appears. He also distinguishes between the surplus value that appears accidentally during the circulation process, *as a result of unequal exchange*, and the surplus value produced in the course of the production process. The

---

4. *Selected Correspondence*, p. 102.

5. See Gino Longo, *Il metodo dell'economia politica*, pp. 120–125, quoting Marx's letter to Lachâtre of March 18, 1872; and also a text by Lenin published in Vol. 38 of his *Collected Works*.

former precedes the rise of the capitalist mode of production, whereas the latter can develop only within it. Marx speaks bluntly of the "swindling in exchange" which accounts for the origin of the profit of merchant capital in pre-capitalist societies.[6] And he does not fail to point out that non-equivalent exchange can reappear under the capitalist mode of production, not merely in the exchange between capital and labor but also in exchange between different nations, in international trade. Hence his pertinent observation, which illuminates both his conception of the cause of crises, radically different from Rosa Luxemburg's,[7] and his conception of capitalist world trade as a means of exploiting less-developed peoples: "Not only individual capitalists but nations may continually exchange among themselves, renewing this exchange on an ever greater scale, without thereby deriving equal advantage from the exchange. One of the nations may continually appropriate part of the other's surplus labor, giving nothing in exchange, but not to the same extent as occurs in the exchange between capitalist and worker." [8]

Some of the most striking passages in the *Grundrisse* relate, as we have mentioned, to the dialectics of "disposable time/labor time/free time." "Every economy is resolved in the last analysis into an economy of time," Marx writes, and he explains that this rule applies to class societies no less than to a society which has brought its production under collective control: "Once given collective production, the determination of time is obviously essential. The less time society needs to spend producing corn, cattle, etc., the more it has at its disposal for other forms of production, material or spiritual. Just as with an individual *the breadth of his development, his enjoyment, and his activity depends on his economy of time* [*Zeitersparung*] . . . Society must allot its time efficiently so as to secure adequate production of its total

---

6. *Grundrisse*, pp. 742–743.

7. See also, in this connection, the passages regarding the need for capital to expand the circle in which it circulates, but not into noncapitalist milieus: "The surplus value which is created at one point needs surplus value to be created at another point, in order that it may be exchanged for this." (*Grundrisse*, p. 311.)

8. Ibid., p. 755.

needs, in the same way as an individual must use his time correctly in order to obtain knowledge in the right proportions, or to satisfy the different requirements of his activity. Economy of time, like planned distribution of labor time among the different branches of production, thus continues to be the primary economic law for a society based on collective production." [9]

Marx goes on: "It [this economy of time] imposes itself as a law to an even greater extent in such a society. *But that is fundamentally different from the measurement of exchange values (labor or products of labor) by labor time.* The labors of individuals in the same branch of labor, and the different kinds of labor, differ from each other not only in quantity but also in quality. What is implied by a merely quantitative difference between things? That they are identical in quality. Quantitative measurement of forms of labor thus [presupposes] that they are equivalent, identical in quality." [10]

Later Marx returns to the fundamental problem of the economy of labor time, introducing the key ideas of "necessary labor time" and "excess, superfluous, disposable labor time": "*The entire development of wealth is based on the creation of disposable time.* The ratio between necessary labor time and superfluous labor time (this is how it appears at first from the standpoint of necessary labor) changes at the different levels of development of the productive forces. At the more productive levels of exchange, men exchange only their superfluous labor time; it provides the measure of their exchange, which extends only to superfluous products. In production based on capital, the existence of necessary labor time is conditioned by the creation of superfluous labor time." [11]

Marx develops this idea in the pages immediately following this passage from the *Grundrisse*, explaining that capitalism actually strives to increase the working population—that is, the number of persons for whom necessary labor time is guaranteed—only to the extent that these people also yield surplus labor, "superfluous labor" from their own point of view. Hence the tendency

9. Ibid., p. 89. (Emphasis mine.—E.M.)

10. Ibid., pp. 89–90. (Emphasis mine.—E.M.)

11. Ibid., pp. 301–302.

of capital to develop both the total size of the population and that of the "superfluous population" (the industrial reserve army), the latter having the task of making sure that the working population will provide "superfluous labor" for capital: the industrial reserve army brings down wages and thereby increases surplus value, which is nothing but "superfluous labor" from the standpoint of the worker.

This is evidently only one aspect of the problem. Marx also stresses the other aspect of "superfluous labor," the fact that it is a source of enjoyment and wealth as regards the development of individuals. But this is so at first only for a *part* of society, and that only on the condition that it becomes forced labor for another part of society: "Society does not at all evolve so that an individual creates plenty for himself from the moment he has satisfied his fundamental needs. But it evolves because an individual or a class of individuals is obliged to work more than is necessary to satisfy his fundamental needs, for while surplus labor appears on the one hand, on the other appear non-labor and extra wealth. In reality, the development of wealth takes place only through these contradictions; from the standpoint of potentiality, however, it is just this development of wealth that makes it possible to abolish these contradictions." [12]

We thus see the dialectics of "necessary labor time/surplus labor time/free time" opening out wider and wider in the successive development and transcendence of all its internal contradictions; for the development of surplus labor also implies, at least under the capitalist mode of production, a huge development of the productive forces—and that is its indispensable "civilizing mission." Only on this basis will a collectivist society be able to reduce to the minimum the overall working day, without thereby having to repress or mutilate the all-round development of each individual's potentialities.

The development of surplus labor by the working class already implies, under the capitalist mode of production, *the development of free time* on the part of the capitalist: "The fact that the worker has to work for an additional time is identical with this

12. Ibid., p. 305.

other fact, that the capitalist does not have to work, and that his time is thus conceived as a negation of labor time; he does not even have to provide necessary labor. The worker has to work during the surplus labor time in order to obtain permission to objectivize, to valorize, the labor time necessary for his reproduction. On the other hand, even the *necessary labor time* of the capitalist is thus *free time*, that is to say, time which need not be devoted to providing his immediate subsistence. Since all *free time* is time for free development, the capitalist usurps the free time that the workers have produced for society, for civilization." [13]

The development of fixed capital, which seems to be the "historical mission" of the capitalist mode of production, is itself an index and a reflection of the degree of social wealth. "The object of production directed immediately toward use value, and also immediately toward exchange value, is the product itself destined for consumption. The part of production directed toward the production of fixed capital does not produce either immediate objects for enjoyment or values for immediate exchange—at least, not exchange values that are immediately realizable. It thus depends on the level already reached by productivity—that is, on the fact that part of production time is enough to provide immediate production, while another, constantly increasing part of this [same] time can be used for producing means of production. That implies that society can wait;[14] that it can divert a large part of the wealth already created, both from immediate enjoyment and from production intended for immediate enjoyment, so that it can be used for work which is not immediately productive (within the process of material production itself).

"This requires that a high level of productivity already be attained, as well as relative plenty, and more precisely it requires a certain level directly related to the transformation of circulating capital into fixed capital. *In the same way as the volume of relative surplus labor depends on the productivity of necessary labor*, so *the volume of labor time used for the production of*

---

13. Ibid., p. 527.
14. This is amazingly reminiscent of Böhm-Bawerk's theory of capital.

fixed capital . . . depends on the productivity of labor time destined for the direct production of the product." [15]

To the extent, however, that capitalism develops this fixed capital, this scientific technology, in an ever richer and more complex way, production becomes more and more independent of human labor in the strict sense. Marx here forecasts what increasingly advanced automation will be like and the rich promise it holds for a socialist mankind: "As large-scale industry develops, the creation of true wealth depends less on labor time and the amount of [living] labor applied than on the power of the agencies that are set in motion during labor time, and which is itself (hence its great efficiency) not related to the immediate labor time that these agencies have cost to produce but rather to the general level of science and the progress of technology, or the application of this science to production. True wealth reveals itself rather—and this is what large-scale industry brings to light —as an enormous disproportion between the labor time applied and what it produces . . . *Labor no longer seems so much to be included in the process of production, but man behaves rather as the supervisor and regulator of the production process.*" [16]

Under the capitalist mode of production this immense step forward appears in the form of an immense contradiction: the more immediate production of human wealth becomes emancipated from human labor time, the more its effective creation is subordinated to the private appropriation of human surplus labor without which the utilization of capital and the whole of capitalist production become impossible. But this contradiction merely announces the breakdown of capitalist production, of commodity production, and of all production not directly aimed at satisfying human needs and the all-round development of individuals: "It is no longer the immediate labor provided by man, nor the time during which he works, but the understanding of nature and the domination of it thanks to the existence [of man] as a social body —in short, it is the development of the social individual that appears as the great fundamental pillar of production and wealth. *The theft of others' labor time, on which the wealth of today is*

15. *Grundrisse*, pp. 594–595.
16. Ibid., p. 592.

based, appears a wretched basis compared to this newly developed basis created by large-scale industry itself. From the moment when labor in its immediate form ceases to be the great source of wealth, labor time ceases, and must cease, being the measure of it, and for the same reason exchange value must cease being the measure of use value. *The surplus labor of the masses ceases to be the condition for the development of general wealth, just as the non-labor of a small minority ceases to be the condition for the development of the general powers of the human intellect.* Thereby, production based on exchange value breaks down . . . The free development of individual personalities [is now the aim], and *not therefore the reduction of necessary labor time in order to create surplus labor, but the general reduction to a minimum of the labor necessary for society*, to which then corresponds the artistic, scientific, etc., cultivation of individuals *thanks both to the time that has become free for everyone* and to the means now available to all." [17]

The contradictions of capitalism are expressed particularly in the fact that capitalism tries as far as possible to reduce the labor time necessary for the production of each commodity, while on the other hand it sets up labor time as the only measure and source of wealth. It follows that capitalism strives to *restrict* as much as possible the necessary labor time and to *extend* as much as possible the duration of surplus labor, "superfluous labor." The conflict between the social development of the productive forces and the private conditions of capitalist appropriation, between the development of the productive forces and the capitalist production relations, thus appears as a conflict between the creation of wealth, which increasingly frees itself from dependence on immediate human labor, and the constant effort to channel these immense powers into the valorization of existing value, through the appropriation of human surplus labor. Marx deduces from this that the nature of the capitalist mode of production is at once enormously productive and enormously destructive, enormously creative and enormously wasteful.

In another passage, Marx shows that in its insatiable thirst for

17. Ibid., p. 593. (Emphasis mine.—E.M.)

profit, capital drives labor to constantly exceed the limits of its *natural* needs and thus creates the material elements of a rich individuality which is as all-round in production as in consumption, and "whose labor no longer appears as labor but as the full and complete development of activity." [18] Marx here repeats one of the basic ideas of *The German Ideology*—contrary to the opinion of certain "Marxologists" who regard the ideas in that youthful work as somewhat "romantic" and "idealistic," transcended in the work of the maturer scholar.

This "historically necessary" aspect of capital and capitalism is one of the themes Marx keeps returning to in the *Grundrisse*. The creation of the world market; the all-round development of man's needs, tastes, knowledge, and forms of enjoyment; the radical and sharp break-through of all the limits that history and a narrow milieu had previously imposed on man's view of nature and of his own potentialities; the frenzied development of the productive forces—all these constitute the "civilizing mission" of capital.

But unlike many of those who call themselves his disciples, Marx sees no contradiction between acknowledging and emphasizing this "historically necessary mission" of capitalism and constantly pillorying whatever is exploitative, inhuman, and oppressive in it. Marx keeps in view all the time the *two contradictory aspects* of the historical reality he has experienced, and steadily steers clear of both reefs, that of subjectivism and that of objectivism.[19]

He does not contrast existing reality with an ideal reality for which the conditions do not yet exist but must be created precisely through the development of capitalism; but neither does he idealize this existing reality. He does not deny that misery is miserable because it is the product of an historically inevitable phase of evolution. This dual character of the Marxist conception

---

18. Ibid., p. 231.

19. This is what Kostas Axelos does not seem to understand when he contrasts Marx's "positivism"—his admiration of the effects of industrialization —with his "romanticism"—his allegedly deploring these same effects. (*Marx, penseur de la technique*, p. 81.) In reality, Marx's judgment *unites* the two contradictory aspects of industry and economic growth under capitalism.

of "historical necessity" is clearly visible in the *Grundrisse*, where some of the sharpest condemnations of capitalism are to be found side by side with pages that recognize its merits from the standpoint of the general progress of human society.

Many other "modern," "contemporary" problems are taken up in the *Grundrisse:* that of the development of services and that of the application of science and machinery to agriculture, for example. The treatment of the limits set on the concentration of capital is interesting as a refutation "in advance" of the theory of state capitalism:[20] "Capital does not exist and *cannot exist* except in the form of a number of capitals, and its self-determination thus appears as the interaction of these many capitals one with another."[21] And he explains: "The production of *capitalists and wage workers* is thus the chief product of the valorization process of capital. Vulgar political economy, which sees only things produced, overlooks this completely."[22] The problem of a capital which needs both to restrict and to stimulate consumption by the workers also has a modern ring. However, this brings up the whole question of the Marxist theory of wages, which constitutes the last big contribution Marx made to his economic theory before the final writing of *Capital*.

Current discussions raise two essential aspects of this dialectic of the *Grundrisse* which I have just outlined: the problem of the "labor time/free time" ratio in capitalist society, and the problem of the development of the productive forces considered as a necessary condition—whether sufficient or insufficient—for the abolition of capitalist production and of commodity production in general.

The reduction in the length of the working day in the most highly industrialized capitalist countries is a fact, a fact whose progressive significance Marx himself hailed on the occasion of the establishment of the ten-hour day in Britain. It is true that the tendency to reduce the working day has slowed down in re-

20. Except, of course, in the form of a regime insuring the survival of a substantial section of the bourgeois class as *rentiers* living on state bonds, as foreseen by Engels in *Anti-Dühring*.

21. *Grundrisse*, p. 317.

22. Ibid., p. 412.

cent decades and that there has even been some backsliding (as in France). The increasing distance the worker has to travel from his home to his place of work counterbalances to some degree the reduction in his working hours. Greater nervous fatigue caused by present-day industrial techniques, along with encroaching noise and air pollution and the ever graver tension underlying all social relations, must also be taken into account. Nevertheless, while it is exaggerated to talk of a "civilization of leisure," it is clear that important groups of wage- and salary-earners today enjoy, it would seem, much more "free time" than in Marx's day.

I say "would seem" to enjoy, because what was bound to happen in this capitalist society, based on a universal commodity economy, has obviously happened. Leisure has been largely commercialized. The equation "increased incomes + more leisure = more freedom" has been shown to be illusory. The proletarian has been unable to recover in the sphere of "leisure consumption" what he lost in the sphere of production.[23] An extensive literature has accumulated, analyzing and emphasizing the "industrial shaping of minds," the mental degradation brought about by the mass media,[24] the yawning boredom that prolongs fatigue and ends by combining with it, in work and in "free time" alike.[25] Things could not be otherwise in a society in which the whole of economic life continues to be focused on the realization of *private profit*, in which every activity tends to become an end in itself and every fresh acquisition brings the danger that it may become a new cause of the mutilation of alienated man.

Does this mean that the extension of leisure is a bad thing and that we should aim rather at a "humanization of work," by way of the communal labor preached by Erich Fromm or through workers' management of their work places?[26] The Marx of the

23. Cf. in particular the articles by Heinz Theo Risse and Walter Dirks in *Gibt es noch ein Proletariat?*, M. Feuersenger, ed., pp. 88–89, 92.

24. See especially Hans Magnus Enzensberger, *Culture ou mise en condition*, pp. 9–18; and Edgar Morin, *L'Esprit du Temps*, among other books.

25. In *Monopoly Capital* (pp. 346–349), Baran and Sweezy emphasize the complete void—"doing nothing"—which is typical of how a large part of the American people spend their leisure.

26. Erich Fromm, *The Sane Society*, pp. 321 *et seq.*

Grundrisse.gives the same answer as the Marx of Volume III of
Capital: it is an illusion to suppose that industrial work, work in
large factories, can ever become "free" work. The realm of freedom begins only where the realm of material production—that
is, the realm of mechanical work—*ends*, assuming that nobody
wants to go back to the level of craft production. The real solution thus lies in such a thoroughgoing reduction in labor time
("necessary time") that the ratio between "work" and "leisure"
is upset completely. The abolition of capitalism is not only a
condition for this, because it will stimulate the growth of the
productive forces and thus make it possible to speed up the reduction of the time spent working; it is also the driving force
behind this change, because it will make it possible to *substantially
reduce surplus labor*, so obviously wasted at present, and to allot
the necessary labor among a much larger number of persons.[27]

The transformation of the quantitative ratio between work and
leisure (say from 1:1 to 1:2 or 1:3, which implies a week of 32
or 24 hours, or, more precisely, half a day's work instead of a
full day's[28]) will give rise to a qualitative revolution, on the condition that it be integrated into a process of progressive disalienation of labor, consumption, and man himself, through the progressive withering away of commodity production, classes, the state,
and the social division of labor.

Leisure will cease to be commercialized when "commerce" itself withers away. The mass media will cease to be instruments
of degradation when higher education becomes universal and
when opinion becomes differentiated and cultivated through the
abolition of every kind of monopoly in the press, radio, televi-
sion, and the cinema. "Free time" will cease to be a source of
boredom and oppression when its "consumers" change from passive spectators to active participants.

These radical changes must *first*, however, be realized in the
sphere of production and political life, before they can take

---

27. Jean Fallot rightly points this out in *Marx et le machinisme*, pp. 183–
188. Planning, too, makes it possible to economize on surplus labor.

28. Even as conformist a writer as George Soule (*The Shape of Tomorrow*, p. 121) acknowledges that a twenty-four-hour work week may be
possible as early as 1990, or at the beginning of the twenty-first century.

effect in the leisure sphere: this is the grain of truth contained in Fromm's false conclusion. "Free time" cannot become a "time of freedom," a means whereby man can realize all his potentialities, except to the extent that he first conquers the material conditions of this freedom through his emancipation from all forms of economic exploitation, all political constraint, and all enslavement to elementary needs.

Are the development of the use of machinery, automation, the productive forces of science and technology necessary and sufficient conditions for making this human freedom possible? Necessary, certainly: Marx's view on this point did not change between *The German Ideology* and the *Grundrisse;* and practical experience has since taught us that it is impossible to establish a truly socialist economic organization—implying in particular the disappearance of commodity production—unless there is an adequate level of technical attainment.

But can we go along with Kostas Axelos when he declares that "Marx's hopes in technique are unshakable," that for him " 'unleashed' production technique [has] . . . the task of solving in practice all problems and puzzles as it develops in the future"? [29] This strangely underestimates the dialectical nature of Marxist thought, which repeats many times, from Marx's youthful writings to the *Grundrisse*, that *the productive forces threaten to become transformed into destructive forces* if capitalist production relations are not overthrown. And with the change in the production relations—once there is a definite level of the productive forces—subsequent technological revolutions will be guided by real *choices* on the part of socialist mankind, for whom the will to secure a many-sided development of *man* will certainly rank higher than the vain temptation to seek to accumulate unceasingly an ever greater quantity of *things*.

In this sense, I agree with Jean Fallot when he writes: "Marxism is not a philosophy of the domination of nature by technique, but of the transformation of social production relations through class struggle" [30]—though for Marx a high level of technique was unquestionably a precondition for such a transformation.

---

29. Kostas Axelos, *Marx, penseur de la technique,* pp. 265, 268.
30. Jean Fallot, *Marx et le machinisme,* p. 40.

In the same way, we ought to include in the tendency for man, for all men, to master *all* their social relations—which is in fact the process whereby they will become individuals and increasingly *human* beings in a socialist society—a tendency to all-round development of scientific aptitudes. This demolishes one of the final arguments brought against the liberating character of socialism by pessimistic contemporary sociologists like Alain Touraine and Hannah Arendt: the alleged inability of contemporary man, faced with an "unleashed" technique which is already breaking out of its terrestrial confinement, to retain his power to act effectively, this power being restricted to learned men or "higher cadres" only.[31] In fact, nothing now stands in the way of progressively transforming all men into scientists and scholars,[32] that is, of that progressive dissolution of productive work into scientific work that Marx foresees in the passage from the *Grundrisse* quoted above, provided that human society so reorganizes itself that every child is surrounded with the same infinite care and attention that are today devoted to preparing nuclear submarines or interplanetary rockets.[33]

---

31. See in particular Hannah Arendt, *The Human Condition*, on men of learning; Alain Touraine, *Traité de sociologie du travail*, Vol. I, pp. 420 *et seq.*, on engineers and higher cadres; Günther Hillmann, "Zum Verständnis der Texte," in *Karl Marx, Texte zu Methode und Praxis, II*, p. 203, on both categories.

32. Cf. J.N. Dawydow (*Freiheit und Entfremdung*, p. 114): "The prospect of the development of communist society is the prospect of creating a society composed of scientists and scholars."

33. See Chapter 11 for a more thorough examination of the relation between technical progress and the classless society.

8

The Asiatic Mode of Production and the Historical Pre-Conditions for the Rise of Capital

It was on June 10, 1853, that Marx first publicly discussed the Asiatic mode of production; he had recently exchanged ideas on this subject with Engels in a letter sent on June 2 to which Engels replied on June 10.[1] In the following months and years he was to return to the subject many times, notably in articles sent to the *New York Daily Tribune* and in the *Contribution to the Critique of Political Economy*. It was in the *Grundrisse*, however, that this idea was most fully developed, under the heading "Pre-capitalist forms of production." [2] The publication of this text in German in 1953, coinciding with the beginning of de-Stalinization, has made it possible to take up again a discussion that had become greatly confused, if not bogged down, in previous years.

It seems well established that Marx held to the idea of an Asiatic mode of production to the end of his life.[3] Engels, however, eliminated it from the succession of "stages" passed through by mankind, as set out in *The Origin of the Family, Private Prop-*

1. The two letters, together with Marx's reply to Engels of July 14, 1853, are in *MEGA*, III, 1, pp. 474–477, 478–482, 483–487. The article of June 10 appeared in the *New York Daily Tribune* on June 25.

2. *Grundrisse*, pp. 375–413. (In English as *Pre-Capitalist Economic Formations*, Eric Hobsbawm, ed.)

3. Maurice Godelier has compiled a provisional bibliography of the writings of Marx and Engels on the Asiatic mode of production, but it omits *Theories of Surplus Value* and passages in the *Grundrisse* other than the section "Pre-capitalist forms of production." (See *La Pensée*, April 1964, pp. 56–66.)

erty, and the State, where he based himself narrowly on Morgan. (He had upheld the idea in *Anti-Dühring*, published six years earlier.) This is what aroused the controversy among Marxists.

Not much use was made of the idea in Western Europe. In Russia Lenin took it up, in the considerably modified form of "Asiaticism," but did not use it to designate a particular socio-economic formation.[4] Plekhanov eventually rejected its relevance to Russia, and even to history in general.[5] Lenin mentioned it again, explicitly, in 1914, as one of the four major socioeconomic formations.[6]

Soon after the Russian Revolution, during the rebirth of Marxist studies which this event stimulated, Ryazanov drew attention once again to the importance of the Asiatic mode of production in an introduction he wrote to three articles by Marx on China and India which were published in the journal *Under the Banner of Marxism*.[7] In the same year Eugene Varga wrote an article on the subject, and in 1928 Madyar published a big book on Chinese rural economy which discussed the idea of the Asiatic mode of production.

China was, of course, fashionable in that period of the climax and defeat of the Second Chinese Revolution. But it was precisely the fact that the strategic and tactical problems of this revolution

---

4. See Karl A. Wittfogel (*Oriental Despotism*, pp. 389–400), where he gives a fairly complete summary of the passages in Lenin relating to "Asiaticism."

5. See in particular G. Plekhanov (*Introduction à l'histoire sociale de la Russie*, p. 4): "We now know not only that Russia, like Western Europe, passed through the phase of feudalism but also that this same phase occurred in the history of Egypt, Chaldea, Assyria, Persia, Japan, and China—in short, in all or nearly all of the civilized countries of the East." On the same page, however, the author writes of the "great despots of the East." In *Fundamental Problems of Marxism* (pp. 68–69) Plekhanov retained the concept of an Asiatic mode of production, while correctly pointing out that it could not be regarded as preceding the ancient (slaveowning) mode of production.

6. Lenin, *Collected Works*, Vol. 21, p. 56.

7. Year I, No. 2, pp. 370–378. Lucien Goldmann has pointed out to me that the concept of the Asiatic mode of production was "re-launched" not by Ryazanov, but by the Hungarian Communists who published the review *Communism* from 1920 onward.

obtruded that put an end to scientific discussion of the Asiatic mode of production. The Stalinist tendency reduced all scientific discussion to a "functional" level, in connection with the factional struggles within the Comintern. To admit that an Asiatic mode of production existed in China was equivalent to underestimating the "anti-feudal tasks" of the Chinese revolution. Accordingly, the concept of the Asiatic mode of production was "denounced" in the Leningrad discussions of February 1931: "E. Yolk observed . . . that the Trotskyists' conceptions, which emphasized the existence of commercial capitalism in China and stressed the anti-capitalist nature of the current revolution, differed from those of the supporters of the Asiatic mode of production but that nevertheless the political consequences of the two conceptions were identical since they implied rejection of the anti-feudal (bourgeois-democratic) nature of the present stage of the Chinese revolutionary movement." [8]

For two decades thereafter, the category of the Asiatic mode of production was doomed, first in the U.S.S.R. and then in the people's democracies and in China, to increasing obscurity, eventually vanishing from the textbooks. [9] In the West, however, a German Communist named Karl August Wittfogel had meanwhile devoted a monumental work to the Asiatic mode of pro-

---

8. Jan Pecirka, "Les discussions soviétiques sur le mode de production asiatique et sur la formation esclavagiste" (1964), in "Premières sociétés de classe et mode de production asiatique," special issue of the review *Recherches internationales à la lumière du marxisme*, May–June 1957, p. 62. See also Eugene Varga, pp. 370–394.

9. Three examples: (1) The textbook by W. I. Avdijev, *Geschichte des Alten Orients,* published in Moscow in 1948 and translated in Berlin in 1953, was based on the views of Academician V.V. Struve and declared (pp. 12–13) that "the peoples of India and China have followed the same road, from gentile society to slaveowning society." (2) In 1950, Kuo Mo-jo was still writing about a "slaveowning society" in ancient China which evolved toward a "feudal society" ("La société esclavagiste chinoise," in *Recherches internationales à la lumière du marxisme*, May–June 1957, pp. 32–33, 41, 51), although what was involved was obviously a society which, while there were slaves present, was nevertheless definitely not based upon a slaveowning mode of production. (3) Similarly, *An Outline History of China,* published in Peking in 1958, speaks (p. 15) of the earliest class society in China (under the Shang Dynasty) as a "society based on slavery."

duction, and this eventually had a lasting effect on the thinking of sociologists.[10] It was also in the West that the discussion of the Asiatic mode of production first re-surfaced, notably in Britain and France. In the people's democracies, the idea was used, as soon as de-Stalinization began, to break out of the mechanistic and anti-Marxist straitjacket of the "four stages" which all mankind was supposed to have necessarily passed through: primitive communism, slaveowning society, feudalism, capitalism. This straitjacket had compelled writers who claimed to be Marxist but who wanted to be accepted as "orthodox" by the Communist parties to assemble under the heading "feudal society" a most variegated collection of socioeconomic formations.[11] It had also brought to a dead end historical research on the empires established by the nomadic and semi-nomadic peoples (Huns, Turks, Ottomans, Mongols) which was of such great importance for the history of Central and Eastern Europe. It was indeed impossible to describe these empires as either "slaveowning societies," or as "feudal societies," or as societies in transition between slavery and feudalism. The differentiation that resulted from the discussion of these problems facilitated the abandonment of the dogma of the "four universal stages" and hastened the re-emergence of the concept of the Asiatic mode of production.[12]

The revived discussion of the Asiatic mode of production is to be welcomed. At the same time, though, one must carefully distinguish what Marx and Engels meant by this expression, the distortion that it subsequently suffered at the hands of some of Marx's disciples and some of his opponents, and the way it is used today by historians and sociologists inspired by Marxism.

---

10. Karl A. Wittfogel, *Wirtschaft und Gesellschaft Chinas*, p. 768.

11. See Maurice Godelier, "La notion de 'mode de production asiatique' et les schémas marxistes d'évolution des sociétés," in *Cahiers du Centre d'Etudes et de Recherches Marxistes*, pp. 26–27; and Eric Hobsbawm, Introduction to *Pre-Capitalist Economic Formations*, pp. 61–63.

12. See in this connection, *inter alia*, A.A. Bernshtam, *Sotsialno-ekonomichesky stroy Orogono-Yeniseiskikh Turok VI–VIII vekov* (The Social and Economic System of the Turks of the Orkhon and the Yenisei from the Sixth to the Eighth Century); S.E. Tolybekov, in *Voprosy Ekonomiki*, No. 1, 1955, even invented a concept of "patriarchal feudalism," endowed with collective ownership of the land!

For this purpose, a brief review of the origin of the idea in the thought of Marx and Engels seems useful.

Without wishing to go back to the origin of the expression "Oriental despotism," which dates from the seventeenth century, or to Montesquieu, who made extensive use of it,[13] it is likely that Marx and Engels worked out their theory of the Asiatic mode of production under the influence of three currents of thought: first, economists like John Stuart Mill and Richard Jones, whom Marx had studied or was studying in 1853, and who employed similar expressions;[14] then, accounts of travels, memoirs, and monographs devoted to Eastern countries, which Marx and Engels read at about this time;[15] finally, special studies they made of village communities in other parts of the world which

---

13. Wittfogel refers to this.

14. In 1848, John Stuart Mill wrote of "Oriental society," and in 1831 Richard Jones had already written of "Asiatic society." (See Wittfogel, *Wirtschaft und Gesellschaft Chinas,* p. 489.) V. Struve, pope of Soviet historiography of the East during the Stalin period, and the authority mainly responsible for the "rejection" of the Asiatic mode of production, found a passage in the writings of Richard Jones in which the latter affirmed that it was the non-agricultural population that carried out large-scale public works in Eastern countries. Bringing this quotation together with two passages in Volume I of *Capital* where Marx points out that the occasional large-scale cooperative effort made by working people in pre-capitalist society was usually due to their serf-like subordination to the ruling power, or to their being slaves, and that the great public works of the ancient East were made possible by "the concentration in one hand, or in a small number of hands, of the revenues on which the workers lived," Struve gaily arrived at "proof" that, for Marx, the Asiatic mode of production was actually a particular form of the slaveowning mode of production! ("Comment Marx définissait les premières sociétés de classe" [1940], in *Recherches internationales à la lumière du marxisme,* May–June 1957, pp. 82–94.)

15. In his Introduction to *Pre-Capitalist Economic Formations,* Hobsbawm gives a fairly complete list of these, which includes Bernier's *Voyages,* Stamford Raffles's *History of Java,* the Rev. C. Foster's *Historical Geography of Arabia,* J. Child's *Treatise on the East India Trade,* etc. In *La Chine future,* Pierre Naville mentions (pp. 89–93) that Bernier's *Voyages* were written to counter a plan by Louis XIV to proclaim all the land in France royal property—or, at least, a plan of this sort that the enemies of absolutism had attributed to him.

led them to recognize the importance of this type of community in the countries of the East.[16]

All of these studies were at bottom by-products of a constant and minute analysis Marx and Engels were making of Britain's foreign trade and economic situation. The markets of the East were increasingly important as outlets for British industry. The expansion of British exports was causing profound upheavals in Oriental society—the Taiping rebellion in China and the Sepoy mutiny in India were reactions, directly or indirectly, to this disintegrating influence. Fascinated by revolutions, whether they occurred in the West or in the East, Marx and Engels set themselves to study the structure of the societies that were being shaken. This was how they came to formulate the working hypothesis of an Asiatic mode of production.

The fundamental characteristics of this mode of production were set out exhaustively enough in the three letters of June 1853 already mentioned, and in four articles published in the *New York Daily Tribune*. They can be summarized thus:

(1) What is above all characteristic of the Asiatic mode of production is the absence of private ownership of land.[17]

(2) As a result, the village community retains an essential cohesive force which has withstood the bloodiest of conquests through the ages.[18]

---

16. Maximilien Rubel points to two studies by Marx, dated 1853, one an article on the village community in Scotland ("The Duchess of Sutherland and Slavery," published in the *New York Daily Tribune* of February 9), and the other a study of the relations between absolute monarchy and administrative decentralization in Spain. (See *Karl Marx: Essai de biographie intellectuelle*, pp. 297–301.)

17. As regards India: "It can be said that private ownership of house-plots and gardens was a recognized fact in the urban and suburban areas by the 6th century B.C. There was no such private ownership of cultivated fields in general." (D.D. Kosambi, *An Introduction to the Study of Indian History*, p. 145.) For China, see Henri Maspero, quoted in Naville, *La Chine future*, pp. 96–98. For the classical Islamic empire and the beginnings of the Ottoman empire, see Reuben Levy, *The Social Structure of Islam*, pp. 13, 401.

18. The ancient Hindu author Kautilya wrote in his *Arthasastra*: "*Samghas* [tribal village communities] are invincible to others because of their unity." (Quoted in Debiprasad Chattopadhyaya, *Lokayata: A Study in Ancient Indian Materialism*, p. 173.)

(3) This internal cohesion of the ancient village community is further increased by the close union of agriculture and craft industry that exists in it.[19]

(4) For geographical and climatic reasons, however, the prosperity of agriculture in these regions requires impressive hydraulic works: "Artificial irrigation is here the first condition of agriculture." [20] This irrigation requires nearly everywhere a central authority to regulate it and to undertake large-scale works.[21]

(5) For this reason, the state succeeds in concentrating the greater part of the social surplus product in its own hands, which causes the appearance of social strata maintained by this surplus and constituting the dominant power in society (whence the expression "Oriental despotism"). The "internal logic" of a society of this kind works in favor of a very great degree of stability in basic production relations.

We find all these characteristics mentioned in the *Grundrisse,* including the importance of hydraulic works.[22] At the same time, however, we find a number of additional ideas which enable us to define more exactly what Marx and Engels meant by the Asiatic mode of production.

In the first place, the quite accidental and secondary develop-

19. See the description of the ancient Indian village in H. D. Malaviya, "Village Communities in India, a Historical Outline," in A. R. Desai, ed., *Rural Sociology in India,* pp. 164–170. The following passage is especially significant: "The original method of remunerating the village servants [i.e., the craftsmen] was either by giving them a grant of land free of rent and sometimes free of revenue, or by giving them definite shares out of the common heap of grain . . ." (p. 170).

20. Engels to Marx, June 6, 1853, in *Selected Correspondence,* p. 66.

21. Cf. Kosambi, *An Introduction to the Study of Indian History,* p. 280, on the Gupta empire.

22. *Grundrisse,* p. 377: "The communal conditions for real appropriation through labor, such as irrigation systems (very important among the Asian peoples), means of communication, etc., will then appear as the work of the higher unity—the despotic government which is poised above the lesser communities." (In English in *Pre-Capitalist Economic Formations,* pp. 70–71.) In *Fundamental Questions of Marxism* (pp. 48–51), Plekhanov ascribes decisive importance to the geographical conditions that make such works necessary. He returns to the subject further on (p. 63): "If these two types [the classical and the Oriental] differed considerably from each other, their chief distinctive features were evolved under the influence of the geographical environment . . ."

ment of the towns in Eastern countries, and their strict subordination to the heads of state or their satraps, are stressed several times.[23] This meant that production remained almost exclusively production of use values.[24] *Now, it is the development of the production of exchange values in the towns that makes possible preparation for the predominance of capital.* When the power of money becomes predominant in non-industrial societies, it leads to the domination of the country over the town.[25] In other words, the distinctive structure of the Asiatic mode of production—the subordination of the towns both to agriculture and to the central authority[26]—implied that capital could not fully develop. That meant not stagnation of the productive forces (which cannot be proved in a case like that of China) but *retarded development*, which in the end proved fatal to the nations based on this mode of production.[27]

---

23. *Grundrisse*, p. 377. And K. S. Shelvankar notes: "It is certain . . . that the merchants and handicraftsmen, the bourgeoisie as a class organized in its guilds, never attained the ascendancy that its European counterpart won for itself when it seized political power in the towns. In India the town was nearly always an outpost of the territorial state, governed by prefects or boards appointed from the *center*." (Quoted in Desai, ed., *Rural Sociology in India*, p. 150.)

24. *Grundrisse*, p. 384. Cf. Desai, ed., *Rural Sociology in India* (p. 25): "In pre-British India, village agriculture mainly produced for meeting the needs of the village population. This subsistence village agricultural economy was transformed into a market economy during the British period."

25. *Grundrisse*, p. 405. (*Pre-Capitalist Economic Formations*, p. 110.) Cf. Leon Trotsky: "Thus, the Russian towns, like the towns under the Asiatic despotisms, and in contrast to the craft and trading towns of the European Middle Ages, played only the role of consumers . . . Where, then, were manufacturing industry and the crafts? In the country, attached to agriculture." (*Results and Prospects*, in *The Permanent Revolution*, p. 47.)

26. Marx stresses (in the *Grundrisse*, pp. 407–408) the importance of a community of free craftsmen in the towns for preparing the work of dissolution that capital carries out upon the ancient communal relations in the countryside. In my *Marxist Economic Theory* (Vol. I, p. 124), I quote a similar view by Stefan Balazs regarding the towns of ancient China, and point out that this idea, usually credited to Max Weber, was actually first put forward by Marx.

27. This does not mean, of course, that the nations of Asia would not have been able to achieve capitalism on their own. It merely explains why Western Europe was able, starting in the sixteenth century, to get further

The dissolving effect which the development of trade and a money economy had on the Asiatic mode of production is shown in numerous examples from the history of ancient Mesopotamia, China, and India. The Hungarian sinologist Ferenc Tökei uses, for China, the expression "pre-capitalist development." It is undeniable that under the Ming dynasty China experienced—like India at the height of the Mogul period—an expansion of luxury production and private trade that brought the country to the threshold of manufacturing and commercial capitalism.[28] But it is the peculiar structure of the Asiatic mode of production that enables us to explain why this threshold was not crossed.

What must we then think of the attempts made by writers such as Maurice Godelier, Jean Chesneaux, Jean Suret-Canale, and P. Boiteau to reduce the Asiatic mode of production to a socioeconomic formation marking the transition from classless society to class society? [29] In order to do this they have had to *suppress*, first and foremost, the key role that Marx and Engels attributed to hydraulic and other large-scale public works in the establishment of this mode of production.[30] Godelier, who follows Suret-

---

and further ahead of the rest of the world. The *present-day* underdevelopment of the nations of Asia is not the result of the Asiatic mode of production but of the retarding and regressive effect that the subordinate situation of these nations, resulting from European penetration, has had upon them. The one Asian nation which succeeded in retaining genuine independence —Japan—has also largely succeeded in escaping "underdevelopment."

28. Ferenc Tökei: "Le mode de production asiatique en Chine" (1963) in *Recherches internationales à la lumière du marxisme*, May–June 1957, pp. 172–173, 180–182. See also Irfan Habib, "Potentialities of Capitalist Development in the Economy of Mughal India" in *Journal of Economic History*, March 1969; and N. B. Jankowska, "Extended Family Commune and Civil Self-Government in Arrapha in the 15th–14th Century B.C." in U.S.S.R. Academy of Sciences, *Ancient Mesopotamia: Socio-Economic History*.

29. Godelier, "La notion de 'mode de production asiatique'"; Jean Chesneaux, "Le mode de production asiatique," in *La Pensée*, April 1964; Jean Suret-Canale, "Les sociétés traditionnelles en Afrique tropicale," in *La Pensée*, October 1964; Pierre Boiteau, "Les droits sur la terre," in ibid. Boiteau even declares that the Asiatic mode of production is a universal phenomenon, a stage through which *all* societies have passed.

30. In "Le mode de production asiatique," Chesneaux states (p. 42): "We have to ask ourselves whether this idea of an 'economic supreme command' does not cover other functions besides those of the upkeep of dikes and

Canale, declares that "the control of inter-tribal or inter-regional trade by tribal aristocracies where the exchange of valuable products was concerned, such as gold, ivory, skins, etc., between Black Africa and White Africa," [31] could have given rise to kingdoms like Ghana, Mali, Songhai, etc. By thus expanding the scope of the idea of the Asiatic mode of production (just as the "dogmatic" Marxist writers who rejected this concept were forced to expand the scope of the idea of "feudalism"), these writers risk losing altogether the specific meaning of the idea.

What they are doing, in fact, is gradually reducing the characteristics of the Asiatic mode of production to those that mark *every* first manifestation of the state and of ruling classes in a society still essentially based on the village community. It can indeed be considered proven that in *every* case we find first of all a voluntary tribute paid by the communities to meet the cost of tasks of common interest (even if this be an imaginary interest, religious or magical in nature[32]); that to an increasing extent a tribal, or inter-tribal, aristocracy takes over first the usufruct and then the ownership of this tribute; and that for a more or less prolonged intermediate period a "democracy at the grass roots," based on the village community, coexists with a government of

---

canals: as, for example, control of the rotation of crops, and the maintenance and supervision of the security of the cultivated fields . . . the military protection of villages against raids by nomads or invading foreign armies; the direct undertaking by the state of certain sectors of industrial production, which were beyond the scope of the peasant communities, as in the case of mining and metallurgy . . .". Here we have a clear case of question-begging, from the moment when the essential reason for the appearance of such an entrepreneur-state is no longer ascribed to "hydraulic works." Why was it that, in other civilizations, groupings of villages, or the earliest urban corporations, or local lords, were able to fulfill the functions that Chesneaux enumerates, whereas under the Asiatic mode of production these were the responsibility of the state?

31. Godelier, "La notion de 'mode de production asiatique,'" p. 30.

32. Thus the collective organization of labor in West African villages, which gradually passes from being collective mutual aid rendered as work in exchange for gifts, to being work done for the benefit of "the most eminent men," and eventually to being barely disguised labor service. (Cf. Claude Meillassoux, *Anthropologie économique des Gouro de Côte d'Ivoire*, pp. 175–185.)

an increasingly "despotic" type at the top, which is an expression of the new ruling class.

Once having stated that the Asiatic mode of production can in the last analysis be reduced to the mere combination of a village community and an exploiting central authority,[33] the authors I have mentioned naturally have no difficulty in discovering, though not without astonishment, this "Asiatic" (*sic*) mode of production in Black Africa and pre-Columbian America, and even in Mediterranean Europe (the Etruscans and the Creto-Mycenean civilization).[34] When, however, this reduction process has been successfully completed, we have to ask what that is specifically Asiatic remains in this expanded category. And the answer is clear: not very much, especially as regards the phenomena that, after all, started Marx and Engels on their analysis —the *hypertrophied and despotic* character of the state, and the absence of private property in land.

Further, the excessive extension of the idea of the Asiatic mode of production to *all* societies "in transition from classless society to class society" does not enable us to account for another, still more important, aspect of this idea as Marx described it. By making the Asiatic mode of production a society that comes in between clan communism and slaveowning or feudal society, one which "breaks up" into either slaveowning or feudal society, these critics once again suppress all that is specific in the history of the East, and return, after a short detour, to the good old rut of universal "slavery" or "feudalism"—after having previously

33. Jean Chesneaux ("Le mode de production asiatique," p. 41): "The Asiatic mode of production seems indeed to be characterized by the combination of the productive activity of the village communities with the economic intervention of a state authority which exploits them."

The Czechoslovak professor Jan Harmatta comes to a similar conclusion in his interpretation of the social structure of the ancient empire of the Huns: "The society of Attila's time was, undoubtedly, a class society; but the production relations that prevailed among the Huns did not correspond to the categories of an established social system like the slaveowning or the feudal system. The characteristic feature of Hunnish society was precisely its transitional nature, as a class society with strong survivals of the former clan organization." ("La société des Huns à l'époque d'Attila," in *Recherches internationales à la lumière du marxisme*, May–June 1957, p. 238.)

34. Godelier, "La notion de 'mode de production asiatique,'" p. 21.

deplored the excessive expansion of these ideas.[35] They do not seem to have reckoned with the fact that in the writings of Marx and Engels, the idea of an Asiatic mode of production is related not just to some "primitive" Indian or Chinese society, lost in the mists of the past, but to *Indian and Chinese society as they were when European industrial capital encountered them in the eighteenth century*, on the eve of the conquest (India) or the massive penetration (China) of these countries by this capital.[36]

---

35. See ibid., p. 33, on the ways in which the Asiatic mode of production "breaks up."

On this point it is interesting to observe that even so profound a Marxist historian as Ernst Werner gives the following definition of "production relations of a purely feudal type": "The preponderance of petty peasant production; the domination of agriculture over the crafts and of the country over the town; land monopolized by a minority; appropriation of the peasants' surplus product by the dominant class." (*Die Geburt einer Grossmacht, die Osmanen*, p. 305.) This definition would apply to the Later Roman Empire of the third and fourth centuries and to feudal Europe of the ninth century, to the China or India of the sixteenth century (since what is mentioned is *monopoly* of land and not *ownership* of land!), to the Ottoman Empire of the eighteenth century, and even to Tsarist Russia at the beginning of the nineteenth century—that is, to societies and states which were profoundly different from each other. Werner forgets the *fundamental* characteristic of feudalism, namely, *private ownership* of the land by the feudal nobility and *labor service* (or rent in kind) exacted from the peasantry (which evolved only later on into money rent). Since he knows the *Grundrisse*, and even quotes from them, his forgetting this point is inexcusable.

36. Let me remind the reader that the sub-chapter of the *Grundrisse* dealing with the Asiatic mode of production is entitled "Pre-*capitalist* forms of production," and that it is part of a chapter devoted to the primitive accumulation of *capital*. The context shows us at once that there is a definite reason for placing the sub-chapter here: the task is to show why, under the Asiatic mode of production, even the very greatest accumulation of sums of money did not lead to a process of capital accumulation. Similarly, Lenin in 1914 described "Asiatic despotism" in these terms: "It is generally known that this kind of state system possesses great stability whenever completely patriarchal and pre-capitalist features predominate in the economic system and where commodity production and class differentiation are scarcely developed." (*Collected Works*, Vol. 20, p. 403.) It is hard to recognize in this description the type of society that fills the gap between tribal communism and a society based on slavery. It is true that in the *Grundrisse* (pp. 380–386) Marx also describes the Asiatic mode of production as one of the forms of collective ownership of the land that issue from

(In this connection, Romesh Dutt quotes the writers of official reports at the beginning of the nineteenth century who confirm that at that time the fields still belonged collectively to the village communities.[37])

If the idea of the Asiatic mode of production is stripped of its specific meaning, it can no longer explain the *special* development of the East in comparison with Western and Mediterranean Europe. It loses its chief usefulness as a tool for analyzing the societies for which Marx and Engels explicitly intended it. It can recover this usefulness only if we go back to the original formulations, and to the function originally intended for it by Marx and Engels—that of explaining the peculiarities of the historical development of India, China, Egypt, and the Islamic world, as compared with the historical development of Western Europe.

Oriental Despotism, Wittfogel's latest *magnum opus*, plainly lacks scientific objectivity;[38] nevertheless it seems to me that it

the decomposition of tribal communism—on the same plane with the collective ownership of the *ager publicus* in Rome or the collective ownership of the land among the Germans and Slavs. This is doubtless the passage that has led some writers astray. In the same context, however, Marx notes that of all these forms of collective ownership that constituted by the Asiatic mode of production is "the one that survives longest and most stubbornly," implying that it has existed down to the beginnings of modern capitalism. (*Pre-Capitalist Economic Formations*, p. 83.)

37. Romesh Dutt, *The Economic History of India*, Vol. I, p. 107.

38. In *Oriental Despotism* (pp. 497–499), Wittfogel argues, without offering any proof, that Marx "mystified" the nature of the "bureaucracy" of the "Asiatic mode of production," for fear of condemning along with it the bureaucracy of the "socialist state" that he wanted to establish. The same motive, according to Wittfogel, led Marx later to play down his idea of the "Asiatic mode of production." Quite apart from the fact that the latter section of this thesis remains quite unsupported by evidence, the former section, which attributes to Marx a bureaucratic-Stalinist conception of the state to be set up after the overthrow of capitalism (whereas Marx had hailed the Paris Commune which, itself the outcome of universal suffrage, abolished the permanent tenure of officials and reduced their salaries to the level of skilled workers' wages, as the model of the "dictatorship of the proletariat" as he understood it), is a rather scandalous falsification of history. Rubel remarks with justification that "this retrospective denunciation of an act of intellectual dishonesty allegedly committed by Marx belongs more to the realm of pathology than to that of scientific discussion." (See the note on p. 1680 of Rubel's edition of Marx's works, *Oeuvres—Economie I*.)

is in his masterpiece of 1931, *Wirtschaft und Gesellschaft Chinas*, that, to this day, one can find the key to understanding the specific character of the Asiatic mode of production, in the twofold sense in which Marx and Engels meant it in the *Grundrisse*. In this book Wittfogel fully describes the amazing prowess of the Chinese peasant, who rapidly made China one of the most densely populated countries in the world. This prowess, however, was dependent on the existence of hydraulic works on such a scale that the communes, or even groupings of communes or of provinces, were incapable of undertaking them.[39] From this arose the objective necessity, the functional role, of a strong central authority, which also made possible the fairly rapid development of large-scale manufacture—much sooner than in Europe[40]—but without engendering a free bourgeoisie, even in the medieval sense of the word. The state was too strong, it imposed too broken a rhythm upon the accumulation of money capital, it subjected too thoroughly all intellectual and scientific life to the requirements of agriculture,[41] to allow for the possibility of a process equivalent to that of the primitive accumulation of capital and the formation of a modern industry with a free proletariat which occurred in Western Europe.

It is necessary to stress that this society is not at all a "primitive" one, in the sense that there are no clearly defined or constituted social classes. On the contrary, alongside the peasants there are not only public functionaries but also landowners (illegally appropriating ownership of the land) and merchants and bankers, often enormously rich. What determines the specific position of these classes in the Asiatic mode of production, however, is that, confronted with the hypertrophy of the state authority, they

---

39. Wittfogel, *Wirtschaft und Gesellschaft Chinas*, pp. 187, 192–193, and especially 285–287.

40. See a striking allusion to the existence of these Chinese manufactories in the *Grundrisse*, pp. 397, 410. (In *Pre-Capitalist Economic Formations*, pp. 98, 116–117.)

41. Wittfogel, *Wirtschaft und Gesellschaft Chinas*, pp. 670–679. Cf. a passage on page 572 of the same book where the writer shows that the Chinese craftsman always remained a servitor, and usually an itinerant one, owing to the Asiatic extent of the landed estates! This passage could be fitted into the *Grundrisse* context I have commented on here.

can never acquire the *social and political power* which, in other countries, gives rise first to feudalism and then to modern capitalism. This is what the concept of the Asiatic mode of production explains.

Here I must answer an objection put forward by Michael Mauke, who devoted himself especially to going more deeply into the idea of class in Marx's writings in connection with a thesis on office workers which he was completing at the time of his sudden death at the age of thirty-seven. Mauke said that under the Asiatic mode of production there was indeed appropriation of the social surplus product by the ruling strata, and they held the right to command surplus labor. "But so long as these two phenomena were still linked with the fulfillment of functions for the *whole* of society (bureaucracy, theocracy, etc.), then, whatever abuses and parasitism there might be, for Marx there could be no question of 'classes' but, instead, of government, domination, and despotism." [42]

Mauke is here generalizing—mistakenly, in my view—a feature of the ruling class which in reality applies only to the capitalist bourgeoisie, for whom the separation between "private interest" and "social function" is almost complete.[43] With all pre-capitalist ruling classes, and *a fortiori* with non-ruling classes like the independent craftsmen of the Middle Ages, this radical separation does not exist. At the level of the demesne, the feudal lord, or the abbot of the abbey, carries out functions "useful for the whole of society" in the same way as is done by the scribe of ancient Egypt or the mandarin of classical China. He sees to the draining of marshes, busies himself with building and maintaining dikes when geographical necessity dictates it, protects the estate against raids by brigands, and so on.[44] None of this prevents him from appropriating the social surplus product in re-

42. Michael Mauke, "Thesen zur Klassentheorie von Marx," in *Neue Kritik*, February 1966, p. 29.

43. Even the bourgeoisie fulfills a useful function from the standpoint of society as a whole, namely, that of developing the productive forces. Marx often reiterates this in the *Grundrisse*.

44. Cf. Marx: "The landowner, such an important functionary in production in the ancient world and in the Middle Ages . . ." (*Theories of Surplus Value*, Part II, p. 44.)

turn for these "services," whereas both pre-history and history show that these same functions can be fulfilled in the service of the community without giving rise to economic privilege.

It is in this sense that it is possible to speak of the appearance of a ruling class under the Asiatic mode of production, a class which appropriates the social surplus product. In the table of ruling classes known to history it is certainly the closest to the primitive functions of the "servants of the community" and the farthest from the bourgeoisie of today.

Economic history shows us, moreover, that, alongside this ruling class, the Asiatic mode of production includes other social classes different from those of the peasants and the lords—in particular a comparatively well-developed merchant class and a class of urban craftsmen working exclusively in the service of the lords.[45]

No other writers have yet put forward in a systematic way a criticism such as I have made of the conceptions of Godelier, Chesneaux, Suret-Canale, and others. It has, however, at least been suggested and partly anticipated in a number of studies.

Thus, in his introduction to the English translation, *Pre-Capitalist Economic Formations,* Eric Hobsbawm prudently steers clear of any mechanistic interpretation of the well-known series of "four main socioeconomic formations" (Asiatic society, slave-owning society, feudalism, capitalism) which Marx lists in the Preface to his *Contribution to the Critique of Political Economy* by describing these as "analytical, though not chronological, stages." [46] Nevertheless, a few pages earlier he puts forward Godelier's idea that "the Asiatic system is therefore not yet a class society, or if it is a class society, then it is the most primitive." [47] The two observations clearly contradict one another. If the sequence is not chronological, if the Asiatic mode of production is not necessarily placed in time *before* slaveowning society (or even feudal society), how can one suppose it to be not even a class society, or at most to be a society with rudimentary classes?

Though he tends, wrongly in my view, to minimize the con-

45. See, in this connection, G. L. Adhya, *Early Indian Economics*, p. 98 for the merchants, and pp. 84–87 for the urban craftsmen.

46. Hobsbawm, *Pre-Capitalist Economic Formations*, p. 37.

47. Ibid., p. 34.

cept of the Asiatic mode of production, especially as regards more developed societies like India and China,[48] Maxime Rodinson does by implication criticize Godelier's idea when he comments thus on the passage in the *Grundrisse* which we are discussing: "Essentially, Marx sees pre-capitalist development in relation to capitalism. What interested him was the appearance in preceding formations of the conditions which make possible the emergence of a capitalist society. Pre-capitalist history is not, as in the vulgar Marxist vision, a succession of universal stages, of economic-social formations ruled by implacable laws which carry them ineluctably toward capitalism and thereby toward socialism . . . It starts from a primitive community with a structure imposed essentially by the conditions of existence of archaic humanity, but which nevertheless present a variety of types. Some of these types carry an evolutionary potential within their particular structure because of their internal contradictions. It is in the course of this evolution over thousands of years that phenomena are produced which, converging in a given place (Europe), in a given time (the sixteenth century), in a given juncture, bring forth capitalist society. Between the point of departure and the point of arrival, there are other phenomena such as slavery and serfdom, particular modes of production[49] (rather than economic-social formations in the strict sense), in which, here and there, socioeconomic relations of domination are crystallized." [50]

The remarkable foreword written by Pierre Vidal-Naquet for the French edition of Karl Wittfogel's *Oriental Despotism* must be mentioned here. Vidal-Naquet accepts, broadly speaking, the

48. Maxime Rodinson, *Islam et capitalisme*, pp. 73–83.

49. In *Studia o marksowskiej teorii spoleczenstwa* (Studies in the Marxist Theory of Society), the Polish sociologist Julian Hochfeld has established the correct distinction between "a mode of production," that is to say, an economic model which is "pure" and therefore abstract, and a socioeconomic formation, that is, a concrete type of society within which a mode of production holds a dominant position. Thus, it would be true to say that the capitalist mode of production developed in Britain from the sixteenth century onward, but to describe Britain as a capitalist "socioeconomic formation" would not be true before the second half of the eighteenth century.

50. Maxime Rodinson, "What Happened in History," in *New Left Review*, January–February 1966, pp. 97–99.

theory of the Asiatic mode of production as applied to the countries to which Marx himself applied this concept, while at the same time emphasizing the weaknesses and exaggerations in Wittfogel's book and insisting on the fact that "an agriculture which requires that large-scale public works be undertaken by the community as a whole . . . is alone capable of giving rise to this type of society." [51]

Finally I must refer to an unpublished paper by Guy Dhuquois, lecturer at the University of Algiers, which the author has kindly sent me.[52] He makes criticisms similar to those I have set out in relation to the theses of Godelier, Chesneaux, and Suret-Canale. Like Maxime Rodinson he comes back to Marx's *purpose*, which was to *contrast* the line of evolution followed by Europe to that which issued from the Asiatic mode of production. He correctly emphasizes, in this connection, the "cohesion and the extremely marked tendency to stability and to 'palingenesis' [regeneration]" which are characteristic of this mode of production. "Trade sometimes creates a beginning of capitalism [it would be more correct to say, of the accumulation of capital—E. M.] but it is destined to satisfy the needs of the aristocrats and the sovereign, who control the surplus product. . . . The towns appear as parasitic growths, living at the expense of the rural world and giving it hardly anything in return; they provide only a narrow basis for the development of urban trade and craft production. The financier works above all for the benefit of the 'despot.' The trader and the financier find themselves in a setting which is from many points of view—economic, sociological, political, cultural—unfavorable to individual initiative of a new type. For example, the social models offered them encourage them to purchase rights over land or to enter their sons in the civil service. Finally, the state, director of the whole of economic life, intervenes to supervise their activities. We see the dominant model continually absorbing these marginal activities." [53]

Dhuquois points out at the same time that, because of this crite-

---

51. Pierre Vidal-Naquet, Foreword to French edition of Wittfogel, *Oriental Despotism*, p. 10.

52. Guy Dhuquois, *Le mode de production asiatique*, p. 13.

53. Ibid., pp. 4–5.

rion, it would be wrong to apply the concept of the Asiatic mode of production to societies like the Later Roman Empire or the Byzantine Empire. In the case of the former the analogy would be out of place "because, in addition to the importance of private property, which, with the great landowners, had set in motion a beginning of feudalization, the state's economic preponderance seems arbitrary in relation to technical needs." [54] It was for this reason that this preponderance did not last long and that it led to a continual worsening of the economic situation and eventually to the breakdown of the state, *without this being followed by a revival* such as was so characteristic in countries like India or China. As for Byzantium, the Byzantine Empire "underwent an evolution that indeed seems to have been inevitable toward a particular kind of feudalism, which finally got the upper hand in this case, whereas, according to our definition, in the Asiatic mode of production it is normal for the state to reappear . . . in its traditional role." [55]

However, the idea of the Asiatic mode of production has not only experienced a happy rebirth in recent years, it has also been subjected to criticism, more serious indeed than that which was made by the dogmatic "Marxists" in Stalin's day. This is particularly so in the case of E. R. Leach, whose study of Ceylon published in 1959 was also a criticism of Wittfogel's book.[56]

Leach's criticism, valid in so far as it attacks the far-fetched formulations—"dogmatism the other way round"—of the Wittfogel of 1958, is far less pertinent when examined in the light of the ideas of Marx and Engels on the subject of the Asiatic mode of production, and of the Wittfogel of 1931. Undoubtedly, *elements* of "feudalism" (that is, of large-scale landed property existing *de facto* if not *de jure*, cultivated by means of labor services, or imposing payment of rent upon peasant farmers) exist under the Asiatic mode of production. According to Leach's description, these elements seem to have been more important in Ceylon than in India or China, but they existed in China too, and in *Wirtschaft und*

---

54. Ibid., p. 7.

55. Ibid., p. 8.

56. E. R. Leach, "Hydraulic Society in Ceylon," in *Past and Present*, April 1959, pp. 2–26.

Gesellschaft Chinas Wittfogel takes them fully into account. There is just this point, though: this feudal class never became the ruling class. Its advances were always regarded as encroachments on the power of the state and the rights of the peasants, and when these encroachments went too far, they periodically caused an economic and political crisis, which usually ended in the overthrow of the reigning dynasty, by way of a peasants' war, and the appearance of a new dynasty which brought the landowners to heel.[57]

Furthermore, it is possible, as Leach suggests in his study, that Ceylon's ancient irrigation system was not really as impressive as it looks today, judging by the size of the ruins. He suggests that it was built up by progressive additions, each generation contributing a certain number of canals and reservoirs, using *decentralized* labor techniques (coordinated at the village level). In that case, though, Leach's conclusion does not really disprove the thesis of the Asiatic mode of production. The latter links the appearance of an hypertrophied despotic state only with the need for *large-scale* hydraulic works. When these works are carried out in their essentials at the village level—as with the system of the *qanats* in Iran[58]—*despotism* does not necessarily result.[59]

---

57. Kosambi, in *An Introduction to the Study of Indian History* (pp. 326–331, 351–365), declares that the Moslem invaders of India established from the eleventh century onward an embryonic feudal class, but this never succeeded in seizing power over the whole territory, being caught between the despotism at the top and the village community down below.

58. See on this, Henri Goblot, "Dans l'ancien Iran, les techniques de l'eau et la grande histoire," in *Annales ESC,* May–June 1963, pp. 500–520.

59. It should be mentioned that in his *Philosophy of History*, Vol. II, which Marx and Engels studied with enthusiasm, Hegel had perceived the essential difference between the historical development of China and Europe: "Similarly there is no hereditary aristocracy in China, no feudal situation, nor is there dependence on wealth as in England, but supreme power is habitually exercised by the monarch." Cf. too, this remarkable definition, which already augurs the analysis of the "Asiatic mode of production": "In China, we have the reality of absolute equality [the village community], and all the differences that exist are possible only in connection with [the imperial] administration . . . Since equality prevails in China, but without any freedom, despotism is necessarily the mode of government." (Ibid., p. 124.)

There are also other passages in the *Grundrisse* where Marx takes up this specific difference between a society *based on the production of use values*—that is, in the last analysis based on agriculture (whether in the Asiatic mode of production, in the antique, slaveowning mode of production, or even in "pure" feudalism)—and a society *based on the production of exchange values*, on commodity production. The appearance of merchant capital (buying in order to sell) "can occur within peoples for whom exchange value has not at all become the condition of production. The movement *appropriates only the surplus* of their production aimed at immediate consumption, and takes place only at its frontiers [i.e., marginally]. Just as the Jews [did] within old Polish society or, in general, in the Middle Ages, entire trading peoples, as in the Ancient World and later the Lombards, can take up this position of intermediary between peoples whose mode of production does not yet include exchange value as its fundamental condition." [60]

And again: "Money as the fortune of merchants, as it appears in the most diverse forms of society and at the most different stages of development of social productive forces, is only the movement of an intermediary between extremes which it does not dominate, and between conditions which it does not create. . . . The majority of the trading peoples or the independent and well-developed trading towns practice the carrying trade, which is based on the barbarism of the producing peoples between whom they play the role of money [of intermediary]. In the first stages of bourgeois society trade dominates industry; in modern society the opposite is the case. Trade will obviously react to a greater or lesser extent on the communities between which it is carried on. It will subject production more or less to exchange value; it will push immediate use value further and further into the background, in proportion as it makes subsistence depend more upon selling than upon immediate utilization of the product. It disintegrates old-established relationships. It thereby increases the circulation of money. It first of all seizes hold of the surplus of production, then increasingly takes over production itself. *But its disintegrating action depends to a great extent on the nature of the productive*

---

60. *Grundrisse*, p. 165. (Emphasis mine.—E. M.)

communities between which it [trade] *is carried on. Thus, it hardly disturbed the ancient communities of India, or Asiatic conditions in general."* [61]

This passage is important because it shows that in 1857–1858 Marx retained his view of 1853 about the resistance that the Asiatic mode of production offered to the disintegrating effect of exchange. It also emphasizes that, for Marx, the entire progressive evolution of the modes of production is based on *a dialectic of the social surplus product* (the surplus) which is merely a dialectic of "necessary time" and "surplus labor," as we have already seen.[62]

It remains to set all these considerations of the Asiatic mode of production in their concrete context, that is to say, in the analysis that Marx made of the historical conditions—in the most abstract sense—of the rise of capital and of capitalism. The reader will already have realized that, following the dialectical method which he delights in using in the *Grundrisse*, Marx only spends time on the "pre-capitalist forms of production" in order to show up, *negatively*, the factors which in Europe have led, positively, to the flowering of capital and capitalism.

Marx brings out above all, in this connection, the need for labor to become really "free"—this not only in the juridical sense but also and particularly in the economic sense, that is, free from all ties with the means of subsistence or with the means of labor. "This means above all that the worker must be separated from the land, which functions as his natural laboratory. This means the dissolution both of free petty landownership and of communal landed property, based on the Oriental commune." [63] This is an idea that recurs in many passages in the *Grundrisse* and which is used particularly in the analysis of the *conditions for colonization*, an analysis which was to be expanded in Volume I of *Capital*. The

---

61. Ibid., pp. 70, 741–742. (Emphasis mine.—E. M.)

62. The Turkish Marxist writer Sencer Divitçioglu is the author of an interesting study entitled "The Asiatic Mode of Production and the Underdeveloped Countries" in which he tries to make a parallel (and establish a line of descent) between the state in the decadent period of the Asiatic mode of production and the "guardian state" in the underdeveloped countries (he obviously has Turkey in mind). See *Recherches internationales à la lumière du marxisme*, May–June 1957, pp. 277–293.

63. *Grundrisse*, p. 375. (In *Pre-Capitalist Economic Formations*, p. 67.)

rise of capitalism is impossible as long as there is still free access to (relatively) plentiful land.[64] This axiom laid down by Marx has been strikingly confirmed in the tragic fate imposed on the peoples of Zimbabwe and South Africa, who have been cut off from their native soil and herded into "reservations" in order that they may be under economic pressure to sell their labor power to capital. It means, furthermore, the separation of the producer from his traditional means of labor (for example, the case of the independent craftsman) and from the consumption fund which he possessed before he even began to produce.[65]

But Marx also shows the other side of the coin: in the primitive communities man is closely integrated into natural conditions of existence and into the community "whose property he is himself up to a certain point." [66] The level of development of the productive forces allows no other social organization. It is only if this development transcends the stage of the primitive community, if the productive forces become *the product of man much more than the product of nature*,[67] that the individual separates himself from the primitive communities: ". . . man is only individualized through the process of history." [68] Exchange is one of the chief instruments of this individualization. At the same time it brings about the alienation of man—but it also creates the conditions needed for his complete flowering as an individual, with all "the universality of needs, capacities, enjoyments, productive powers, etc., of individuals . . . ," [69] which is absent in the primitive communities and repressed in bourgeois society.

We thus see how unfair is the reproach often hurled at Marx, according to which he is said to have sought to achieve a com-

---

64. K. S. Shelvankar notes that even in the eighteenth century land was still abundantly available in the Ganges region of India. (See Shelvankar in Desai, ed., *Rural Sociology in India*, p. 149.)

65. *Grundrisse*, p. 397. (In *Pre-Capitalist Economic Formations*, p. 98.)

66. Ibid., p. 395. (In *Pre-Capitalist Economic Formations*, p. 95.)

67. Cf. the almost identical formula used in the *Economic and Philosophic Manuscripts:* "Man produces himself." *Man Makes Himself* is the title of an excellent summary of pre-history and ancient history written by the late, lamented Gordon Childe.

68. *Grundrisse*, p. 395. (In *Pre-Capitalist Economic Formations*, p. 96.)

69. Ibid., p. 387. (In *Pre-Capitalist Economic Formations*, p. 84.)

plete integration of the individual in the community and the socialization he wanted is said to mean a complete socialization of the individual.[70] The opposite is true. If Marx attached such great importance to the development of the productive forces, if he was to a certain degree "in love with technical progress"—without ever underestimating the dangers of fragmentation and alienation of labor that result from it—the reason is precisely because he understood that only this development of the productive forces could create the necessary conditions for *an ever greater individualization of man,* which will be ultimately achieved in socialist society.[71]

---

70. Cf. for example, François Perroux's Preface to the Pléiade edition of Marx's works, *Oeuvres—Economie I,* p. xxii: "The socialized man of ultimate communism is man only in the social whole, in the totality that constitutes communist society. The individual is objectivized in and through belonging to this society . . ." Similarly on p. xxiii: "This man who has become truly himself in and through the social whole, this man who remains truly himself only in and through the social totality, is not described as an original and unique subject essentially capable of free activity and free speech. He is not truly himself through the unconquerable spontaneity of his mind, the source of his personal activity and speech, but through his participation in the social whole: only in and through this totality has he become and can he continue to be a man . . ." The quotation from the *Grundrisse* which we have just given shows how little the picture Perroux draws of "socialist man," or "communist man," according to Marx, conforms with Marx's own conception. On the contrary, Marx assigns to the future society the task of insuring "the free development of individualities," which is essentially an "artistic, scientific, etc.," development. (*Grundrisse,* p. 593.) This passage—like that on pp. 599–600 where the idea is taken further in a discussion of the reciprocal action of "free time," which transforms man into "another subject," capable of experimenting and creating freely, and the development of the productive forces—shows how contrary to the truth is another idea of Perroux's (p. xvii), according to which Marx thinks that "a small number of masters of the machines" will continue to exist even in communist society.

71. This does not at all contradict the sixth of Marx's theses on Feuerbach, which declares that "the human essence is no abstraction inherent in each single individual. In its reality it is the ensemble of the social relations." What is meant is, in fact, infinitely richer social relations which will enable socialist man to assert himself.

9

The Final Shaping of the Theory of Wages

As we have seen, the first work that Marx devoted especially to wage labor, *Wage Labor and Capital*, was still partly based on a faulty theory of wages, taken over wholesale from Ricardo. The same theory of wages is found in other writings of Marx's belonging to the same period, notably in *The Poverty of Philosophy* and in the *Communist Manifesto*.

What is the point here? Ricardo's theory of wages was largely inspired by Malthus and describes a movement of supply of and demand for workers which is essentially a result of the *demographic* process. An increase in wages causes the workers to have more children—or, if one wishes to speak more circumspectly, it causes a decline in infant mortality—which results in an increase in the supply of hands, and so a fall in wages. On the other hand, a fall in wages reduces the size of workers' families—or what comes to the same thing, increases the rate of infant mortality—and so decreases the supply of hands. At a certain moment, therefore, the demand for workers must exceed the supply, resulting in an increase in wages. These two movements of the pendulum tend to even out the level of wages, but at the lowest level, just sufficient to keep a worker with an "average" family alive (in order to insure a demographic movement corresponding exactly to capitalist industry's need for workers).

It is obvious that this is an extremely primitive theory.[1] The

---

1. It must be added, however, in Ricardo's defense, that he was not unaware of the effect of capital accumulation on wages: though at first he supposed that the increased use of machinery would tend to raise wages,

reasoning is weak in the first place because, while Ricardo defines wages as resulting from the fluctuations in the supply and demand for workers, he in fact confines himself to studying the fluctuations in supply (and even those only partially), leaving out of account fluctuations in demand. As far as the supply of workers is concerned, he examines only what follows from the demographic movement among the workers, leaving aside one of the most significant processes in capitalism, the proletarianization of producers who previously had direct control of their means of production or exchange (peasants, craftsmen, small shopkeepers, and small businessmen), but who appear on the labor market in increasing numbers.

Finally, in that part of the reasoning that seems to be more valid —namely, the fluctuations in infant mortality governed by the average standard of living of working-class families—a crude mistake is made: the time factor is overlooked. In reality, a decline in infant mortality does not immediately produce an increase in the supply of hands: the increase only occurs ten to fifteen years later (the length of the interval depending on the volume of child labor and the average age at which young workers are hired). In order to know whether this increase in the supply of workers will or will not cause a fall in wages, it is necessary, at the very least, to consider what the tendency of the demand for workers is from one decade to the next. The Malthus-Ricardo theory of wages thus in fact tacitly presupposes a *long-term stagnation* of demand for workers (decade after decade!), something which does not conform to the actual phenomena of the industrial revolution, of industrialization, and of economic growth under capitalism in general. This theory was espoused, in its crude form, only by various "utopian" socialists and by Lassalle, in his famous "iron law of wages." [2] Marx and Engels never upheld it, but it did undoubt-

---

he later modified this view and acknowledged that the spread of machinery might have a harmful effect on wages. (See Piero Sraffa's Introduction to *The Works and Correspondence of David Ricardo*, Vol. I, p. lvii.) But Ricardo was too greatly hypnotized by his own theory of rent, and the hypothesis of a general and permanent rise in the cost of food, to be able to break decisively with Malthus's ideas.

2. "The iron economic law that determines wages under present-day conditions, in the name of supply and demand of labor, is the following: that

edly influence them in formulating their first, faulty theory of wages, which implies, like the Ricardo-Malthus theory, a tendency for wages to decline toward the physiological minimum living wage and stay there.

It was the "brilliant sketches" by the young Engels, the *Outlines of a Critique of Political Economy*, that provided the wage theory the two friends were to maintain, broadly speaking, until Marx's second exile in England. In the *Outlines*, Engels denounces Malthus's doctrine as "vile" and "infamous," but nevertheless adopts its conclusions: ". . . only the very barest necessities, the mere means of subsistence, fall to the lot of labor . . ."[3] He deduces this not from a *demographic* movement (though he says that it "constitutes Malthus's merit" that he showed "that population is always pressing on the means of employment"[4]) but from an economic fact: the *universal competition* in which the workers are weaker than the capitalists, and are all the weaker because they can be replaced by machines.

This last argument, which seems somewhat marginal in the *Outlines*, was to take first place in the wage theory Marx and Engels held in their youth. Thus, in his reading notes of 1844, Marx had already added the following comment to his excerpts from Ricardo and Adam Smith: "In all industrial countries, the number of workers is now greater than the demand, and can be added to daily from the *unemployed* proletariat, just as these workers in their turn increase the numbers of the proletariat. Thus, accumulation also has the converse result that the worker's wage gets pushed down farther and farther."[5] In the first of the *Economic and Philosophic Manuscripts of 1844*, Marx says that capitalism will react against any increase in wages by trying to cut down the de-

---

the average wage always remains no higher than the level of subsistence necessary for existence and reproduction, in accordance with the given habits and customs of a people." (Ferdinand Lassalle, "Offenes Antwortschreiben an das Zentralkomitee zur Berufung eines Allgemeinen Deutschen Arbeiterkongresses zu Leipzig," April 24, 1863, in *Gesammelte Reden und Schriften*, Vol. III, p. 58.)

3. *Economic and Philosophic Manuscripts*, p. 223.

4. Ibid., p. 220.

5. It is interesting to observe that the young Marx here uses the word "proletariat" to mean not the working class as a whole, but exclusively the unemployed, by analogy with the proletariat of ancient Rome.

mand for workers *by replacing workers with machines*: "Since the worker has sunk to the level of a machine, he can be confronted by the machine as a competitor." [6] It is this inherent tendency that capitalism has to substitute dead labor for living labor that becomes, in the writings of the young Marx, the driving force both of capital accumulation and of the tendency of wages to decline.[7]

The conclusion Marx derives, at this stage, from this law is that he considers that the more the worker produces, the less he consumes; he thus assumes an absolute decline in wages. The fact that wages cannot rise, in a given situation, without causing profits to fall, is already clearly brought out in the second of the manuscripts of 1844.[8]

Thus, our two young writers were developing a theory of wages *that essentially starts not from population movements but from the movement of the accumulation of capital.*

In the *Economic and Philosophic Manuscripts*, Marx notes that it is the period of expansion, of high conjuncture, that is the most favorable to the workers, because in such a period the demand for workers exceeds the supply, and competition among the capitalists is intensified. These two factors cause wages to rise. Marx adds, however, that the logic of the capitalist system quickly brings about the opposite result. The high conjuncture stimulates capital accumulation, and then capitalist concentration, which in turn causes a number of independent producers to fall into the ranks of the proletariat, and this means an increase in the supply of workers and a fall in wages.[9]

In *The Poverty of Philosophy*, in the "Arbeitslohn" manuscript, in *Wage Labor and Capital*, and in the *Communist Manifesto*, Marx and Engels remain wedded to the idea that the general tendency of wages under capitalism is to fall absolutely and to sink to the physiological subsistence minimum. I have mentioned above their reservations and qualifications, which were to help them

6. *Economic and Philosophic Manuscripts*, p. 69.

7. Two years later Marx was to write to Annenkov: "Since 1825, the invention and application of machinery has been simply the result of the war between workers and employers." (In *Selected Works*, Vol. I, p. 521.)

8. *Economic and Philosophic Manuscripts*, p. 79.

9. Ibid., p. 68.

substantially in overcoming what was amiss in their theory. The two driving forces of this tendency for real wages to fall are, on the one hand, the replacement of workers by machines (that is, a form of capital accumulation that does away with more jobs than it creates), and, on the other, *the growing competition among workers*, as a result of this permanent and increasing unemployment.

When he wrote his "Arbeitslohn" notes in Brussels in 1847, Marx still believed that the objections to trade unions made by economists (claiming that the unions could not prevent wages from falling because their activity inevitably provoked new forms of division of labor, the shifting of capital from one sector to another, the introduction of new machines, and so on) were basically well founded. Marx nevertheless defended these "associations" of workers, taking the view that it was in them that the workers learned to prepare themselves for the overthrow of the "old society." [10] He was to revise and amplify this opinion, too, some years later.

In short, during the whole of this period Marx's fundamental idea on wages was that the "natural price" (the value) of labor (of labor power) is the minimum wage, this being conceived as a physiological notion. [11] When and how did he revise this conception? It is not easy to establish this with precision, but it was doubtless his study of the cyclical fluctuations of the economy and of trade-union activity in Britain that led him to form more correct views. [12]

---

10. *Kleine ökonomische Schriften*, pp. 246–247.

11. See the well-known passage in the *Communist Manifesto:* "The cost of production of a workman is restricted, almost entirely, to the means of subsistence that he requires for his maintenance, and for the propagation of his race. But the price of a commodity, and therefore also of labor, is equal to its cost of production. In proportion, therefore, as the repulsiveness of the work increases, the wage decreases." (In *Selected Works*, Vol. I, pp. 114–115.)

12. Nevertheless, it should be noted that as early as 1847, in his "Arbeitslohn" notes, Marx considered that the minimum is not an absolute physiological notion; that different elements can be introduced into it, or deducted from it; that the bourgeoisie itself includes in it "a little rum, tea, sugar and meat"; and that the workers themselves include in it their trade-union subscriptions. (*Kleine ökonomische Schriften*, p. 247.)

In the *Grundrisse*, written in 1857–1858, exactly ten years after the passages just quoted,[13] Marx already held a more dialectical, more finished, and more mature view of the wage problem, a view that was to remain practically unchanged down to the writing of *Capital*. Thus in the *Grundrisse* Marx observes that the only thing that distinguishes the worker from the slave is that he can *expand* the range of his enjoyment during a period of economic prosperity, that he can "take part in higher forms of enjoyment, even spiritual forms, can agitate for his own interests, buy newspapers, listen to lectures, educate his children, develop his tastes," in short, "participate in civilization" in the only way that remains open to him, *by increasing his needs.*[14] Now here Marx is saying by implication that this increase in consumption, this expansion of needs, is possible for the worker, at least in periods of high conjuncture, and that the value of labor power thus includes *two* elements: a more or less stable physiological element, and a variable element, regarded as necessary for the reproduction of labor power *in accordance with the increasing needs acquired by the worker.*

A few pages farther on in the *Grundrisse* Marx points out that capital has a tendency to drive the worker to replace his "natural [i.e., physiological] needs" with "historically created" needs.[15] This idea had already been dealt with in an earlier passage, where Marx emphasized that the worker is also regarded as a *consumer* by the capitalist, who therefore tends to seek to stimulate consumption, except on the part of his own workers.[16] This idea is also developed in the analysis of the production of relative surplus value, where the *two contradictory effects of the accumulation of capital on the value of labor power and on the evolution of wages* are explained.

On the one hand, the accumulation of capital, the replacement of living labor by machines, and the increasing productivity of

13. See Engels: "In the 1840's Marx had not yet finished his critique of political economy. This took place only toward the end of the 1850's." (Introduction to the 1891 edition of *Wage Labor and Capital*, in *Selected Works*, Vol. I, p. 142.)

14. *Grundrisse*, pp. 197–198.

15. Ibid., p. 231.

16. Ibid., pp 194, 198

labor, all tend to lower nominal wages (the same amount of food-stuffs, or of commodities in general, is now produced in a shorter period of time) and even real wages (under the pressure of growing unemployment). On the other hand, however, the accumulation of capital implies the creation of new branches of industry—and thus the creation of new jobs—as well as *the creation of new needs* and the spreading of these needs in wider and wider circles.[17] In this way it tends to increase the value of labor power (because this value now includes the prices of the new commodities purchased to satisfy these new needs) as well as its price (when unemployment declines). The real movements of wages are thus no longer determined by mechanical and simple laws, but depend on the dialectical interaction of this *dual effect* of capital accumulation on the value of labor power.[18]

In *Theories of Surplus Value*, written in 1862–1863, Marx explains that the accumulation of capital, while constantly replacing living labor by machines, can reproduce wage labor on an expanded scale—that is, can increase the absolute number of wage earners even if the total amount of wages declines relative to the total amount of capital.[19] Elsewhere he notes that in a period of high conjuncture the workers "play an important role as consumers," and as "consumers of their own products" (consumer goods).[20]

But it was in his address to the General Council of the First International, on June 20 and 27, 1865, that Marx fully set out his theory of wages. He summarizes this theory in the following passage: "But there are some peculiar features which distinguish

17. Ibid., p. 312.

18. Ricardo had a presentiment of these complex effects when he emphasized that the fall in the price of many commodities might make it possible for workers to buy them. He added, however, that this would be on condition that there is a disparity between the prices of raw materials (and of labor power) and those of finished goods, and on condition that the workers *sacrifice part of their income intended for the purchase of food*. As Marx stresses, by abolishing this "disparity," free trade would at the same time abolish the source of the expansion of workers' needs. (*Grundrisse*, Appendix, pp. 817–818.)

19. *Theories of Surplus Value*, Part II, p. 572.

20. Ibid., Vol. III, p. 221.

the *value of the laboring power, or the value of labor*, from the values of all other commodities. The value of the laboring power is formed by two elements—the one merely physical, the other historical or social. Its *ultimate limit* is determined by the *physical* element, that is to say, to maintain and reproduce itself, to perpetuate its physical existence, the working class must receive the necessaries absolutely indispensable for living and multiplying. The *value* of those indispensable necessaries forms, therefore, the ultimate limit of the *value of labor*. . . .

"Besides this mere physical element, the value of labor is in every country determined by a *traditional standard of life*. It is not mere physical life, but it is the satisfaction of certain wants springing from the social conditions in which people are placed and reared up. . . .

"By comparing the standard wages or values of labor in different countries, and by comparing them in different historical epochs of the same country, you will find that the *value of labor* itself is not a fixed but a variable magnitude, even supposing the values of all other commodities to remain constant." [21]

Marx here deduces that while the minimum limit of wages can be more or less exactly defined, there is no maximum limit. Or, more precisely: the maximum wage is whatever permits the maintenance of a sufficient level of profit, below which capital will no longer be interested in hiring workers. Between this minimum and this maximum the concrete determination of the level of wages depends on "the respective powers of the combatants," that is, upon the vicissitudes of the class struggle. This was, indeed, what Marx was striving to show, since his address was above all aimed at refuting the view that trade-union activity was useless and even harmful to the workers.[22]

But these "respective powers of the combatants" are in their turn determined, at least in part, by objective factors. Among these Marx mentions first and foremost the fluctuation in the supply and demand of labor, which gives him occasion to explain that, in

21. *Wages, Price and Profit* (also known as *Value, Price and Profit*), in *Selected Works*, Vol. II, pp. 71–72.

22. See his letter to Engels of May 20, 1865, in *Selected Correspondence*, p. 202.

relatively underpopulated overseas countries like the United States where the labor market is "being continuously emptied by the continuous conversion of wage laborers into independent, self-sustaining peasants," [23] the law of supply and demand favors the worker and enables him to obtain higher wages than in Europe. Marx had noted some years earlier, in a polemic against Ricardo, that the comparative shortage of population in the United States had stimulated both a rise in wages and a remarkable extension in the use of machinery.[24]

How do the supply and demand of labor evolve in countries that are already largely industrialized? By the constant replacement of workers by machines, the constant increase in the organic composition of capital. Marx believed that the long-term tendency is thus one of imbalance between supply and demand in favor of the capitalists and to the disadvantage of the workers: ". . . the general tendency of capitalist production is not to raise, but to sink the average standard of wages. . . ." [25]

Are we to understand this expression in the absolute sense or in the relative sense, as the lowering of the *value* of labor power or as the lowering of the *purchasing power of wages?* There are many reasons for thinking that the relative sense is closer to Marx's thought than the absolute sense. Indeed, Marx points out in the same address I have been quoting that a fall in the value of labor power can, if productivity is increased, coincide with the maintenance of the level of real wages, and he adds: "Although the laborer's absolute standard of life would have remained the same, his *relative* wages, and therewith his *relative social position*, as compared with that of the capitalist, would have been lowered." [26]

---

23. *Wages, Price and Profit*, in *Selected Works*, Vol. II, p. 73.

24. *Theories of Surplus Value*, Part II, p. 574. Cf. a similar observation made in December 1846 in the letter to Annenkov: "Finally, in North America the introduction of machinery was due both to competition with other countries and to lack of hands, that is, to the disproportion between the population of North America and its industrial needs." (In *Selected Works*, Vol. I, p. 521.)

25. *Wages, Price and Profit*, in *Selected Works*, Vol. II, p. 74.

26. Ibid., p. 66. Marx attached great importance to the idea of "relative wages" and considered it to be one of Ricardo's "scientific achievements" to have established the category of relative or proportional wages. (See

Now, these conditions of increasing productivity have undoubtedly been the most "normal" in capitalist countries for nearly a century. Marx immediately adds, following the passage just quoted: "If the working man should resist that reduction of relative wages, he would only try to get some share in the increased productive powers of his own labor, and to maintain his former relative position in the social scale." [27]

This possibility even implies a tendency for real wages to rise, with a decline in the relative share of the newly created values going to the worker. And in his *Theories of Surplus Value* Marx seems to indicate that this is a general tendency and that "the workers cannot prevent, to be sure, the decline of wages [in value], but they do not let themselves be reduced absolutely to the minimum, instead wresting, quantitatively, a certain participation for themselves in the progress of general wealth." [28]

In any case, the conclusion regarding the tendency of average wages to fall needs to be qualified by two observations. It applies only to capitalist society taken as a whole, that is, on the *world* scale; and it may well find concrete expression in a tendency for average wages in the industrialized countries to rise, since there the accumulation of capital takes place on such a scale that employment constantly expands, in comparison with the growth of population, *because the abolition of jobs implied by this movement takes place not so much inside these countries as outside them, in the countries of the "Third World."* It may be tempered, too, by the fact that alongside the increasing use of machinery there is also an increase in the number of jobs in the service sector, and a "new middle class" develops which prevents continual growth in the industrial reserve army—phenomena which Marx had foreseen long before they occurred, in two passages in *Theories of Surplus Value.*[29] And large-scale migratory movements, such as the emigration of some 70 million Europeans to America and other over-

---

Theories of Surplus Value, Vol. II, p. 417.) Marx actually emphasized the importance of the idea himself as early as 1847. (See *Wage Labor and Capital*, in *Selected Works*, Vol. I, pp. 150–174.)

27. *Wages, Price and Profit*, in *Selected Works*, Vol. I, p. 66.
28. *Theories of Surplus Value*, Vol. III, p. 309.
29. Ibid., Vol. II, pp. 571–572, 573.

seas regions during the nineteenth century, may eventually profoundly alter the tendencies in the evolution of supply and demand of labor.

At the same time, the useful effect of trade-union activity is that it abolishes, to a large extent at least, that famous competition among the workers that had seemed to the young Marx to be the reason for the inevitable decline of wages to the minimum level.[30] In *Wages, Price and Profit*, Marx expresses himself more scientifically when he says that when there is abundant supply on the "labor market," especially in a period of economic crisis and large-scale unemployment, labor power may actually be sold *below its value*. The workers' coalition, the abolition of competition among workers, collective bargaining on wages, trade-union activity—all these in the last analysis are meant to insure that, on the average, labor power is sold at its value and not below it. And Marx thus considers these forms of action absolutely indispensable, since without them the working class "would be degraded to one level mass of broken wretches past salvation." [31] But the *objective possibilities* of successful trade-union activity depend in turn on the *relative* size of the industrial reserve army which, as Marx was to say later on, in *Capital*, is the regulator of wages. It is only when unemployment tends to remain stable or even decline over a long period that a long-term rise in real wages can be achieved.[32]

Marx's essential concern was to bring out the *relative* impoverishment of the proletariat, the fact that even when wages rise they rise much less than the wealth of capital. As early as *Wage Labor and Capital* we find, in this connection, the metaphor of the house, which "may be large or small," beside which a palace rises. Twenty years later Marx was to write in *Capital*: "The lot of the laborer, be his payment high or low, must grow worse." The same denunciation of relative impoverishment underlies these two formulations.[33] All the evidence we have presented shows

---

30. See in particular *Wage Labor and Capital* in *Selected Works*, Vol. I, pp. 171–173.

31. *Wages, Price and Profit*, in *Selected Works*, Vol. II, p. 75.

32. Cf. my *Marxist Economic Theory*, Vol. I, p. 145 *et seq.*

33. *Wage Labor and Capital*, in *Selected Works*, Vol. I, p. 163; *Capital*,

clearly that in his mature works Marx never expounded any "law" of the *absolute* impoverishment of the workers, though he regarded their relative impoverishment as inevitable.

Eliane Mossé[34] quotes the well-known passage from Volume I, Chapter XXV, of *Capital* in which Marx speaks of the "accumulation of wealth at one pole" being "at the same time accumulation of misery, agony of toil, slavery, ignorance, brutality, mental degradation, at the opposite pole, i.e., on the side of the class that produces its own product in the form of capital." [35] But she does not seem to notice that, if one takes into account the context— the sentences that lead up to this passage—Marx's formulation is intended not to apply to the employed workers but to "the lazarus-layers of the working class," that is, to the mass of unemployed who make up the industrial reserve army. This is further emphasized by the preceding passage in which Marx explains "the absolute general law of capitalist accumulation": "The relative mass of the industrial reserve army increases therefore with the potential energy of wealth. But the greater this reserve army in proportion to the active labor army, the greater is the mass of a consolidated surplus population, whose misery is in inverse ratio to its torment of labor. The more extensive, finally, the lazarus-layers of the working class, and the industrial reserve army, the greater is official pauperism.[36] *This is the absolute general law of capitalist accumulation.* Like all other laws it is modified in its working by many circumstances, the analysis of which does not concern us

---

Vol. I, p. 645. The whole question of Marx's theory of wages is the subject of a remarkable study by Roman Rosdolsky, "Der esoterische und der exoterische Marx," in *Arbeit und Wirtschaft* (the Austrian trade-union journal), November 1957 and January 1958.

34. Eliane Mossé, *Marx et le problème de la croissance dans une économie capitaliste*, p. 60.

35. *Capital*, Vol. I, p. 645.

36. In the *Communist Manifesto*, Marx and Engels had already made use in an unclear and ambiguous way of the well-known formula "the laborer . . . becomes a pauper" ("der Arbeiter wird zum Pauper") since this formula could be taken to refer no less to the decline in the wages of the workers still in employment (which the *Manifesto* declares to be inevitable) than to the workers ousted from the production process. In *Capital*, the term "pauperism" is used only in relation to this "lazarus-layer" of the proletariat.

here." [37] There is therefore nothing to be deduced from this passage as far as the evolution of *wages* is concerned, especially as almost immediately afterward comes the observation already referred to: "It follows therefore that in proportion as capital accumulates, the lot of the laborer, be his payment high or low, must grow worse."

Many studies confirm the existence of these "lazarus-layers of the working class" in all the capitalist countries. The most striking example is provided by the country with the highest wage level, the United States, where the "absolute general law of capitalist accumulation" has been verified in dramatic fashion. Since the publication of Michael Harrington's book *The Other America*, it is generally accepted in the United States that a quarter of the nation, 50 million Americans, are poor and bear the stigmata of poverty.[38] And if this figure is not higher, it is due in part to the fact that between 1940 and 1957 the percentage of married women employed, or in receipt of wages, increased from 15 to 30 percent, which implies, in a country whose social services are notoriously underdeveloped, "the impoverishment of home life, of children who receive less care, love and supervision." [39]

Emile James is closer to Marx's thinking than Eliane Mossé when he writes in his Preface to her book: "The conclusion is that, in conformity with Marx's views, there has indeed been both an 'absolute' and a 'relative' impoverishment of the working class during the period of France's expansion. As regards the 'relative' impoverishment, in Marx's sense of the word, Mlle Mossé's demonstration seems convincing. But what would be important would be to prove that there has been 'absolute' impoverishment. I have no hesitation in saying that my reading of Mlle Mossé's work has not convinced me on this point." [40] Actually, "absolute" impoverishment does not form part of Marx's views in his mature years.

An even more conclusive proof exists that Marx and Engels did not maintain any hypothesis of the "absolute impoverishment" of

---

37. *Capital*, Vol. I, p. 644.

38. Michael Harrington, *The Other America: Poverty in the United States*, pp. 177–178.

39. Ibid., p. 174.

40. Emile James, Preface to Eliane Mossé, *Marx et le problème de la croissance dans une économie capitaliste*.

the proletariat. In his critique of the Erfurt Programme of the German Social-Democratic Party, Engels commented on the sentence, "The number and the misery of the proletarians increase continually" in the following manner: "This is incorrect when put in such a categorical way. The organization of the workers and their constantly growing resistance will possibly check the *increase of misery* to a certain extent. However, what *certainly* does increase is the insecurity of existence. I should insert this." [41]

One can nevertheless conceive that, for Marx, relative impoverishment does not only refer to the ratio between society's total income and the share that falls to the workers; it also refers to the inadequacy of wages in relation to the needs newly aroused by capitalist production.

For Marx it is a question of comparing wages with the total wealth created by labor, and "wealth, considered from a *material* standpoint, consists only in variety of needs." [42] Now, the evolution of industrial production tends to make common and necessary needs that previously were considered luxuries. But, under the capitalist mode of production it does this in a contradictory way "in so far as it sets only a fixed social criterion for necessity as against luxury." [43] In other words, only some of the new needs are satisfied by being included in the calculation of wages for the workers, while others remain luxuries to which the workers have no access despite the fact that large-scale industry could satisfy these needs as well were it no longer developed on the basis of private appropriation.

When he completed his detailed analysis of the wage problem, Marx had in reality finished the analytical work that was to make it possible for him to write *Capital*. "I am now working like a horse, as I must use the time in which it is possible to work, and the carbuncles are still there . . . ," he wrote to Engels on May 20, 1865.[44] Those carbuncles, as he remarked on another occasion, would long be remembered by the bourgeoisie.

41. *Critique of the Erfurt Programme*, in *Selected Works*, Vol. III, p. 431.

42. *Grundrisse*, p. 426.

43. Ibid.

44. *Selected Correspondence*, p. 202.

10

From the *Economic and Philosophic Manuscripts* to the *Grundrisse:* From an Anthropological to a Historical Conception of Alienation

The time has come to conclude. I have described the genesis of Marx's economic ideas. How can one sum up the evolution of these ideas between 1843–1844—when Marx began systematically studying political economy—and the completion of the *Grundrisse?*

Marx first approached economic problems as a philosopher, still soaked in Hegel and Feuerbach, broadly accepting Feuerbach's materialist criticism of Hegel, but starting to criticize Feuerbach on the basis of Hegel, because Hegel's contribution added a historico-social dimension to anthropology that was lacking in Feuerbach.[1] Thus the *Economic and Philosophic Manuscripts* present us with a fascinating "encounter" between philosophy and political economy, a source both of a new awareness and of a contradiction for Marx, and a source of problems and disputes for those who study his work today.

1. See Herbert Marcuse, *Reason and Revolution: Hegel and the Rise of Social Theory*, pp. 271–272. See also Emile Bottigelli's remark, in his Introduction to the Editions Sociales edition of the *Economic and Philosophic Manuscripts* (p. lxix): "Marx took from Hegel the idea of man's historical evolution. From Feuerbach he took materialism, concrete man, and the equation 'humanism means naturalism.' His own conception, however, is something quite different from a mere synthesis of these elements. It transcends them in an original way, even when it seems to speak the language of those whose thought inspired it." Plekhanov had already pointed out that, "If Marx began to elaborate his materialist explanation of history by criticizing Hegel's philosophy of right, he could do so only because Feuerbach had completed his criticism of Hegel's speculative philosophy." (*Fundamental Problems of Marxism*, p. 31.)

And yet this bringing together of philosophy and political economy was nothing new in the history of human thought. It is found in Aristotle and in Thomas Aquinas; the liberal theoreticians of natural law practiced it on a grand scale.[2] Through his critique of Hegel's philosophy of right, Marx had already discovered that the state, in defending the interests of the property owners, does not serve the interests of society as a whole. It was enough to confront the reality of bourgeois society with the hypotheses of the theoreticians of natural law to see that equality of opportunity and the affirmation of every individual personality are deceptions in a society based on private property.

It was, however, Hegel's philosophy of labor that provided Marx with the conceptual tools with which to undertake his first struggle with political economy.[3] This philosophy of labor, whose foundations were laid down in the *System der Sittlichkeit* (System of Morality), developed in the *Realphilosophie* (Philosophy of the Real), firmly established in the *Phenomenology of Mind*, and defended in the *Philosophy of Right* and the *Science of Logic*,[4] is at the same time a veritable anthropology.

It was as early as 1805–1806 that Hegel established the relationship between man's purposeful strivings and the causality of nature, which man uses in his labor (that labor which Hegel was to present in his *Science of Logic* as the original form of human praxis). And in his *Phenomenology of Mind* Hegel defined labor as "desire restrained and checked" (*gehemmte Begierde*).[5] He developed a real dialectic of needs and labor and thus arrived at a twofold definition of labor as alienating and alienated: alienating because labor is, *by its nature*, the externalizing (*Veräusserung*) of a human capacity, which means that man loses something that previously belonged to him; and alienated because

---

2. See my *Marxist Economic Theory*, Vol. II, pp. 693–697, 700–703, and Jürgen Habermas, *Theorie und Praxis*, p. 79.

3. See in this connection the excellent chapter on Hegel's philosophy of labor in Pierre Naville, *De l'aliénation à la jouissance*.

4. Georg Lukacs, in *Der junge Hegel*, devotes himself above all to analyzing the *System der Sittlichkeit*, in which Hegel takes as his point of departure the first dialectical triad: needs—labor—enjoyment; and the *Realphilosophie*, written in Jena.

5. Hegel, *Phenomenology of Mind*, p. 238.

needs always run ahead of production and the latter can never fully satisfy the former.[6]

The anthropological nature of the idea of "alienated labor" as it appears in Hegel does not lie in the fact that Hegel had no inkling of the social contradictions produced by bourgeois society. There is a passage in the *Philosophy of Right* that reads like an anticipation of the more famous passage in *Capital* regarding the general tendencies of capitalist accumulation: ". . . [large] profits are derived. . . . The other side is the subdivision (*Vereinzelung*) and restriction (*Beschränkung*) of particular jobs. This results in the dependence and distress of the class tied to work of that sort . . ."[7] In his *Aesthetics*, Hegel describes strikingly the contrast between poverty and wealth and the alienation of *all* classes of society which results from this, in the following passage: "Here there appear within this industrial formation and the reciprocal employment of the other formations, together with their repression, partly the severest ferocity of poverty and partly, if misery is to be held at bay, of the individuals who have to seem rich, so as to be freed from work to meet their needs and to be able to devote themselves to higher interests. In this abundance the constant reflection of a ceaseless dependence has been eliminated, and man is all the more remote from all the risks of earning his living because he is no longer integrated in the milieu closest to himself, which no longer appears to him as his own work. All that surrounds him is no longer his own creation but is . . . produced . . . by others than himself."[8] The anthropological and mystifying nature of the theory lies in the fact that, on the one hand, Hegel regards this alienation as rooted in *human nature*, if not in nature in general, and on the other hand, he does not see that the contradiction which results from the contrast of wealth and poverty can lead to elimination of this alienation

6. Hegel, *Philosophy of Right*, paragraphs 190–195. This is the crucial argument used by numerous economists to deny the possibility of socialism. A Yugoslav Communist theoretician, Branko Horvat, uses it today to "refute" the possibility of a withering away of commodity production, even under communism. (*Toward a Theory of Planned Economy*, p. 132.)

7. Hegel, *Philosophy of Right*, paragraph 243.

8. Hegel, *Aesthetik*, Book I, pp. 255–256.

through a transformation of the social structure as soon as a certain level of development of the productive forces has been reached.[9]

This was the position Marx started his questioning from, at the same time as he began questioning the foundations of classical political economy by comparing them with the anthropology of Feuerbach and Hegel. The tools of his analysis *seem* to be the same, but the results are different. In this sense we cannot agree with Louis Althusser when he declares: "For this encounter of Marx's with political economy is . . . an encounter of *philosophy* with Political Economy. Naturally, not of any philosophy: of the philosophy erected by Marx through all his practico-theoretical experiments . . . This is the philosophy which resolves the contradiction of Political Economy by *thinking it*, and through it, by thinking the whole of Political Economy and all its categories, with a key-concept as starting-point, the concept of alienated labor." [10] There is much more reason to say, with Marcuse: "The transition from Hegel to Marx is, in all respects, a transition to an essentially different order of truth, not to be interpreted in terms of philosophy. We shall see that all the philosophical concepts of Marxist theory are social and economic categories, whereas Hegel's social and economic categories are all philosophical concepts. Even Marx's early writings are not philosophical. They express the negation of philosophy, though they do so in philosophical language." [11]

The point is that, from the start, Marx states clearly his *critical* position as regards political economy, no less than as regards

---

9. See in this connection the well-known dialectic of master and bondsman, which is resolved not by the *actual* abolition of servitude but merely by the declaration that, *spiritually*, the bondsman becomes freer than his master. (*Phenomenology of Mind*, pp. 234–238.)

10. Louis Althusser, *For Marx*, pp. 157–158.

11. Marcuse, *Reason and Revolution*, p. 258. See also Habermas, *Theorie und Praxis*, p. 279: "Marx does not want to philosophize according to the assumptions of philosophy, but rather according to the assumptions resulting from the fact that he has transcended it—that is, he wants to criticize. Absorbed in this way, the categories are transformed, together with the problems of philosophy, and along with them the instrument of reflection is also itself transformed."

philosophy.[12] His starting point in this critique is by no means the "concept" of alienated labor; on the contrary, it is *his practical observation of the misery of the workers*, which increases parallel with the increase of the wealth that these same workers produce. His conclusion is by no means a philosophical conclusion, on the plane of thoughts, ideas, intellectual work. On the contrary, he concludes that: "In order to abolish the *idea* of private property, the *idea* of communism is completely sufficient. It takes *actual* communist action to abolish actual private property." [13] The call to revolutionary action, to be carried out by the proletariat, is already substituted for the resignation of the "philosophy of labor."

Does this mean that in the *Economic and Philosophic Manuscripts* Marx had already rid himself of all the philosophical slag from a way of thinking that thenceforth became rigorously social and economic? This is obviously untrue. What we have here is the *transition* of the young Marx from Hegelian and Feuerbachian philosophy to the working out of historical materialism. In this transition, elements from the past are inevitably combined with elements belonging to the future. Marx combines in his own way—that is, by profoundly modifying them—the dialectics of Hegel, the materialism of Feuerbach, and the social facts established by political economy.[14] This combination is not a coherent one; it does not create a new "system," a new "ideology." It presents us with scattered fragments which contain many contradictions.[15] Nor must we forget that this was a manuscript that

---

12. See Marx, Preface to the *Economic and Philosophic Manuscripts*, pp. 63–64.

13. Ibid., p. 154.

14. Naville, *De l'aliénation à la jouissance*, p. 136.

15. Here we put our finger on the source of Louis Althusser's mistake when he vainly tries to present the *Economic and Philosophic Manuscripts* as a work with a finished ideology, "forming a whole." He is right to oppose the analytico-teleological method which examines the work of a young writer exclusively in order to see how close it comes to the "goal," meaning the writer's mature work. But he is wrong to set against this a method that arbitrarily cuts up into ideologically coherent slices the successive phases in a writer's evolution, on the pretext of regarding every ideology as a whole. (*For Marx*, p. 60.) A rich and living totality (the thought of a

was "not merely unfinished but also partly destroyed." [16] It is precisely in the light of the concept of alienated labor that the contradictions contained in the *Economic and Philosophic Manuscripts* can be most clearly revealed.

After having successively discovered alienation in the religious sphere (in the appendix to his doctoral thesis) and in the juridical sphere (private interest alienates man from the community), Marx had realized, in his criticism of Hegel on constitutional law, that private property was a general source of alienation; and then, in his *Contribution to the Critique of Hegel's Philosophy of Right*, that human alienation was fundamentally alienation of human labor.[17] By subjecting political economy to systematic criticism

---

writer taken as a whole, evolving all the time under the pressure of its internal contradictions, an evolution which is determined, in the last analysis, by the dynamic of the socioeconomic context in which the writer lives) is thus sacrificed in favor of a meager and static totality. It is not accidental that Althusser is led to speak of the "mutations" of a writer's thinking— that is, the more or less arbitrary leaps—and that the idea of *internal contradictions* in this thinking, as the driving force of its evolution, completely disappears. Althusser's objection that this conception would mean "putting Marx back into Hegel," since Marxism would then appear as having been "born from the internal contradictions of Hegelianism," is baseless. It is not a matter of the contradictions of Hegel but of those in the thinking of Marx *when he combined elements borrowed from Hegel with new knowledge* arising from new experience and new practice in a new social and economic context of history.

16. Naville, *De l'aliénation à la jouissance*, p. 131. See also this view expressed by Paul Kaegi: "It is thus advisable first to examine carefully the remains [of these sketches] taken separately. That will save us from combining them too readily, letting ourselves imagine that we have before us a sketch of something entire, and overlooking the essential differences between the various pieces." (*Genesis des historischen Materialismus*, p. 218.) Bottigelli says the same thing in his Introduction to the *Economic and Philosophic Manuscripts* (pp. xxxvii–xxxviii): "*The Manuscripts of 1844* do not come before us as a finished work. In the first place, we do not possess all of them . . . Again, they terminate without coming to a conclusion, their writing having doubtless been stopped by external circumstances. Finally, the separate parts lack homogeneity."

17. Wolfgang Jahn, "Der ökonomische Inhalt des Begriffs der Entfremdung der Arbeit in den Frühschriften von Karl Marx," in *Wirtschaftswissenschaft*, No. 6, 1957, p. 850. Jahn takes this idea from Auguste Cornu (*Karl Marx, Die ökonomisch-philosophische Manuskripte*), who writes (p.

he discovered that it tends to *conceal* the social contradictions, the misery of the workers, which are, so to speak, epitomized in the phenomenon of alienated labor.

Here, however, Marx's thinking hesitates on the brink of great discoveries. In one of the fragments of the *Economic and Philosophic Manuscripts* Marx gives a remarkable explanation of alienated labor as the product of *a particular form of society*. He explicitly declines to let himself push the problem back into the mists of the past. He declares: "We proceed from an economic fact of the present. The worker becomes all the poorer the more wealth he produces . . . The worker becomes an ever cheaper commodity the more commodities he creates. With the *increasing value* of the world of things [of commodities] proceeds in direct proportion the *devaluation* of the world of men. Labor produces not only commodities: it produces itself and the worker as a *commodity*—and this in the same general proportion in which it produces commodities." [18]

I will not go on quoting; but everything remains coherent within the context indicated by Marx himself. In *present-day society*, alienated labor, that is, the labor that no longer owns its own products, is the labor that enriches others with its products, the labor that becomes forced labor, labor for the benefit of those who do not work. In other words, alienated labor is here clearly reduced to the division of society into classes, the contrast be-

---

9), very much to the point: "The fundamental problem for him remains the emancipation of mankind; but he raises it now from the standpoint of the proletariat, and this leads him to conceive of the abolition of alienation, which he continues to regard as the fundamental condition for human emancipation, no longer in its politico-social form, as abolition of the human essence in the state, but in its economico-social form, as abolition of the alienation of human activity, human labor . . ." It can thus be seen how wrong Jacques Rancière is to declare that, at least in the first manuscript, "it [economic alienation] appears no longer as the fundamental alienation to which other alienations can be reduced . . . The different forms of alienation are presented at first as being all on the same level." (In *Lire le Capital*, Vol. I, p. 102.) This is in complete contradiction with the text: "All these consequences result from the fact that the worker is related to the *product of his labor* as to an *alien* object." (*Economic and Philosophic Manuscripts*, p. 108.)

18. *Economic and Philosophic Manuscripts*, p. 107.

tween capital and labor, private property, and, perhaps, in a rather obscure passage, to the division of labor and the beginning of commodity production.[19]

However, the manuscript stops abruptly without following this path. The thought diverges and gives us a passage in which the origin of alienated labor is no longer sought in a *specific* form of human society but in *human nature* itself, or more precisely in *nature in general*;[20] alienated labor is contrasted to the qualities of generic man, as a "species being" (*Gattungswesen*), and alienation can be understood at first sight, if not as *externalization* in the Hegelian sense then at least as the negation of an "ideal human being" such as has never existed.

Even here, however, Marx is already transcending Hegel, for, as Naville puts it: "What is noteworthy here is that alienation is not merely rooted in society, it is also rooted in nature; but the natural relations may recreate what human relations have destroyed, human re-appropriation depends on maintaining them. In fact, nature is *one*, and its internal 'rending,' as Hegel showed, is therefore only relative, not absolute. So that it is just because alienation is also natural that it is a transitory discord within nature itself, which can be overcome and which natural appropriation can restore." [21]

Nevertheless, this anthropological conception of alienation, though it goes further than Hegel because it issues in a solution, remains largely philosophical and speculative. It lacks empirical foundations. It has not been proved. Moreover, it is not to be found in the other manuscripts, particularly in the remarkable passage about needs, where Marx explicitly contrasts the alienation of consumers, under the regime of private property, from enjoyment, the source of development of man's universal capaci-

19. It may be objected that there is a passage in the *Economic and Philosophic Manuscripts* (pp. 116–117) in which Marx declares that alienated labor is the *cause*, and private property the *result*. But Jahn correctly observes that Marx is not dealing here with the problem of the *historical origin* of private property but rather with the problem of its nature, of how it reappears daily in a mode of production based on alienated labor. (Jahn, "Der ökonomische Inhalt," p. 856.)

20. *Economic and Philosophic Manuscripts,* pp. 110–114.

21. Naville, *De l'aliénation à la jouissance,* p. 152.

ties.[22] There is thus indeed a *contradiction* within the *Economic and Philosophic Manuscripts*[23] which no amount of casuistry can conjure away, either by arbitrarily interpreting the socioeconomic passages in a philosophical sense or by interpreting the passage mentioned above as though it described a *socially determined* alienation.[24]

We know how Marx subsequently solved this contradiction. Resolutely abandoning the concept of generic man, the "species being" (a year later, in *The German Ideology*, he was to blame Stirner for holding on to it), he found the precise historical roots of the exploitation of man by man, and thus outlined its origins, the reasons for its development, and the conditions for its withering away.

In *The German Ideology*, the source of alienated labor is explained as being the division of labor and commodity production, an idea already present in the third of the *Economic and Philosophic Manuscripts*.[25] And in *Capital* the fetishism of economic categories is reduced to commodity relations, that is, to private property and competition, which isolate the individual producers (and property owners) from each other as soon as petty commodity production arises, even before the coming of capitalism.[26]

The evolution of Marx's concept of alienated labor is thus clear: from an anthropological conception (Feuerbacho-Hege-

---

22. *Economic and Philosophic Manuscripts*, pp. 147–151.

23. This contradiction is further reinforced by the fact that in the last of the manuscripts, "Critique of the Hegelian Dialectic and Philosophy as a Whole," Marx declines to follow Hegel when the latter identifies objectification with alienation. (*Economic and Philosophic Manuscripts*, pp. 175–176.) Marx distinguishes, to use a phrase of Roger Garaudy's (in *Dieu est mort*, p. 69), between alienated objectification and human objectification.

24. "The passage on alienated labor, the end of which was unfortunately destroyed, was preceded by the . . . remarks on the excerpts from James Mill. One can truly see here, 'from life,' how Marx came to apply the metaphor of Hegel and Feuerbach about alienation to economic phenomena, and thus to make a fruitful means of proof of it, and how this means of proof became transformed imperceptibly into a means of knowing . . ." (Kaegi, *Genesis des historischen Materialismus*, pp. 231–232.)

25. *The German Ideology*, pp. 41–44; *Economic and Philosophic Manuscripts*, pp. 159–160.

26. *Capital*, Vol. I, p. 71 *et seq.*

lian) before the *Economic and Philosophic Manuscripts,* he advances toward a historical conception (starting with *The German Ideology*). The *Economic and Philosophic Manuscripts* constitute a transition from the first to the second, with the anthropological conception surviving here and there, though it already marks a considerable advance on Hegel's conception, first because it is no longer based on a dialectic of needs and labor that issues in the impossibility of a solution,[27] and second because it already implies the possibility of transcending alienation through the communist struggle of the proletariat.

There has been great controversy around Marx's concept of alienation practically since the *Economic and Philosophic Manuscripts* were first published in German in 1932. This controversy is far from over. It has even been revived in France with the appearance in 1965 of Louis Althusser's *Pour Marx (For Marx),* which has attracted a number of critical commentaries.

The starting point of this controversy was the attempt by a number of bourgeois or revisionist philosophers to "reinterpret" Marx in the light of the writings of his youth.[28] But the lines of

27. Heinrich Popitz blames Marx for abandoning, in *The German Ideology,* Hegel's postulate of "needs inevitably exceeding the level of development of the productive forces." (*Der entfremdete Mensch,* p. 151.) He does not see (1) that Marx had already given it up in the third of his manuscripts of 1844; (2) that this postulate is worth only what all "philosophical postulates" are worth, that is, not much; (3) that a concrete analysis of human economic history shows that for tens of thousands of years human needs have not exceeded, or have hardly exceeded, the given level of development of the productive forces; (4) that this generalized and institutionalized "excess" of needs is only the product of a generalized commodity economy, that is, of the capitalist mode of production, which would not be able to carry on without the permanent reproduction of "unsatisfying demands"; and (5) that this mode of production creates at the same time the premises for transcending the "dialectic of needs and labor," by creating the material premises of plenty.

28. The antecedents of this attempt are to be sought in the striving of bourgeois ideology to "integrate" Marx, after having vainly striven to ignore him or to declare him finally outdated. N. I. Lapin (*Der junge Marx im Spiegel der Literatur,* p. 12) notes that the number of academic writings devoted to Marx and Marxism rose rapidly after 1895 (20 before 1883; 66 between 1883 and 1895; 214 between 1895 and 1904). It was obviously the upsurge of the labor movement that accounted for this effort at integra-

the discussion have combined and been superimposed to such an extent that today it is possible to distinguish three different positions:

(1) The position of those who try to deny that there is any difference between the *Economic and Philosophic Manuscripts* and *Capital*, and find the essentials of the theses of *Capital* already present in the *Manuscripts*.

(2) The position of those who consider that compared to the Marx of *Capital*, the Marx of the *Manuscripts* sets out in a more "total" and "integral" way the problem of alienated labor, especially by giving an ethical, anthropological, and even philosophical dimension to the idea; these people either contrast the two Marxs or else "re-evaluate" *Capital* in the light of the *Manuscripts*.

(3) The position of those who consider that the conceptions of the young Marx of the *Manuscripts* on alienated labor not only contradict the economic analysis of *Capital* but were an obstacle that made it difficult for the young Marx to accept the labor theory of value. For the extreme representatives of this school, the concept of alienation is a "pre-Marxist" concept which Marx had to overcome before he could arrive at a scientific analysis of capitalist economy.

The first school unites, oddly enough, official Communist writers, fiercely anti-Communist socialist writers like Erich Fromm and Maximilien Rubel, and Catholic writers like Father Bigo, Father Calvez, and H. Bartoli.[29] Fromm, for example, writes: "It

tion. The direct ancestor of the philosophers and sociologists who have tried to reduce Marx to Hegel is Johann Plenge (*Marx und Hegel*, Tübingen, 1911, pp. 16–17), who declared that Marx had remained all his life what he had become while a student at Berlin, namely "a dialectical realist and realistic dialectician." We shall see later that Plenge, though he did not know the *Economic and Philosophic Manuscripts*, foreshadowed most of the arguments of those who set the "young Marx" against the "mature Marx." Instead, however, of contrasting these two phases in Marx's thought, Plenge saw the matter as a contradiction inherent in Marxism. What is put more delicately and with more subtlety by writers today appears bluntly and crudely in Plenge's work: his whole thesis is based on denying the principal *materialist* aspects of historical materialism, which constitutes an obvious falsification.

29. See particularly Palmiro Togliatti, "De Hegel au marxisme," pp. 36–52 in *Recherches internationales à la lumière du marxisme*, No. 19, 1960;

is of the utmost importance for the understanding of Marx to see how the concept of alienation was and remained the focal point in the thinking of the young Marx who wrote the *Economic and Philosophic Manuscripts* and of the 'old' Marx who wrote *Capital*." [30] Fromm refers explicitly in this connection to the idea that for Marx alienation implies alienation of man from nature. But it is clear that this conception is quite absent from *Capital*.[31] Similarly, the attempt to equate the concept of alienation of labor in the *Economic and Philosophic Manuscripts* with the concept of alienation and mutilation of the worker that we find in Marx's later works, ignores the real problem, namely, the juxtaposition in the *Manuscripts* of an anthropological and a historical conception of alienation which are logically and practically irreconcilable. If alienation is indeed rooted in the nature of labor, and labor is indispensable to man's survival, as Marx was later to declare in a well-known letter to Kugelmann,[32] then alienation will never be overcome. In a precise comparison of two passages, one from the *Manuscripts* and the other from *Capital*,[33] Fromm does not notice that in the former what is being discussed is labor and products of labor *in general*, whereas the latter begins with these very words: "Within the capitalist system . . ."

For his part, Rubel declares that with the idea of alienated la-

---

Roger Garaudy, *Dieu est mort;* Erich Fromm, *Marx's Concept of Man;* Maximilien Rubel, *Karl Marx: Essai de biographie intellectuelle;* R. P. Bigo, *Humanisme et économie politique chez Karl Marx;* R. P. Jean-Yves Calvez, *La Pensée de Karl Marx.* I include the last two works in this first category with some reservations; though their writers stress the continuity of Marx's economic thought, from the *Economic and Philosophic Manuscripts* to *Capital,* they nevertheless tend to re-evaluate the latter somewhat in the light of the former.

30. Erich Fromm, *Marx's Concept of Man,* p. 51.

31. The question of the evolution of Marx's idea of nature has been studied in great detail by Alfred Schmidt, *Der Begriff der Natur in der Lehre von Marx,* who also shows that the more mature Marx gave up the naïve hope "of solving the conflict between man and nature" which is still found in the *Economic and Philosophic Manuscripts.*

32. "Every child knows that a nation which ceased to work, I will not say for a year, but for a few weeks, would perish." (Letter of July 11, 1868, in *Selected Works,* Vol. II, p. 418.)

33. Fromm, *Marx's Concept of Man,* pp. 51–52.

bor in the *Manuscripts,* "we are at the very heart of the Marxist
critique and vision, we hold the key to the entire subsequent work
of the economist and sociologist. . . . The concept of alienated
labor would henceforth occupy a central position in Marxist sociology and ethics." [34] How can the "key" to the economist's
subsequent work be discovered elsewhere than in the labor theory
of value and the theory of surplus value? At most one might agree
with the idea that Marx's basic *motivation* is revealed in the
Manuscripts; that from then on he was trying to criticize effectively an "inhuman political economy." But between the motivation of his criticism and the *actual content* of the latter there
is a world of difference, to which Marx himself drew attention
and to which we shall return in the concluding part of this study.

Nor can we accept the view expressed by Palmiro Togliatti
that in the *Manuscripts* "economic categories are reduced to the
necessary expression of a real dialectical process. The road is
open to the critique of bourgeois society as a whole, a critique
that would be made in the years and in the works that were to
follow, culminating in *Capital,* but *which we can say was already
largely complete.*" We agree still less when he writes: "Despite
the form, which is not simple, we indeed sense that *all Marxism
is already contained here.*" [35] All Marxism—without the labor
theory of value, without the theory of surplus value, without the
understanding that the conflict between the level of development
of the productive forces and the relations of production is the
driving force of social revolutions?

It is interesting to note the identity of the views of Togliatti
and Father Calvez: "There have been . . . plenty of commentators who have accepted the view that the economic categories
of *Capital* do not spring from the same way of thinking as the
philosophical categories in Marx's youthful writings. . . . I have
come to a conclusion that runs absolutely contrary to any attempt
of this sort to dissociate the two. The whole of Marx's argument
is based on the connection between the various alienations." And
again: "There is a genuine unity in all Marx's work: the philo-

---

34. Maximilien Rubel, *Karl Marx: Essai de biographie intellectuelle,* pp.
121, 135.

35. Togliatti, "De Hegel au marxisme," pp. 48–49. (Emphasis mine.—E.M.)

sophical categories of alienation which he took from Hegel in his youth were to form the framework of the great achievement of his mature years." [36] Unfortunately for this hypothesis, the "philosophical" categories taken from Hegel had already been "stood on their feet," that is, transformed into socioeconomic categories, from the *Manuscripts* onward, and they represent at most the motivation of *Capital*, not its "framework," which is provided by a critique of the categories of bourgeois political economy, and by the perfecting of the theories of value and surplus value.

Nor can I agree with the following observation by Jean Hyppolite: ". . . Marx's original theses are to be found in *Capital* and provide the best means of understanding the full significance of the theory of value." [37] By saying this, Hyppolite is actually suggesting that Marx's theory of value is not to be understood except as an expression of its author's moral indignation when faced with the phenomena of alienated labor. The real dialectic of Marx's evolution is both more complex and richer. There is conformity between the ethical motivation and the conclusions of the economic analysis; the one does indeed coincide with the other. But this economic analysis has an *independent value of its own*. It results from a strictly scientific study. The theory of surplus value corresponds to an *objective reality;* though it reinforces Marx's moral indignation regarding capitalism, it is independent of that feeling.

A similar confusion is to be found in some writers who nevertheless emphasize the differences between the *Manuscripts* and *Capital*. Thus, Adoratsky writes in his introduction to the first Soviet edition of the *Manuscripts* that "the real contradictions of the capitalist social order are here strikingly revealed in the situation of the working class." [38] Instead of saying "revealed" it would have been much more correct to say "suggested" or "foreshadowed." The *Manuscripts* are far from giving an analysis of the real contradictions of capitalism, and even the description of the

---

36. Calvez, *La Pensée de Karl Marx*, pp. 316–317, 319. See also a similar idea in Bigo, *Humanisme et économie politique chez Karl Marx*, p. 30.

37. Jean Hyppolite, *Studies on Marx and Hegel*, p. 129.

38. *MEGA*, I, 3, p. xiii.

workers' situation is seriously hindered by the presence of the theory of "absolute impoverishment" that Marx was later to abandon.

Even a writer like Wolfgang Jahn, who erects an absolute dogmatic screen between the concept of alienation and that of labor value, tries to find a theory of "production relations in general" in the *Manuscripts*, whereas no such theory can be found there.[39] Similarly, Heinrich Popitz, though he stresses the differences between the "young Marx" and the "mature Marx," sees in the *Manuscripts* a sign of the discovery of the conflict between the level of development of the productive forces and the relations of production,[40] even though in 1844 Marx was clearly still only on the threshold of discovering this conflict—a threshold he had not yet crossed.[41]

The second school of thought—which either contrasts the young Marx with the richer and more "ethical" mature Marx or else reinterprets the latter in the light of the former—has so far made itself the most widely heard. Beginning with Landshut and Mayer's Introduction to the German edition of the *Economic and Philosophic Manuscripts*, it has produced a large number of works, some of which are of undoubted interest.[42] All the same,

---

39. Jahn, "Der ökonomische Inhalt," p. 854.

40. Popitz, *Der entfremdete Mensch*, p. 161.

41. The analysis of the *Economic and Philosophic Manuscripts* made by Wolfgang Heise, on the whole excellent, nevertheless includes some elements of an excessive idealization of the text. (Über die Entfremdung und ihre Überwindung," in *Deutsche Zeitschrift für Philosophie*, pp. 690–692.)

42. In particular, Popitz, *Der entfremdete Mensch*; Heinrich Weinstock, *Arbeit und Bildung*; Jakob Hommes, *Der technische Eros*; Erich Thier, *Das Menschenbild des jungen Marx*; Victor Leemans, *De jonge Marx en de Marxisten*; Karl Löwith, *Von Hegel zu Nietzsche*; in part also Herbert Marcuse, *Reason and Revolution*; Hendrik De Man, "Der neu entdeckte Marx"; Kostas Axelos, *Marx, penseur de la technique*; Robert Blauner, *Alienation and Freedom: The Factory-Worker and His Industry*. Etc. In *The Sane Society*, an earlier work than his *Marx's Concept of Man*, Erich Fromm also contrasted the young Marx with the "old Marx" who was exclusively preoccupied with the "purely economic analysis of capitalism" and a prisoner of the "traditional view of the importance of the state and political power." (See *The Sane Society*, pp. 263, 259.)

one can agree with Jürgen Habermas that the error common to them all is that they do not see the difference between the anthropological and the historical conception of labor:[43] "Materialist dialectics means, therefore, understanding the dialectical logic that starts from the context 'labor,' from the metabolism of men with nature, without conceiving labor in a metaphysical way (either theologically, as being necessary for salvation, or anthropologically, as being necessary for survival)." [44] The Marx of 1844 still retains, in part, such a metaphysical conception of labor; the Marx of *Capital* has long since given it up.

Karel Kosic also emphasizes the difference between the conception of labor, which is characteristic of Hegelian philosophy and of classical philosophy generally, and that of Marx in his mature years, which coincides with the notion of praxis: "The division of human activity into labor (sphere of necessity) and art (sphere of freedom) grasps only *approximately* and only in certain aspects the problematic of labor and non-labor. It starts from a *historical*, determined, form of labor as from a hypothesis which has not been analyzed closely and has thus been adopted in an uncritical way. On this basis, the division which has *developed* historically between material-physical labor and mental labor is petrified. Concealed in this distinction, however, is an essential characteristic of labor as human praxis, which, to be sure, does not abandon the sphere of necessity but which does tend *to go beyond* this sphere, and which creates within itself the real pre-conditions for human freedom." [45] But Kosic does not then deal with the problematic of Marx's youthful writings.

An analysis of these works enables us to note the contradictions and paradoxes that inevitably result from a fundamental misunderstanding of Marx's intentions in the *Manuscripts* and of the nature of the concepts he uses. I will here confine myself to a few examples.

43. Underlying this difference is obviously a difference of method, that between idealist apriorist dialectics and materialist experimental dialectics, which seeks out the specific logic of the specific object. (Galvano Della Volpe, *Rousseau e Marx*, pp. 150, 153.)

44. Habermas, *Theorie und Praxis*, pp. 318–319.

45. Karel Kosic, *Die Dialektik des Konkreten*, pp. 206–207.

In the preface to the Landshut and Mayer edition, Landshut considers the *Manuscripts* to be "the revelation of genuine Marxism . . . Marx's central work, the crucial point in the development of his thought in which the principles of economic analysis follow directly from the idea of man's true reality." [46] Kostas Axelos postulates: "The *Manuscripts of 1844* are and remain the richest in thought of all Marx's writings and all Marxist works." [47] Hendrik De Man declares (in that same year, 1932) that, "however highly we may esteem Marx's later writings, they nevertheless show a certain inhibition and weakening of his creative potentialities [!], which Marx was not always able to overcome by a heroic effort." [48] It is enough to mention that the theory of surplus value was discovered and the labor theory of value perfected fourteen years *after* the writing of the *Manuscripts* in order to appreciate the full "depths" of this "weakening."

Erich Thier equates "externalization" of the worker with alienated labor and declares that "alienation is present as a tendency, *potentially* [in labor]; the worker himself 'produces' the nonworker. . . . Not Hegel but Marx thus allows private property to appear as flowing from the analysis of the concept of externalized labor and to move toward further alienations." [49] Thier does not seem to remember that he had himself previously declared that Marx's critique of Hegel's *Phenomenology of Mind*, included in the *Economic and Philosophic Manuscripts*, is essentially a critique of Hegel's conception of alienation—which Thier has just now attributed entirely to Marx;[50] Marx explicitly rejected the identification of externalization with alienation in the fourth manuscript of 1844! Nor has he noticed that, apart from the single passage mentioned earlier, the *Manuscripts* do not derive alienation from an anthropological conception of "the externalization of the worker" but from *precise historical condi-*

46. Siegfried Landshut and Gustav Mayer, eds., *Der historische Materialismus, die Frühschriften*, Vol. I, p. xiii.

47. Axelos, *Marx, penseur de la technique*, p. 47.

48. Hendrik De Man, "Der neu entdeckte Marx," pp. 275–276.

49. Thier, *Das Menschenbild des jungen Marx*, pp. 69–70.

50. Ibid., p. 25.

tions: the production of a surplus, the division of labor, the beginnings of commodity economy, private appropriation of the means of production, etc. Thier has not studied the context and so cannot show that the sole passage which does not conform to this concept can really be regarded as expressing a general idea of Marx's about alienation. And above all he has not noticed that even in the "anthropological" passage of the *Manuscripts,* the idea of alienation is derived not from the *concept* of "externalized labor," but from the analysis (faulty, or at least incomplete) of the worker's *activity* in nature. The young Marx has been transformed back into a Hegelian pure and simple; which does not help in understanding the *Manuscripts.*[51]

Similarly, when Thier states that in Marx's writings "anthropology can be fully developed, and starting from this it is possible to understand Marx's purpose in its full scientific and political bearing, without the law of value and its problems having been thought of," [52] he is obviously muddled. For the fact must be faced that, given the inadequacy of his knowledge in 1844, Marx was not able to *have more than an inkling* of the real contradictions of the capitalist mode of production; he was not in a position to analyze them fully, thoroughly, and satisfactorily.[53] His aim, from the time he began writing the *Manuscripts,* was

---

51. Father Bigo has made the same attempt to reduce Marx to an Hegelian pure and simple: "The phenomenology of mind is merely [!] changed into that of labor, the dialectics of human alienation into that of capital, the metaphysics of absolute knowledge into that [!] of absolute communism." (Bigo, *Humanisme et économie politique chez Karl Marx,* p. 34.) In order to do this, Father Bigo has to ignore Marx's hard empirical work in the sphere of political economy, and to present his becoming aware of these new ideas as the result of a mere "brilliant intuition" (pp. 36–37).

52. Thier, *Das Menschenbild des jungen Marx,* p. 71.

53. Cf. the correct observation made by Leonid Pajitnov: "Marx's basic ideas [in the *Manuscripts of 1844*] are still in the process of becoming; and alongside some remarkable formulations, the seed of his future world-conception, we can also find, frequently, ideas that are not yet ripe, bearing the mark of the theoretical sources Marx used as his material for thought and the starting point for the working out of his doctrine." ("Les manuscrits économico-philosophiques de 1844," in *Recherches internationales à la lumière de marxisme,* No. 19, 1960, p. 98.)

to formulate a "critique of political economy"; he was not fully able to achieve this aim until he had mastered and brought to perfection the labor theory of value.[54]

In Popitz's work, though it is more fundamental and more profound than Thier's, there are a number of misunderstandings of the same sort. He declares that in the *Manuscripts* Marx "criticizes determined social relations and reduces them to an undetermined[!] center which he calls 'the essential human being.' This is the conceptual substratum of the empirically observed relations. . . . Marx attributes a dialectical schematism to social phenomena and strives to give it grounds by means of the genesis of a human 'essential being.' The latter thus plays the role of the world spirit or the folk spirit in Hegel." [55] Here we have an obvious misunderstanding: Marx is simply transformed back into Hegel. The fact that alienation has been deduced from an analysis of the empirical conditions of bourgeois society is forgotten. Also forgotten is the whole historico-social context of the origins of alienation as given in the *Manuscripts:* economic surplus, division of labor, commodity production, separation of capital and labor, etc. We are in fact rather a long way from Hegel's *Weltgeist.*

Popitz likewise attributes to Marx a "postulate" of the progressive productivity of the human race,[56] whereas all that Marx writes about is the progressive productivity *of the capitalist mode of production,* and this, moreover, is not derived from some "theory of needs" but from competition. Popitz's idea that the famous passage in *The German Ideology* about the necessary abolition of the division of labor is "anti-technical" or "romantic," [57] shows an amazing failure to grasp a process of reasoning that had already been broadly outlined in the *Manuscripts.*

---

54. In the same way, it seems to me to be going too far to say, as T. I. Oiserman does, that in the *Economic and Philosophic Manuscripts* Marx attributes alienation to the insufficient level of development of the productive forces. (See *Die Entfremdung als historische Kategorie,* p. 83.) At most one can say that he *had an inkling* of this idea, which he did not set forth clearly until *The German Ideology.*

55. Popitz, *Der entfremdete Mensch,* p. 88.

56. Ibid., p. 152.

57. Ibid., p. 160. Adam Schaff, in *Marxism and the Human Individual,* expresses a similar idea.

By this reasoning, the alienation of labor arises historically from a too limited surplus, the appearance of which leads to simple exchange, then to the progressive division of labor, and so to developed exchange, commodity production, generalized commodity production, and capitalism. What is needed to overcome it, therefore, is a surplus big enough to make pointless "the base appropriation of other men's labor," and this is just what results from the development of mechanization and science!

Why should it be "romantic" to suppose that, within the framework of automation imagined by Marx, the abundance of goods and the making general of higher education, together with the constant extension of "free time," will bring about the conditions for a full and entire flowering of humanity, really freeing itself from the slavery of the social division of labor and freely practicing technical, scientific, artistic, sporting, social, and political forms of activity, one beside the other? [58]

Another remark of Popitz's should also be noted: he states that it is impossible to "distinguish phenomenologically" between the

---

58. In a passage I have already criticized from another angle, Perroux finds himself perfectly capable of imagining a social life in which "the economy is wholly and fully automated," so that a way of life becomes possible which is entirely free, "everyone doing what he likes when he likes." The only objection that Perroux has to this vision is that it implies a withering-away of the state, whereas, in his view, "fundamental contradictions [will continue to exist] between the individual members of this society," contradictions between "masters of machines" and "supervisors and inspectors." However, Perroux does not show why such social contradictions must survive under conditions of plenty. (See Perroux, Preface to Karl Marx, *Oeuvres—Economie I*, p. xvii.) Rolf Dahrendorf similarly declares that in "any society" there must always be "differentiation into positions of domination and positions of subjection" and that "it is hardly possible to imagine a society in which there is no differentiation of roles in terms of legitimate *power*." (*Class and Class Conflict in Industrial Society*, p. 219.) The atrophy of Dahrendorf's social imagination is evidently not a scientific argument. As for Marx, far from wishing to maintain any "commanding elites," he presupposes, on the contrary, that the constant extension of "free time," in the real sense of the term, will develop to the full the scientific and creative capacities possessed by the great majority of men and women and will make them all capable of carrying out *technical* functions of administration (administration of things instead of administration of human beings).

use and employment of the productive forces, on the one hand, and the production relations determined by the latter on the other.[59] Here Popitz is being much more "deterministic" than Marx himself, but in a narrowly mechanistic way. What Marx explains, particularly in the Preface to the *Contribution to the Critique of Political Economy*, is that when there is a *conflict* between a certain level of development of the productive forces and production relations which have objectively been outgrown, a period of social revolution begins—a period which may last a long time and during which *two types of production relations* may coexist with an equivalent level of development of the productive forces (Western Europe in the years 1770–1830, or Central Europe in 1914–1964).

In short, what all these writers fail to grasp is that the Marx of the *Economic and Philosophic Manuscripts*, while he has not yet fully developed the theory of historical materialism, has advanced beyond Hegel and no longer reasons in absolute ideas or philosophical concepts, but *tries to criticize a particular ideology (political economy) through real social contradictions observed empirically*. These writers mix up the *aim* of Marx's researches and preoccupations with the tools and language he uses in order to reach this aim.

There remains the third school of thought, which is represented above all by writers defending the official point of view of the Communist parties during the 1940's and 1950's. Jahn sets forth their thesis most succinctly; Auguste Cornu puts forward broadly the same idea in the second volume of his biography of Marx and Engels.[60] Emile Bottigelli partly endorses it in his Introduction to the edition of the *Manuscripts* published by Editions Sociales;[61]

---

59. Popitz, *Der entfremdete Mensch*, pp. 164–165.

60. Jahn, "Der ökonomische Inhalt"; Auguste Cornu, *Karl Marx und Friedrich Engels: Leben und Werke*, Vol. II. Cornu had already expressed the same view in *Die ökonomisch-philosophische Manuskripte*.

61. Emile Bottigelli, ed., *Manuscrits de 1844*. Bottigelli's Introduction, which is in general careful and sensible, notes (p. lx) that "the problem of the identification of the subject with the object, which Hegel had resolved by the dialectic of the Absolute Idea, was resolved by Marx concretely. With the coming of communism, 'the necessary form of the near future,' man will take possession of his true nature, and the world, to which all his

Manfred Buhr defends it with conviction.[62] It can be summarized thus: the *Manuscripts* are an important but transitory stage in Marx's intellectual history; he had already succeeded in grasping the chief contradictions of bourgeois society, but was still expressing them in Feuerbachian, humanistic language. The concept of alienated labor is the most obvious expression of this. It was a concept that hindered Marx's acceptance of Ricardo's labor theory of value. He had to overcome it before he could formulate his own theory of value and of surplus value.[63] It is no longer found in the writings of his mature years.

This argument is never accompanied by a logical demonstration: it is left unclear why it should have been the concept of alienated labor that hindered Marx from accepting Ricardo's labor theory of value. The real reasons that delayed Marx's acceptance of this theory have been examined in Chapter 3 of this book. Experience has shown that it is perfectly possible to combine a theory of alienation with the labor theory of value in its perfected form: Marx, in fact, did this in 1857–1858.

The argument put forward by Jahn, Cornu, Bottigelli, and Buhr is above all lacking in any empirical proof to support it. These authors do not in the least succeed in showing that Marx gave up the concept of alienation after he accepted the labor

---

practical activity opposes him in the age of alienation, will become once more the world of man, the extension of his own essence. Thus the problem of the return to unity which haunted all German thought from the end of the eighteenth century to the beginning of the nineteenth, is resolved not in a mystical way but in favor of man, by affirming his freedom and his right to the free deployment of his faculties." We are all the more astonished to read, a few pages farther on (p. lxvii), that in the *Manuscripts*, "it is still the essentially Hegelian idea of the development of the contradictions that leads to [?] the transition from one social order to another." In reality, in the *Manuscripts* Marx does not base himself on any "idea" at all, but on a concrete analysis of *social* contradictions; and communism, from then on, is for him no longer the result of "the idea of the development of the contradictions," but of *the practical struggle of the proletariat*.

62. Manfred Buhr, "Entfremdung—Philosophische Anthropologie—Marx-Kritik," in *Deutsche Zeitschrift für Philosophie*, No. 7, 1966, pp. 806–834.

63. Jahn, "Der ökonomische Inhalt," p. 683; and Cornu, *Karl Marx und Friedrich Engels*, p. 152.

theory of value. Jahn restricts himself to noting that Marx and Engels come back to it in *The German Ideology* in order to give it "a new content" (which is true), but immediately adds: "In his subsequent writings [the problem of alienation] no longer plays an important part" [64]—which is false. Bottigelli says: "Once he had finished his struggle against the Left-Hegelians, the expression 'alienation' never appears again, to my knowledge, except in the Preface to the *Contribution to the Critique of Political Economy*. . . This is the last [text] in which he argued as a philosopher in the classical sense of the word." [65] It seems to me out of place to say that in the Preface to the *Contribution to the Critique of Political Economy*, one of the most remarkable of his writings from the methodological standpoint, Marx "argues as a philosopher." But it is in any case untrue that the concept of alienation no longer appears in Marx's works after 1857. It is also untrue to allege, as Manfred Buhr does, that Marx "largely abandoned using this term" in his later writings, though Buhr recognizes that Marx never lost sight of the problem underlying this concept.[66] As for Louis Althusser, he has recently ventured even further by announcing that "the ideological concept of alienation" is a "pre-Marxist" concept.[67]

Unfortunately for all these writers, in the *Grundrisse*, written

64. Jahn, "Der ökonomische Inhalt," pp. 863–864.

65. Bottigelli, Introduction to *Manuscrits de 1844*, pp. lxvii–lxviii.

66. Buhr, "Entfremdung—Philosophische Anthropologie—Marx-Kritik," p. 813.

67. Althusser, *For Marx*, p. 239. See also what the same author writes on p. 159: "One day we shall have to study this text in detail and give a word-by-word explanation of it; discuss the theoretical status and theoretical role assigned to the key concept of *alienated labor;* examine this notion's conceptual field; and recognize that it does fill the role Marx then assigned it, the role of *original basis;* but also that it can only fill this role so long as it *receives it* as a mandate and commission from the whole *conception of Man* which can derive from the *essence of Man* the necessity and content of the familiar *economic concepts.* In short, we shall have to discover beneath these terms imminently awaiting a future meaning, the meaning that still keeps them prisoners of a philosophy that is exercising its last prestige and power over them. . . . I should almost say . . . the Marx *furthest* [*sic*] *from Marx* is this Marx . . ." What is to be said, then, of the Marx of the *Grundrisse?*

in tempore non suspecto[68] after the famous Preface to the *Contribution to the Critique of Political Economy*, at a date which Althusser himself makes the beginning of the period of Marx's "maturity," Marx returns well and truly to the concept of alienation and even dwells on it! Passages relating to alienation are plentiful in the *Grundrisse*, and they reduce to ashes the thesis of Jahn, Cornu, Bottigelli, Buhr, and Althusser. Not only is the concept of alienation not "pre-Marxist," it forms part of the *instrumentarium* used by Marx when he had arrived at full maturity. When reading *Capital* with attention, one comes upon it there as well, though sometimes in a slightly modified form.[69]

This is how Marx introduces the problem of alienated labor in the *Grundrisse*, in the chapter on money: "It has been said,

---

68. The *Grundrisse* were written *after* the famous Preface to the *Contribution to the Critique of Political Economy*, which, according to Althusser ("L'objet de *Capital*," in *Lire le Capital*, Vol. II) constitutes the quintessence of mature Marxist method. (See *Grundrisse*, Foreword, pp. vii, viii.)

69. See, however, the following passages: "Hence, the character [*Gestalt*] of independence and estrangement [Marx uses the word *entfremdet*, i.e., "alienated"] which the capitalist mode of production as a whole gives to the instruments of labor and to the product, as against the workman, is developed by means of machinery into a thorough antagonism." (*Capital*, Vol. I, p. 432.) "We saw in Part IV, when analyzing the production of relative surplus value: within the capitalist system all methods for raising the social productiveness of labor are brought about at the cost of the individual laborer; all means for the development of production transform themselves into means of domination over, and exploitation of, the producers; they mutilate the laborer into a fragment of a man, degrade him to the level of an appendage of a machine, destroy every remnant of charm in his work and turn it into a hated toil; they estrange [*entfremden*] from him the intellectual potentialities of the labor process in the same proportion as science is incorporated in it as an independent power . . ." (Ibid., p. 645.) "Since, before entering on the process, his [i.e., the worker's] own labor has already been alienated [*entfremdet*] from himself by the sale of his labor power, has been appropriated by the capitalist and incorporated with capital, it must, during the process, be realized in a product that does not belong to him [*in fremdem Produkt*]." (Ibid., pp. 570–571.) "Capital comes more and more to the fore as a social power, whose agent is the capitalist. This social power no longer stands in any possible relation to that which the labor of any single individual can create. It becomes an alienated [*entfremdet*], independent, social power, which stands opposed to society as an object, and as an object that is the capitalist's source of power." (*Capital*, Vol. III, p. 264.)

it can be said, that what is fine and great [in commodity economy] is based precisely upon this interconnection, this material and spiritual metabolism, independently of the knowledge and will of the individuals involved; and presupposing precisely their mutual independence and indifference. And this objective interconnection is certainly preferable to a lack of interconnection, or to a purely local interconnection, or to one based on something narrow and primitive such as a blood relationship, or relations of domination and slavery. It is likewise certain that individuals cannot take control of their social interconnections before they have created them. But it is foolish to think of this merely *objective interconnection* as an interconnection that is *ab origine* impossible to dissociate from the nature of individuality (in contrast to reflected knowledge and will) and immanent in it. It is its product—a historical product. It belongs to a definite phase of its evolution. The alien character and independence that it retains in this regard merely show that it [the individuality] is still in the process of creating the conditions of its social life, instead of having started from these conditions in the first place. It is the original interconnection between individuals within the framework of definite, limited, production relations. Individuals with an all-around development whose social relations have been subjected to their own collective control as their own collective relations, are not a product of nature but of history. The degree and universality of the development of the capacities [of the productive forces] which makes *such individuality* possible, presupposes precisely production based on exchange values, which produces, along with generality, *the alienation of the individual from himself* [my emphasis—E.M.] and others, but also the generality and universality of his relations and capacities. At earlier stages of evolution, the single individual seems to be fuller precisely because he has not yet developed the fullness of his relations and because he has not yet opposed them to himself as social forces and relations which are independent of him. Just as it is absurd to desire a return to this original fullness, so it is absurd to believe that we have to remain fixed at this complete void [that exists today]. . . ." [70]

70. *Grundrisse*, pp. 79–80.

In order to complete the picture, we must add to this passage others in the *Grundrisse* in which Marx describes the total subjection of "living labor" to "objectified labor" ("dead labor," fixed capital),[71] and the remarkable passage in which Marx explains the difference between "repulsive" labor, the labor of the slave, the serf, and the wage worker, on the one hand, and "free labor," "attractive labor," on the other.[72]

There are also other passages in the *Grundrisse* in which the concept of alienation reappears explicitly. In particular there is the very important passage in which Marx returns to the distinction between *objectification* and *alienation:* "The bourgeois economists are to such an extent prisoners of the concepts of a particular historical phase in the development of society that the necessity of the *objectification* of social labor power seems to them inseparable from the necessity of the *alienation* of this labor power in relation to living labor. . . . No special intelligence is needed to understand that, given the free labor that had emerged from serfdom, or wage labor, machines could not effectively *be created* otherwise than as property which was alienated from them [the workers] and which appeared to them as a hostile power, that is, which was bound to confront them as capital. It can be understood just as easily, however, that machines will not cease to be agencies of social production when they become, for example, the property of the associated workers." [73]

And, above all, there is the following passage which recalls almost word for word the *Economic and Philosophic Manuscripts:* "But if capital appears as the product of labor, the product of labor appears, in the same way, as capital—not merely as just a product, nor merely as an exchangeable commodity, but as *capital:* labor objectified as domination, as the power to dominate living labor. It thus appears so much a product of labor that its product appears as an *alienated* quality [my emphasis—E.M.], an independent mode of existence with which living labor is confronted, a value existing for itself, and the product of labor is crystallized as an *alien power* [my emphasis—E.M.] in relation

---

71. Ibid., pp. 582–592.
72. Ibid., p. 505.
73. Ibid., pp. 716–717.

to labor. From labor's own standpoint, labor appears as being active in the production process in such a way that it at the same time detaches from itself its own realization . . . as an alien reality, and thus presents itself as a capacity for labor which is without substance, filled exclusively with needs, confronted with the *alienated reality* [my emphasis—E.M.] which does not belong to it but to others." [74]

No more quotations. From all these passages a *Marxist theory of alienation* emerges which is both the coherent development of that contained in *The German Ideology* and the dialectical transcendence of the contradictions contained in the *Economic and Philosophic Manuscripts*.

In primitive society the individual directly contributes social labor. He is harmoniously integrated into his social setting, but if he seems "fully developed" this is only because of the extremely limited range of needs that he has become aware of. In reality, the material poverty of society, the helplessness of men before the forces of nature,[75] are sources of alienation, especially social (from men's *objective* potentialities), ideological, and religious alienation.[76]

---

74. Ibid., pp. 357–358.

75. The passage from the *Grundrisse*, pp. 79–80, which I quoted above shows clearly that there was no question of Marx idealizing primitive man or presenting him as non-alienated. Henri Lefebvre is therefore mistaken when he writes of "the wonderful equilibrium of the village community," in which man could give himself up "to his elemental vitality." (*Critique de la Vie quotidienne*, Vol. I, p. 221.) Lefebvre here follows Engels, who expressed similar notions in *The Origin of the Family, Private Property and the State*. Lefebvre had also written: "Alienation has stripped life of everything that formerly, in man's primitive weakness, endowed him with joy and wisdom," in the first version of his *Critique de la Vie quotidienne* (1947), p. 242. In other respects, this work provides one of the best accounts of the Marxist theory of alienation. See also, on the same subject, Gajo Petrović, "Marx's Theory of Alienation," in *Philosophy and Phenomenological Research*, pp. 419–426.

76. George Novack, "Basic Differences Between Existentialism and Marxism," in *Existentialism versus Marxism*, George Novack, ed., p. 337. See also T. I. Oiserman, *Die Entfremdung als historische Kategorie* (p. 8): "Man has increasingly taken control of the elemental forces of nature, and at the same time he has become increasingly enslaved to the elemental forces of social evolution." In 1970, Merlin Press (London) published a book by Istvan

With the slow progress of the social productivity of labor, an economic surplus progressively comes into being. It creates the material conditions for exchange, for the division of labor, and for commodity production. In the last, the individual is alienated from the product of his labor and from his productive activity, and his labor increasingly becomes alienated labor. This *economic alienation*, which is now added to *social, religious, and ideological alienation*, is essentially the result of the social division of labor, of commodity production, and of the division of society into classes. It produces *political alienation*, with the rise of the state and the phenomena of violence and oppression that characterize the relations between men. Under the capitalist mode of production, this multiple alienation reaches its climax: "The transformation of all objects into commodities, their quantification in fetishistic exchange values [becomes] . . . an intense process which affects every objective form of life." [77]

Economic alienation acquires an extra aspect in *technical alienation*, because the worker is not merely alienated from his instruments of labor but finds them opposed to him as an alien and hostile power which enslaves and stifles him and deprives him of his elementary potentialities of self-development.[78] But this same mode of production creates, with the universality of exchange relations and the development of the world market, the universality of human needs and human capacities, and a level of

---

Mészaros entitled *Marx's Theory of Alienation*, which generally follows a reasoning similar to ours on the subject, but in much greater detail.

77. Georg Lukacs, *Geschichte und Klassenbewusstsein*, p. 187. Lukacs's book, written before the author could have read the *Economic and Philosophic Manuscripts* or the *Grundrisse*, is a masterly reconstitution of Marx's thought on problems of alienation and reification, in spite of certain idealistic excesses in his conclusions.

78. A typical (and tragic) example of the mutilating effects of capitalist technique is provided in what may seem a marginal field of social life, the evolution of toys. By making dolls that speak, the toy industry risks drying up one source of the development of the imagination, language, and intelligence of children, which is found in the dialogue, spontaneously discovered and progressively extended, between the little girl and her doll. Play thus loses its spontaneous character and becomes something mechanical, remote-controlled, and pre-determined by the manufacturer.

development of the productive forces that makes it objectively possible to satisfy these needs and bring about the all-around development of man.[79] Ending the capitalist order then makes possible the progressive withering away of commodity production, of the social division of labor, and of the mutilation of human beings. *Alienation will not be "abolished" by a single event, any more than it appeared all at once. It will wither away progressively, just as it appeared progressively.* It is not rooted in "human nature" or in "man's existence," but in *specific* conditions of labor, production, and society. It thus is possible to glimpse the conditions necessary for it to wither away.

I do not share the view of Gajo Petrović that alienation means non-realization of human potentialities that have already been *historically created*.[80] If that were so primitive man (who actually did realize the potentialities that existed in his time) would indeed have been a non-alienated man, contrary to what Petrović himself says. The following observation by Helmut Fleischer seems to define the problem better: "Some of the relationship of alienation revealed by Marx may be born of previously integrated unities; but in its general anthropological sense, alienation cannot be a loss of something that has already been, in its essentials, previously possessed; the concept must have a forward-looking rather than a backward-looking meaning; it could signify that one lags behind in relation to what is already possible, rather than that one has lost what one once already possessed. For the positive notion (contrasted with that of alienation) of what is proper to man cannot be conceived, according to Marx's premises, as a Platonic idea or an Aristotelian entelechy, but rather as an anticipation or projection which is rooted in nature and linked with a historical situation, and more precisely as a completed

79. A typical instance of alienation in the field of needs is provided by the deliberate attempt American bourgeois society is making to "bring back into the home" the woman who has been to university. The aim is to stimulate the sale of domestic appliances, furniture, and so on; the effect is to bring about a veritable atrophy of women's intellectual capacities, a "progressive dehumanization" of women. (On this see Betty Friedan, *The Feminine Mystique*.)

80. Gajo Petrović, "Marx's Theory of Alienation," pp. 422 ff.

projection which starts from the horizon of the given social problematic . . ." [81]

However, these concepts of "anticipation" and "projection" should not be confined within that of what is already historically possible, as the writer seems to confine them in the first part of the passage quoted. For one of the special features of man's capacity for anticipation is precisely that he *can* set himself problems long before the conditions for solving them have matured. The hope of a society free from oppression and exploitation, without class divisions or alienation, could arise in classical antiquity or in the Middle Ages, long before the conditions for creating such a society had become "historically possible." The fact that this dream could arise gives expression, however, to a subjective awareness of alienation, just as much as it reflects an objective reality. The same is true, *mutatis mutandis,* of primitive religions.[82]

Some writers have spoken of a transformation of the primitive Marxist theory of alienation into a "general theory of the fetishistic character of commodities." [83] I do not think this formulation

---

81. Helmut Fleischer, "Umrisse einer 'Philosophie des Menschen,'" in *Hochschul-Informationen der Zentralstelle für Gesamtdeutsche Hochschulfragen*, No. 2, 1967, p. 19.

82. Cf. Gramsci, in a passage which seems to anticipate Althusser's problematic: "They do not deal with this fundamental point: how does the historical movement come to birth on the basis of structure . . . This is the crucial point in all the questions that have arisen around the philosophy of praxis, and without solving this question it is not possible to solve the other question, regarding the relations between society and 'nature.'" ("Il Materialismo Storico e la Filosofia da Benedetto Croce," in *Quaderni del Carcere I*, p. 129.)

83. E.g., Freddy Perlman, "Essay on Commodity Fetishism," a hitherto unpublished essay the author has kindly made available to me. Perlman makes a reference to a similar opinion expressed in a Marxist work, now forgotten, but which deserves to be republished, by the eminent Soviet Marxist I. I. Rubin entitled *Essays on the Marxist Theory of Value*. See also Karl Korsch, *Karl Marx*, pp. 99–100. Neither Rubin nor Korsch was acquainted with the *Grundrisse*, and they could therefore not be aware that Marx had in that work taken up the thread of his thinking on alienation, which he had first begun to weave in the *Manuscripts of 1844*. Korsch writes, in the passage I have just mentioned: "The principal difference between this philosophical critique of economic self-alienation [in the *Manuscripts of 1844*] and its subsequent scientific presentation consists in the fact that Marx gave his

is correct. It is true that Marx reduced human alienation in society based on commodity production essentially to the reification of human and social relations caused by commodity relations. But, in the first place, he made this reduction only so far as the essence of the matter was concerned, and not for all aspects of alienation; for even in bourgeois society the concept of alienation embraces a wider field than that of "reification" or of "commodity fetishism" (e.g., alienation on the plane of consumption, alienation of the individual's capacities for development, alienation of socially possible knowledge, etc.). And, furthermore, Marx continued to speak of alienation in primitive society, as we see from the *Grundrisse* passage quoted above, though in that society there was neither commodity production nor, *a fortiori*, commodity fetishism.

The *social* significance of the three mystificating interpretations of the relationship between the *Economic and Philosophic Manuscripts* and *Capital*, the three mistaken interpretations of the relationship of the mature Marx with the anthropological concept of alienated labor, can now be better understood. They reflect certain *historical conditions* and *definite social and economic contexts* which explain their appearance, over and beyond the accidental fact of the publication of the *Manuscripts* in 1932.

For the bourgeoisie it is a question, after the remarkable rise of the Marxist-inspired labor movement, of "integrating" Marx by reducing him entirely to Hegel. At the same time, the bourgeoisie tries to "de-fuse" the explosive revolutionary significance of Marx's teaching in order to integrate him, as "thinker" and "philosopher," into a capitalist world conceived, if not as the best of worlds, then at any rate as the least bad of all possible worlds.

Reformist social-democracy marches in step with the bourgeoisie. But it has more difficulty in identifying the Marx of the

economic critique in *Capital* . . . a deeper and more general significance by reducing all the other alienated categories of the economy to the fetishistic character of the commodity." This is only partly true. Analysis of the fetishistic character of commodities undoubtedly does enable us to reveal in a scientifically more exact way the fundamental features of the capitalist mode of production, and thus also of alienation within this mode of production. But it is not identical with analysis of the wider problem of alienation.

youthful writings with the Marx of *Capital*. For a long time it strove to hide the revolutionary character of Marx's work by upholding a mechanistic interpretation: the task of overthrowing the capitalist mode of production was entrusted to the "inexorable development of the productive forces" rather than to the action of the organized proletariat.

When, however, the economic crisis of 1929–1933 and the rise of Fascism showed everyone that there was no *inevitable* cause-and-effect relationship leading from the undoubted conflict between the level of development of the productive forces and capitalist production relations, on the one hand, to the coming of socialism, on the other, social-democratic ideology was obliged to change its approach. After having for a long time disdained the works of Marx's youth,[84] social-democracy suddenly sought inspiration in them to counterpose an "ethical message" to hopeless capitalist reality, to the socialist revolution for which it had no enthusiasm, and to the degeneration of that revolution in the Soviet Union in the Stalin period, which provided a welcome foil. Hence the vogue enjoyed by the *Economic and Philosophic Manuscripts* for the last quarter of a century in social-democratic circles, along with a deliberate attempt to blunt the edge of the revolutionary message contained in the *Manuscripts*.[85]

Marx, as inheritor and transcender of German classical philosophy, is "cleared" of responsibility for the misdeeds of Stalinism in so far as the "anthropological humanism" of the young Marx is contrasted with the "economism" of the "mature" Marx. Marx is "rehabilitated" so that he can be used against the international communist and revolutionary movement.

---

84. N. I. Lapin, *Der junge Marx im Spiegel der Literatur*, pp. 72–75. It is interesting to observe that this tradition of rejecting Marx's youthful works as "too Hegelian," "too lacking in maturity," and "too romantic," also has bourgeois roots. It is especially to be found in the writings of bourgeois economists like Schumpeter. Today it continues to drift along among the neo-Stalinists.

85. Victor Leemans (*De jonge Marx en de Marxisten*, pp. 126–130 *et seq.*) does not bother to take the oratorical precautions incumbent on social-democrats and sees in Marx's will to revolutionary *action*, and even in his political praxis, his original sin and the fundamental contradiction in his youthful writings. It is impossible to speak more plainly than this.

From another angle, Soviet reality in the Stalin epoch was such that the concept of alienated labor inevitably gave rise to its being identified with the current face of that reality. For this reason the concept appeared unacceptable—because too explosive—to the leaders and ideologists of the Stalinist regime: "In Soviet society there was no longer, there could no longer be, any question of alienation. The concept therefore had to vanish, by orders from above, for reasons of state." [86] Hence the attempt to mutilate the youthful writings like the *Manuscripts*, starting with the attempt to avoid reproducing them in full in a single edition.[87] Hence the attempt to minimize the concept of alienation, or flatly to declare it "pre-Marxist."

Those who had degraded Marxism to the level of vulgar apologetics for the policy of the Stalin regime were at the same time totally powerless to answer the challenge of the idealist or existentialist interpreters of the *Economic and Philosophic Manuscripts*. As for those Marxists who recognized the mystificating character of this attempt but who strove to retain their positions within official orthodoxy, they got out of their difficulty by "finding" the whole of the mature Marx already there in the young Marx—thus frequently arriving at results similar to those of bourgeois pseudo-criticism.

86. Henri Lefebvre, Preface to the second edition of Volume I of his *Critique de la Vie quotidienne*, p. 63.

87. Louis Althusser complains with justification that no economist has studied the *Economic and Philosophic Manuscripts* as a philosopher and no philosopher has studied them as an economist. But this breaking up of the interpretation of the work into separate pieces is not unconnected with the fact that in the German Democratic Republic the first three manuscripts were for a long time published separately from the fourth, and that in the U.S.S.R. the first complete edition of the *Manuscripts* in Russian did not appear until 1956. (Günther Hillmann, "Zum Verständnis der Texte," in *Karl Marx, Texte zu Methode und Praxis, II*, pp. 203–204, 240.)

Progressive Disalienation Through the Building of Socialist Society, or the Inevitable Alienation in Industrial Society?

Thus the ideological and mystificating distortion of the Marxist theory of alienation has specific social sources in the reality of our time. Furthermore, it fulfills obvious apologetic functions. The ideologists of the bourgeoisie try to present the most repulsive features of contemporary capitalism as eternal and inevitable results of the "human drama." They endeavor to reduce the socio-historical conception of human alienation to an anthropological conception, bearing the mark of resignation and despair. As for the Stalinist ideologists, they strive to reduce the "valid kernel" of the theory of alienation to specific features of the *capitalist* exploitation of labor, in order to "prove" that alienation no longer exists in the Soviet Union and cannot exist in any society in transition from capitalism to socialism (nor, *a fortiori*, in any socialist society).

Conversely, the glaring survival of phenomena of alienation in Soviet society serves as a basis for bourgeois ideologists to demonstrate triumphantly the absolute inevitability of alienation "in industrial society." And the obstinacy with which official Soviet ideology denies the evidence—that is, the survival of phenomena of alienation during the transition from capitalism to socialism—risks eliciting similar conclusions from Marxist theoreticians in countries with a socialist economic basis who are sincerely seeking to discover the reality under the veil of official lies.

An analysis of the Marxist theory of alienation is thus incomplete as long as it does not enable one to formulate a *Marxist theory of progressive disalienation* and does not defend this successfully against the myth of "inevitable alienation" in any and every "industrial society."

A Marxist concept of alienation and disalienation clearly does not fit in with the apologetic assertions of writers like Jahn, according to whom "the domination of an alien power over men is done away with when private property is abolished by the proletarian revolution and the building of communist society, since here men find themselves freely facing their own products . . ." [1] A similar view is upheld by Manfred Buhr, who writes that alienation is "eliminated only with the socialist revolution and the formation of the dictatorship of the proletariat, in the process of building socialist society." [2] The author adds, to be sure, that all the phenomena of alienation do not vanish spontaneously on the morrow of the socialist revolution. But he refers in this connection to vague ideological and psychological "survivals" from the capitalist era, bourgeois individualism and egoism, without revealing their material and social roots.

In a later work, Buhr declares quite clearly: "Just as the social phenomenon of alienation is a phenomenon of historical origin and will cease to manifest itself as history advances, the concept of alienation that reflects it is likewise an historical concept and cannot be applied significantly to any but capitalist conditions." [3] There is obviously no causal relationship between the first and second parts of this sentence. The fact that alienation is an histor-

---

1. Wolfgang Jahn, "Der ökonomische Inhalt," p. 864.

2. Manfred Buhr, "Entfremdung," in *Philosophisches Wörterbuch*, Georg Klaus and Manfred Buhr, eds., p. 140. It must be emphasized that, despite this weakness regarding the problem of disalienation, Buhr's text represents an advance over the way the question of alienation had previously been dealt with in the German Democratic Republic.

3. Buhr, "Entfremdung—Philosophische Anthropologie—Marx-Kritik," p. 814. In a footnote, Buhr admits that disalienation is a *process* which merely *begins* with the overthrow of capitalist society. But he concludes that it is not possible to deduce from these premises that phenomena of alienation are still to be found in socialist society (more precisely, in the epoch of transition from capitalism to socialism). Everything in socialism that is referred to "commonly and carelessly" as alienation is at most only "externally similar" to capitalist alienation. The apologetic aspect of this casuistry stares one in the face.

ically limited phenomenon does not in the least imply that its validity is limited to the capitalist epoch alone.

T. I. Oiserman expounds his argument on a higher plane: "Under socialism [the writer here refers explicitly to the "first phase of socialism," defined by Marx in *The Critique of the Gotha Programme*] what Marx called the essence, the content, of alienation does not exist and, in the strict sense, it cannot exist under socialism: this content being the domination of the producers by the products of their labor, alienation of productive activity, alienated social relations, subjection of the personality to the spontaneous forces of social evolution." [4]

Unfortunately, all the phenomena Oiserman lists not only can survive in the epoch of transition from capitalism to socialism, but they even survive *inevitably*, in so far as commodity production, the exchange of labor power for a strictly limited and calculated wage, the *economic obligation* to effect this exchange, the division of labor (and in particular the division of labor between manual work and mental work, and so on), continue to survive. In a transitional society which is bureaucratically distorted or degenerated, these phenomena may even acquire greater and greater scope.

This is clear from an analysis in depth of the economic reality of the countries with a socialized economic basis. It is plain that the workers' needs as consumers are not at all completely met: does that not imply alienation of the worker in relation to the products of his labor, especially when these products are goods he wants to obtain, and the inadequate development of the productive forces (not to mention the bureaucratic distortion of the distributive system!) prevents him from doing so? It is also plain that the division of labor (the negative effects of which are reinforced by the bureaucratic organization of the economy) often alienates the worker and citizen from productive activity. The number of candidates for university places who are not accepted and who are therefore compelled to engage in activities whose *sole purpose is to earn a living* are so many witnesses to this alienation. One could add to the list indefinitely. In Czechoslovakia a Communist writer

---

4. Oiserman, *Die Entfremdung als historische Kategorie,* p. 135.

named Miroslav Kusy has not hesitated to draw attention to the new phenomena of alienation caused by the bureaucratization of institutions which alienate themselves from the people.[5] This is a subject that could be developed at great length. Even a writer as subtle as J. N. Dawydow prefers to ignore this problem and prudently restricts himself to an analysis of the conditions of disalienation in the second phase of socialism—a noteworthy analysis, to which I shall return later.

Under these conditions one can only applaud Henri Lefebvre when he states flatly that "Marx never restricted the sphere of alienation to capitalism." [6] And one must acknowledge the courage of Wolfgang Heise when he declares: "Overcoming alienation is identical with the development of the conscious socialist individual and the collective power to create. It is realized through the building of socialism and communism. Thus it is an aspect of the whole historical process whereby the marks of the old society are overcome in all the relations and activities of life. It begins with the emancipation of the working class, the struggle for the dictatorship of the proletariat, *and ends with the realization of social self-management in its most complete form.*" [7] This seems to me broadly correct, even if we must criticize Heise for his analysis of the *concrete* aspects of alienation and of the process of disalienation in the epoch of transition from capitalism to socialism.

In any case, this point must be kept firmly in mind: for Marx, the phenomenon of alienation is older than capitalism. It is connected with the inadequate development of the productive forces, with commodity production, money economy, and the social division of labor. As long as these phenomena continue to exist, the survival of human alienation in some form or other is inevitable.[8]

---

5. Quoted by Günther Hillmann in "Zum Verständnis der Texte," pp. 216–217.

6. Lefebvre, Preface to the second edition of *Critique de la Vie quotidienne*, Vol. I, p. 74.

7. Wolfgang Heise, "Über die Entfremdung und ihre Überwindung," p. 701.

8. A variant of the apologetic conception is offered by E. V. Ilenkov, who says that only "the antagonistic division of labor," "the bourgeois division of labor," has the effect of mutilating man. (*La dialettica dell'astratto e del*

The Yugoslav Communist theoretician Boris Ziherl admits its existence in "socialist society" (I should call it, more correctly, society in transition from capitalism to socialism), and this is entirely to his credit. But he does this only to remonstrate with those Yugoslav philosophers who call for beginning disalienation by beginning the withering away of the commodity economy, or who lay emphasis on the unnecessary and alienating forms of constraint that continue to exist in Yugoslav society.[9]

The position of the official Yugoslav theoreticians on this question is highly contradictory. They say that material conditions are not ripe for the withering away of the commodity economy and the alienation that results from it. But are material conditions ripe for the withering away of the state? In their struggle against Stalin and his followers, the Yugoslav Communists appealed to Lenin who had shown in *State and Revolution* that in order to conform with the advance toward socialism the withering away of the state must begin "on the day after the proletarian revolution," that the proletariat must build a state "which is no longer a state in the strict sense of the word." They proclaimed, and rightly, that refusal to take this road, far from preparing "the maturation of objective conditions," would inevitably set up *extra obstacles* in the way of a future withering away, which could not, after all, develop out of a constant reinforcement of the same state!

But this reasoning, which is correct as it applies to the state, is equally correct in relation to commodity economy.[10] The proletariat cannot deprive itself of this immediately after the overthrow of capitalism; it is linked with a historical phase in the development

---

concreto nel Capitale di Marx, p. 32.) For Marx, *all* division of labor that condemns man to do one job only—and therefore the division of labor that continues to exist in the U.S.S.R.—is alienating.

9. Boris Ziherl, "On the Objective and Subjective Conditions of Disalienation Under Socialism," in *Socialist Thought and Practice* (Yugoslavia), January–March 1965, pp. 122, 129–130.

10. Heise ("Über die Entfremdung," pp. 700–711) analyzes in detail a number of factors which hold back the process of disalienation during the phase of the building of socialism—in reality, the phase of transition from capitalism to socialism. But he does not even mention, in this context, the survival of commodity economy and money economy, though this is one of the essential sources of alienation, according to Marx!

of the productive forces which has far from been outgrown in what are called the "developing" countries (and all the countries with a socialized economic basis, except the German Democratic Republic, were in this category when they began to build socialism). The state can and must be used, within the framework of a planned economy, in order to perfect the planning of the economy and hasten the development of the productive forces, without which its ultimate withering away would be a utopian prospect.

At the same time, however, it must *begin to wither away* or its extension will create fresh obstacles, both objective and subjective, in the path of its future withering away. The nature of these fresh obstacles is revealed in tragic fashion in Yugoslavia, where the commodity has produced a social contradiction whose principle it harbors, namely, unemployment, with all the consequences that also follow for man's consciousness.[11] No more can the state miraculously wither away all at once after being constantly reinforced in the preceding period than can the commodity economy miraculously wither away after being constantly consolidated and extended in the period of transition between capitalism and socialism.

The Yugoslav philosophers who bring up the problem of the survival and reproduction of phenomena of alienation in their country[12] are thus more "Marxist" in relation to this problem than

---

11. Completely forgetting the connection between alienation and commodity production, the Yugoslav economist Branko Horvat sees the road leading to the abolition of alienation in self-management. He writes: "Control of production without the state as intermediary means control by direct producers, which in turn means that the equality of proletarians is turned into the equality of masters. The process of human alienation . . . comes to an end . . . (*Toward a Theory of Economic Planning*, p. 80.) Strange "masters" indeed, who may find themselves on the street, without work or income worthy of the name!

12. I will mention, among others: Rudi Supek, "Dialectique de la pratique sociale," in *Praxis*, No. 1, 1965; Gajo Petrović, "Marx's Theory of Alienation," and also "Man as Economic Animal and Man as Praxis," in *Inquiry*, 1963; Predrag Vranicki, "Socialism and the Problem of Alienation," in *Praxis*, No. 2–3, 1965, and "La signification actuelle de l'humanisme du jeune Marx," in *Annali dell'Istituto Giangiacomo Feltrinelli*, 1964–1965; Zaga Pesić-Golubović, "What Is the Meaning of Alienation?" in *Praxis*, No. 5, 1966.

the official theoreticians—even if they are sometimes led, under the influence of their own bad experiences, to put a question mark over the Marxist theory of the complete disalienation of man in communist society. The possibility of this disalienation is also challenged in two recent works by Henri Lefebvre[13] in which the author can see nothing more than a continual swinging to and fro between alienation, disalienation, and re-alienation. He says, rightly, that it is necessary "fully to particularize," "historicize," and "relativize" the concept of alienation.[14] If, though, in relativizing this concept we do away with the possibility of completely negating it, we tend to make it absolute again. Thus, Lefebvre's attempt to "historicize" alienation must be regarded as a failure, since it has produced the opposite dialectical result, transforming alienation into a concept which is immanent in human society, even if it presents itself in a different form in each type of society.

The sources of this historical skepticism are obvious: they are the negative phenomena that have accompanied the first historical endeavors to build a socialist society[15]—the results of Stalinism—which have outrageously and uselessly intensified the phenomena of alienation and which cannot but continue to exist in the period of transition from capitalism to socialism.

Thus, the neo-skepticism of a Lefebvre or of a Pesić-Golubović is only a negative reaction in face of the Stalinist experience, just as the apologetic writing of Buhr, Jahn, Oiserman, and Ilenkov is only a product of the same experience, an attempt to gloss over the negative aspects of social reality in the countries with a socialized economic basis. Once thinking outgrows apologetics of this sort, in a new political context in Eastern Europe, it may either take

---

13. Lefebvre, *Critique de la Vie quotidienne*, Vol. II, and *Introduction à la modernité*.

14. *Critique de la Vie quotidienne*, Vol. II, p. 209.

15. "*Today* we are less convinced than Marx was that there can be an absolute end to alienation." (Lefebvre, *Introduction à la modernité*, p. 146. Emphasis mine.—E.M.) By referring to *present-day* conditions in order to justify this conclusion, Lefebvre seems to forget the premises of Marx's argument: the withering away of commodity production, money economy, and the social division of labor, on a world scale, and on the basis of a very high level of development of productive forces.

the path of a return to the original conception of disalienation as we find it in Marx—disalienation conceived of as a process depending on a material and social infrastructure which does not yet exist in the period of transition from capitalism to socialism—or else the path of skepticism about the possibility of complete disalienation.

But the task for scientific thought is to analyze the social and economic sources of the continued existence of phenomena of alienation during the period of transition between capitalism and socialism and during the first phase of socialism, and to discover the driving forces of the process of disalienation during these historical phases. This means undertaking an analysis that begins by putting aside those factors reinforcing and aggravating alienation as a result of the bureaucratic distortion or degeneration of a society in transition, and then later on integrating these special factors in a more concrete analysis of the phenomena of alienation in countries like the U.S.S.R., the "people's democracies," and so on.

The general source of the continued existence of phenomena of alienation during the transition period and in the first phase of socialism is the inadequate level of development of the productive forces and the resulting survival of bourgeois norms of distribution.[16] The contradiction between the socialized mode of production and the bourgeois norms of distribution—the chief contradiction of the transition period—brings factors of alienation into production relations. The workers continue to suffer, even if only partially, from the effects of an objective and elemental social evolution which they do not control (the survival of the "laws of the market" in the sphere of consumer goods; the survival of a selection procedure for jobs which does not permit full development of all the aptitudes of every individual, etc.).

When to *these* circumstances we add the hypertrophy of bureaucracy, the lack of socialist democracy on the political level, the lack of workers' self-management on the economic plane, the lack of freedom to create on the cultural plane, *specific fac-*

---

16. See the expression used by Marx in *Critique of the Gotha Programme,* in *Selected Works,* Vol. III, pp. 19–20. See also my *Marxist Economic Theory,* Vol. II, p. 565.

tors of alienation resulting from bureaucratic distortion or degeneration are added to the inevitable factors mentioned in the previous paragraph. The bureaucratization of the transitional society tends to aggravate the contradiction between the socialized mode of production and the bourgeois norms of distribution, particularly by intensifying social inequality. The generalization of a money economy works in the same way.

Wolfgang Heise makes a very subtle analysis of this problem. While collective ownership of the means of production and socialist planning *in principle* overcome social helplessness in relation to the evolution of society as a whole, this does not mean that this social helplessness is immediately overcome for every individual. It is necessary to take into account not only the ideological slag of the capitalist past, of the members of the former ruling classes who are still around, of the inadequate level of education of part of the proletariat, and so on; we have also to realize that this helplessness is overcome in practice only when individuals *realize* their identity with society through social activity based on a large number of free decisions.[17] This implies not only complete self-management by labor at the level of the economy taken as a whole (not merely in the production process but also in distribution and consumption), but also a withering away of the state and the disappearance of all human relationships based on constraint and oppression.

Thus far, Heise's analysis seems to me to be correct. But in stating that the process of disalienation cannot be a spontaneous phenomenon but must be guided by the Party, he begins by saying that the risk of bureaucratization—of seeing the machinery of government become independent in relation to the purposes of society as a whole—can best be neutralized by Party action.[18] This is to take an idealistic view and lose sight of the fact that there are *two objective sources* of bureaucratization: on the one hand, the survival of spontaneous economic processes (the survival of norms of commodity distribution and of elements of a commodity economy, the survival of the division of labor, of cultural privileges, and of delegations of authority, all of which

---

17. Heise, "Über die Entfremdung," pp. 702–703.
18. Ibid., p. 704.

cause the machinery of government to become independent and transform itself from the servant into the master of society), and, on the other hand, the centralization of the social surplus product and the right to dispose of it freely that belongs to the state machine. The dual process of disalienation in relation to these specific phenomena of alienation thus consists in the progressive withering away of the commodity economy and of social inequality and the replacement of the system of state management of the economy by a system of workers' self-management, democratically centralized. Thereby the material infrastructure of bureaucratization is destroyed, and it is only under these conditions that the subjective activity of the Party—and the broadening of socialist democracy on the political plane, which implies abandonment of the dogma of the single party—can be freed from the bureaucratic grip which subjugates it.[19]

Heise rightly insists on the importance of a sufficient level of development of the productive forces in order to make possible the unleashing of all these processes of disalienation. However, after having first sinned by voluntarism, he goes on to sin by a mechanistic deviation. Such a development of the productive forces demands "an extraordinarily high level of organization and differentiation of social functions"; for this reason it would be "senseless to demand direct democracy in production or the abandonment of authoritarian central planning . . . as a condition for overcoming alienation. . . . This would be a demand running counter to the real needs of rational production, to economic and technical logic . . ."[20]

It is noteworthy that, when pushed back into its last entrenchments, an apologia for the lack of workers' self-management in the German Democratic Republic makes use of the same argument—"the high level of differentiation of social functions"—used by bourgeois ideologists to show that alienation is inevitable, not merely under capitalism but in any "industrial society." I shall come back to this point later. It is also noteworthy that Heise cannot conceive of central planning except as authoritarian

---

19. It is well known that in the U.S.S.R. in Stalin's time the Party was the chief vehicle of bureaucratization.

20. Heise, "Über die Entfremdung," p. 706.

planning and that, like the Yugoslav writers already mentioned, he remains caught in a dilemma: either anarchy of production (market economy) or authoritarian planning. The possibility of *democratically centralized* planning, the outcome of a congress of workers' councils managing the enterprises, seems to elude him. What he calls "the lowering of the level of organization of society" means for him (as for the Stalinist and bourgeois writers) the abolition of authoritarian structures. As if the "associated producers," to use Marx's expression, were incapable of raising the level of social *organization* by substituting, at least among themselves,[21] freely accepted discipline for a hierarchy of persons giving and receiving orders!

But the basic weakness of Heise's argument lies still deeper. On the one hand, he appeals to the primacy of Party activity (against tendencies both to spontaneity and to bureaucracy); on the other, he invokes the primacy of economic growth (against democratizing the life of the enterprises). He does not seem to realize that the power of the bureaucracy is reflected *subjectively* in this economic argument, and that by accepting it one paralyzes in advance any subjective activity directed against the bureaucracy. For does not the latter claim to personify "competence" and "specialization" as against the ignorant masses? Nor does Heise notice that *objectively* the bureaucracy remains all powerful as long as it can dispose with sovereign authority of the social surplus product (whether by way of the authority it possesses, as in the U.S.S.R., or through the medium of the "laws of the market," as in Yugoslavia).

This is why he calls for plenty of "correctives" to "mistakes," in the form of an "increasing right of control by the community"; this is why he recognizes that in the long run the centralization of authority in the state machine must be overcome by "socialist democracy" and the "development of conscious activity by the masses"[22]—but without drawing what is from the Marxist standpoint the obvious conclusion, namely that the decisive step toward

---

21. Coercion obviously continues to be inevitable where other social classes are concerned, but the degree of this coercion depends on the violence of social contradictions.

22. Heise, "Über die Entfremdung," pp. 706–707.

this democracy is one which subjects the management of production and the possibility of disposing of the social surplus product to the workers as a whole—to the "associated producers."

J. N. Dawydow attempts a much more profound analysis of the mechanisms of disalienation in the building of communism than does Heise. To Marx—according to Dawydow—the capitalist division of labor had led to the complete elimination of freedom from the sphere of material production; this freedom will be restored by communism, because the needs of technique themselves require increasing functional mobility among the producers, who will have become the principal productive force through their scientific knowledge. The individual personality with an all-around development becomes possible on this technical basis, which, indeed, insists upon it, since from the standpoint of this "political economy of communism" everyone who has not become a "fully developed individual" constitutes a serious economic loss.[23]

But this means that under increasingly general conditions of abundance of material goods, the principal goal of production becomes that of producing "fully" developed individuals, creative and free.[24] In proportion as man becomes the "principal productive force"[25] through the enormous extension of scientific technology, he is less and less directly "integrated" into the production process. In proportion as "living labor" is expelled from the production process, it acquires new significance as the organizer and controller of this process. And in proportion as there thus take place, side by side, the production of an abundance of material goods and the production of men with all-around development, the domination of "dead labor" over "living labor" disappears and freedom is "restored" in material production.[26]

The whole of this analysis, which is essentially based on the passages in the *Grundrisse* which I quoted earlier, seems a con-

23. J. N. Dawydow, *Freiheit und Entfremdung*, p. 114.

24. Ibid., p. 117.

25. Cf. Marx, in the *Grundrisse*, p. 593: "It is the development of the social individual that [now] appears as the great fundamental pillar of production and wealth."

26. Dawydow, *Freiheit und Entfremdung*, pp. 117, 131.

tribution to a fundamental clarification of the problem.[27] Its chief weakness is that it jumps in one leap from capitalist society to *communist* production relations, without analyzing the necessary and inevitable intermediate historical stages—without describing the concrete driving forces of progressive disalienation in the transitional phase, during the building of socialism. Workers' self-management, democratic-centralist central planning, the progressive withering away of commodity production, the generalization of higher education, a radical reduction in the working day, the development of creative activity during "free time," the progressive interpenetration of consumer habits on a world scale, the psychological revolution brought about by these successive transformations, and in particular by the withering away of commodity production:[28] none of this is included in Dawydow's analysis, and they are needed in order to complete it and remove from his work a touch of platitudinism which his bourgeois and dogmatist critics may wrongly use against him.[29]

The point is that, in order to be logical the analysis of the progressive disalienation of labor and of man under socialism must be combined with an exhaustive analysis of alienation in the transition period. Without this, such an analysis becomes arbitrary. It looks like a "flight into the future" which irritates those who give priority to a more pragmatic approach to immediate reality. At least, though, this "flight into the future" has the merit of clarity and precision in its view of future developments. It remains faithful to Marx's teaching, which repudiates any "anthropological" conception of alienation.

The same merit cannot be accorded to the disillusioned conclusions Adam Schaff draws from his confrontation with present-day Polish reality. He recognizes that the phenomena of alienation

---

27. See the series of quotations given in Chapter 7 of this book.

28. I have devoted a large part of Chapter 17 of my *Marxist Economic Theory* to these problems.

29. Several aspects of Dawydow's argument have already begun to be verified empirically, in particular the need for a greater degree of mobility of labor and the ability to perform tasks within functional teams which is resulting from the advance of automation in large-scale industry. (See Friedmann and Naville, eds., *Traité de sociologie du travail*, pp. 380–381.)

are still to be found in socialist society, but solves the problem by casting doubt on the possibility of achieving, even in communist society, the withering away of the state, the disappearance of the division of labor (which he conceives mechanistically: a reading of Dawydow should change his view of this!), and the abolition of commodity production.[30] This skeptical and misanthropic revision of Marx has been criticized by the leaders of the Polish Communist Party[31]—not by calling for a frank analysis of the obstacles to disalienation imposed by the bureaucratized social reality of their country, but by simply denying, in the usual manner of apologetics, that the problem exists at all. Schaff, who has at least tried to draw up a "program of action" against alienation, is by comparison more sincere.[32] But both they and he are incapable of recalling what Marx taught, and therefore cannot check the rise of non-Marxist philosophy and sociology in Poland.

An example of this is the statement by sociologist Stanislaw Ossowski that the classical concept of social class formulated by Marx applies only to a type of society characterized by the capitalism of free competition. Today not only the appropriation of the means of production but also that of consumer goods permits, he says, the establishment of "economic domination over men." There are also new forms of "domination of man by man, domination which results either from ownership of the means of production, or from ownership of the means of consumption, or from ownership of the means of violence, or from a combination of

---

30. "I merely mention this problem, especially because it may be supposed that commodity production will have vanished from fully developed communist society, though this supposition seems problematic [!] in the light of present-day experience." (Schaff, *Marxismus und das menschliche Individuum*, p. 177.)

31. *Nowe Drogi*, December 1965.

32. Schaff admits that the socialization of the means of production can only begin the process of disalienation. But he stresses socialist education rather than changes in economic conditions (especially the necessary withering away of bourgeois norms of distribution) as the means for completing this process. His plea for a "moderate egalitarianism" and greater freedom of opinion and of criticism in relation to "the elite in power" is to his credit, but does not go to the heart of the matter.

these different ownerships." [33] Here we plainly pass from a sociology based on the ideas of social class and social surplus product to a sociology based on the concept, infinitely vaguer and less operative, of "dominant groups." [34] And a bridge is thus established between critical but revisionist sociology (and philosophy) in the so-called socialist countries and the academic sociology of the capitalist countries, which rejects Marxism in favor of a division of society into "those who command" and "those who obey."

There is no need to underline the apologetic character of this conception of "industrial society" as set out by various writers. What is specific to the capitalist mode of production is attributed to every society in the epoch of large-scale industry.[35] The results of a type of *social* organization are attributed to a form of *technical* organization.

Most Western sociologists draw pessimistic conclusions from this mystificating identification of social relations with technical relations. They revive the old myth of Hobbes's Leviathan and see modern man as inevitably crushed beneath the machine that has issued from his own brain. The alienation of labor, the crushing of the worker by his own product, is said to be the inevitable result of large-scale industry, and this alienation, we are told, will relentlessly worsen as the technical apparatus is perfected.

It must be admitted that the bureaucratic degeneration of the U.S.S.R., especially in the Stalin era, has furnished plenty of arguments for supporters of this pessimistic view. But what is char-

---

33. Stanislaw Ossowski, *Klassenstruktur im sozialen Bewusstsein*, pp. 227–228.

34. Ossowski's ideas are close to those of François Perroux or Rolf Dahrendorf, quoted earlier, or to the concepts of the conservative anthropologist Arnold Gehlen: functional authority is said to be increasingly replacing the division of society into classes. (*Anthropologische Forschung*, p. 130.) Ossowski himself indicates (p. 223) that it is the incapacity of the dogmatic and apologetic "Marxism" of the Stalin era to explain the phenomena of social privilege in societies with socialized means of production that lies at the root of his skeptical revisionism.

35. See in particular Raymond Aron, *Dix-huit leçons sur la société industrielle*; Reinhard Bendix, *Work and Authority in Industry;* Dahrendorf, *Class and Class Conflict in Industrial Society.*

202 The Formation of the Economic Thought of Karl Marx

acteristic of most of them is the absence from their writings of an analysis in depth which would bring out the *laws of development* of social reality from a purely phenomenological description of it.

By stating that there will always be "those who command" and "those who obey," that there will always be scarce goods and the necessity of an alienating method of alloting them, these authors raise to the level of an axiom not the conclusions but the premises of their argument. They think they are basing themselves on empirical facts, but in reality they are refusing to recognize a *tendency* that is going in the opposite direction. For it is hard to deny that the potential wealth of society, the degree of satisfaction of rational needs, and the possibility of thereby eliminating the coercive mechanisms in the social and economic organization, have been advancing with giant strides for a whole century—and especially in the last quarter of this century—in what is called "industrial" society. Why should it be supposed that this tendency cannot result in a qualitative "leap," by which man's enslavement to the necessities of a "struggle for existence" would wither away and his capacity to dominate his own social organization, no less than he dominates the forces of nature, would come to full flower?

It must be recognized that technical development is not heading in the direction foreseen by the pessimists. Georg Klaus correctly distinguishes between *two* types of automation, the second of which, much less rigid than the first and based on cybernetics, creates the infrastructure for the withering away of alienating labor and is the precondition for all-around creative labor. And a scientist like A. G. M. Van Melsen honestly admits that technique is still in the primitive stage, with many of its brutalizing aspects resulting precisely from this primitiveness: "When the primary needs have really been satisfied, it is perfectly possible, partly as a result of technical progress itself, to produce many small series and to incorporate original artistic projects in each of these series. Moreover, the shorter and shorter length of time needed for 'obligatory labor' helps to make possible the blossoming of all those things that demand so much personal care and love. . . . No doubt they will come back in the form of free arts practiced by those who will have been liberated by technique." [36] It goes without saying that technique cannot play this liberating role until it has been freed from the grip of private profit and the exploitation of capital.

The pronounced pessimism of the supporters of the thesis that alienation is inevitable in "industrial society" is explained by their confusing the *real sources of authority* with the *functional articulation of authority*.[37] The board of directors of a capitalist company can decide to close down its enterprises, destroying the entire bureaucratic hierarchy patiently built up, without ever having previously encroached on the "growing independence" of the research laboratories or the technological planning department. But its decision to dissolve the company, made from considerations of profit-making, shows how the previous delegation of authority was limited to particular functions and how it is that private property remains the real source of authority. Why could a workers' council not delegate some technical authority in the same way, without thereby ceasing to be able to make (or even to cause the collective groups of workers to make) the basic decisions of *economic management?*

It is not the technical inevitability of this functional articulation that makes it impossible to "democratize the enterprises." It is not the complexity and the increasing differentiation of tasks that hinder this democratization. The insurmountable obstacle under capitalism is the ultimate right of making the final decisions

---

36. Georg Klaus, *Kybernetik in philosophischer Sicht*, pp. 414–415; A. G. M. Van Melsen, *Science and Technology*, p. 321.

37. Typical in this connection are the thoughts of Alain Touraine on the increasing decentralization of decisions within large "bureaucratized" enterprises, in Friedmann and Naville, eds., *Traité de sociologie du travail*, Vol. I, pp. 420 *et seq.* One of the first to use this argument was Johann Plenge, the true ancestor of present-day bourgeois criticism of Marx: "Modern technique implies mental work, it implies the subordination of disciplined manual work in the enterprise as a whole," and so the exercise of power by the manual workers is impossible. (*Marx und Hegel*, p. 134.) This passage should be set beside that taken from Wolfgang Heise, above, concerning the impossibility of democracy within an enterprise owing to the "differentiation of social functions." We see that the apologia for the bourgeois hierarchy in the factory provides the main argument in the apologia for the bureaucratic hierarchy.

which the big shareholders and their allies and representatives, the managers, want to keep for themselves.[38] Once this obstacle has been swept away by the socialist revolution there is no *a priori* reason to suppose that "fresh alienations" must arise from technical necessities within enterprises under democratic-centralist self-management.

The same pessimism also results from inadequately distinguishing between the *apparent automatism of the mechanisms* and the *human decisions inspired by social and economic motives* which are characteristic of what is called "industrial" society. When writers like Norbert Wiener fear that machines will eventually make decisions independently of any judgment by men (themselves mechanized),[39] they forget that in capitalist society the tendency to mechanize labor at the lower levels is accompanied by an unprecedented concentration of *power to decide* at the top, where a handful of men—aided by an enormous mass of information and relying on the entire functional articulation of authority which immensely strengthens its striking power—remain the sole masters who, in the final instance, decide whether a particular line of action *suggested* by the computers will actually be adopted or not.[40] What Marxist theory illuminates is the *motives* that ultimately inspire these men: not arbitrary motives, or irrational ones, or mere speculation, but the overall defense of class interests as these are understood by the most powerful stratum of the class concerned.

If, then, this is how matters really stand, it is clear that it is enough to transfer this power of decision from a small handful of men to the mass of "associated producers" for these same

38. François Bloch-Laîné brings this out strikingly in *Pour une réforme de l'entreprise* (pp. 41, 43–44, 100): He argues for greater participation by the trade unions and the workers in the management of *certain* aspects of the activity of the enterprises. But he immediately emphasizes that this "participation" leaves untouched the single supreme authority, the master hierarchy which alone retains the right to take the key economic decisions.

39. Norbert Wiener, *The Human Use of Human Beings*, pp. 158–160.

40. The case of the American war machine, which is highly mechanized (especially as regards the warning system, guided by computers), but which culminates in the President of the United States, who alone has the right to press certain buttons, is symbolic of the entire mechanism of the capitalist regime.

machines to be made to *serve* society to the same extent that today they seem to *enslave* it.[41]

Alongside these pessimistic mystifications, however, there are also some optimistic ones. The alienation of labor, it is said, is indeed an inevitable result of "industrial society," but it can be overcome without the necessity of overthrowing capitalism. It will be enough to give back to the workers a "sense of participation," or even a "work ethic"—thanks to human relations being given back their value within the enterprise—for the workers no longer to feel alienated.[42] It will be necessary, say others, to insure the existence of means of communication, dialogue, and creation which give back to the worker his sense of personality and his freedom in work and leisure.[43]

The first of these theses is plainly apologetic in character. I will even say that it undoubtedly serves big capital in a direct way, since its avowed aim is to reduce social conflicts *under the existing regime*. What the specialists in "human relations" try to abolish is not the reality of alienation but the workers' awareness of this reality. Their pseudo-disalienation would be alienation carried to an extreme, with the alienated worker alienated from awareness of his own condition as a mutilated human being.[44]

---

41. Here is a striking example of the confusion between the *socioeconomic power of decision* and technical authority, taken from the German bourgeois newspaper *Frankfurter Allgemeine Zeitung* of August 16, 1967. A writer argues that with all the demands for self-management we hear nowadays, why not demand that a "patients' council" have the right to dictate to doctors about diagnoses and treatments?

42. Elton Mayo, *The Human Problems of an Industrial Civilization*, pp. 158–159, 171 *et seq.*; Bendix, *Work and Authority in Industry*, pp. 448–450.

43. François Perroux, "Aliénation et création collective," in *Cahiers de l'ISEA*, June 1964, pp. 92–93.

44. Bendix correctly classifies the theory of "human relations" in the larger category of "ideology of management" (I should call it, rather, capitalist ideology concerning the enterprise). It would be easy to show that the evolution of this ideology, over a century, reflects not only the evolution of the structure of the capitalist enterprise itself but also and above all the evolution of the balance of strength between bourgeoisie and proletariat. Nothing is more revealing in this connection than the change from the haughty Puritanism and social Darwinism of the age when the capitalist was all-powerful to the hypocritical plea for association between capital and labor which nowadays abound.

Alienation thus acquires additional dimensions through the attempt made by bourgeois society to manipulate not merely the thinking and the habits but even the unconscious of the producers.[45] There is little chance, however, that the technicians of "human relations" will in the long run be able to prevent the workers from becoming aware of the state of oppression in which they find themselves.

The second thesis, a more subtle one, is above all ambiguous. It is formulated as a moral imperative, apparently independent of the "form taken by institutions" (that is, the mode of production). But François Perroux explains that "it is not within a rigid framework of institutions, consecrating the wrong and injustice in society as a whole, that specialized institutions can fulfill their function." [46] Is a society based on the *obligation* of the worker to sell his labor power and to carry on brutalizing work in order to obtain the means to live not a "rigid framework consecrating wrong and injustice"? How can one give the worker, within that framework, "the feeling that he is participating in collective creation," or "the opportunity and the means to become conscious of himself" during his leisure hours? Under the capitalist mode of production this would be nothing but a crude deception. Carrying out this program requires overthrowing capitalist society. From that moment onward, however, Perroux's program would undergo a remarkable expansion. It would no longer be a question of giving the worker the "feeling" of participating in collective creation, but of making him a real creator. It would no longer be a matter of giving him the opportunity and the means to "become conscious of himself" in his leisure hours, but of giving him the opportunity to realize himself through free crea-

---

45. Vance Packard, *The Hidden Persuaders*. While C. Wright Mills fears the development of indifference in the face of alienation (*The Marxists*, p. 113), Bloch-Laîné stresses, more realistically, with regard to this same alienation or at least its most striking aspect (the absence of workers' power within the enterprises): "The calm is deceptive. Behind it lie many special and individual dissatisfactions, which are ready to break out into revolt at the first downward turn of the general economic situation." (*Pour une réforme de l'entreprise*, p. 25.) See some bibliographical references on the state of mind of the working class in Chapter 1.

46. "Aliénation et création collective," p. 44.

tion, without external constraint. It would no longer be a matter of allowing "beneficent zones" of "disinterested curiosity" to develop, but of attaining complete self-management by men in all spheres of social activity.

For that is where the key to ultimate disalienation really lies. It results from the abolition of labor (in the sense in which Marx and Engels mean this in *The German Ideology*),[47] or, in other words, the replacement of mechanical and schematic labor by really creative labor which is no longer labor in the traditional sense of the word, which no longer leads to a man's giving up his life in order to insure his material existence, but has become man's all-around creative activity.[48]

A critique of the apologetic conceptions of the bourgeoisie and the bureaucracy thus sends us back to the splendid vision of a classless society which Marx evoked in the *Grundrisse* and which reproduces, on a higher plane because enriched with scientific knowledge and coherent socioeconomic proof, the similar vision he had already outlined in the *Economic and Philosophic Manuscripts* and *The German Ideology*.

And it is in the transformation of the theory of alienation from an anthropological conception, metaphysical and resigned, into a historical conception, dialectical and revolutionary, that lies, in brief, the significance of the enormous amount of work in the field of political economy that Marx carried out between his first reading of the classical economists in 1843–1844 and the writing of the *Grundrisse* in 1857–1858.

We can thus end by answering a question which has been discussed ceaselessly by commentators on Marx—the question of *Marx's specific character as an economist.* Two theses confront each other. On the one hand, there are those who, like Rubel, or

---

47. *The German Ideology*, pp. 85, 95, 236, 242.

48. Cf. Georg Klaus: "In order to develop all man's creative powers, it is necessary to free him to a large extent from the obligation to contribute schematic labor . . ." "Cybernetics and automation are the technical conditions for this situation [communism], because they enable man to free himself from all non-creative, schematic work . . . They give him above all the time for an all-around scientific and technical education, that is, for truly creative labor at the contemporary level of production." (*Kybernetik in philosophischer Sicht*, pp. 457, 464.)

to a lesser extent Father Bigo, actually deny that Marx did the work of an economist, and declare that he arrived at his fundamental theories by "brilliant intuition,"[49] or who say even more clearly: "Marx was by no means the promoter of a new economic theory but was, rather, one of the pioneers of scientific sociology."[50]

On the other hand, there are those who recognize, with Emile James, that Marx was the greatest economist of the nineteenth century,[51] or, with Jean Marchal, that he was the economist who enabled economic science to obtain "the great vision of an immanent evolution of economic processes."[52]

In my view, Marx had earlier given the answer to both parties in a definition of his method which was at the same time a criticism of Lassalle's: "He [Lassalle] will learn to his cost that to bring a science by criticism to the point where it can be dialectically presented is an altogether different thing from applying an abstract ready-made system of logic to mere inklings of such a system."[53] And already in the *Economic and Philosophic Manuscripts* Marx had included the following warning in the Preface: "It is hardly necessary to assure the reader conversant with political economy that my results have been attained by means of a wholly empirical analysis based on a conscientious critical study of political economy."[54]

Marx began by wanting to make a general critique of bourgeois society taken as a whole. This led him to formulate some general laws on the evolution of *all* human societies. One of these laws

---

49. R. P. Bigo, *Humanisme et économie politique chez Karl Marx*, pp. 36–37. Rubel's thesis on the ethical character of Marx's work had already been set forth in 1911 by Karl Vorlander in *Kant und Marx*, p. 293. It involved Vorlander in a famous controversy with Max Adler.

50. Maximilien Rubel, *Karl Marx: Essai de biographie intellectuelle*, p. 12.

51. Emile James, *Histoire sommaire de la pensée économique*, p. 167.

52. Jean Marchal, *Deux essais sur le marxisme*, p. 80. See also Ernest Teilhac: "Marx, following in the footsteps of the classical economists, intended to place himself strictly within the economic framework, to formulate a strictly economic theory, and to do the work of an economist." (*L'Economie politique perdue et retrouvée*, p. 106.)

53. *Selected Correspondence*, p. 103.

54. *Economic and Philosophic Manuscripts*, p. 63.

was that production relations in a sense constitute "the anatomi-
cal system" of the given society. In order to formulate this law
effectively Marx had to master all the empirical data of the economic science of his time (together with many of the data of
the other human sciences).[55] And in order to complete his work
of total criticism in relation to bourgeois society he had to go
deeply into the history of economic doctrines,[56] whose development follows an internal logic, even if it is determined in the last
analysis by social and economic evolution as a whole. This dual
obligation led him to occupy himself with the subject matter of
economic science, as an economist endowed with a special awareness of the impossibility of separating this economic science from
the other human sciences.[57] Marx was therefore "one of the pioneers of scientific sociology" only in so far as he did independent
work as an economist. Without his own discoveries as an economist, his whole social theory would have had an essentially utopian character, voluntarist and "philosophical" in the negative
sense of the word.[58] It was only thanks to his economic discov-

---

55. "Marx always refers to the totality of empirical data, to intuition socially realized." (E. V. Ilenkov, *La dialettica dell'astratto*, p. 13.)

56. "The researcher must always try to find the total and concrete reality,
even if he knows he will not be able to achieve it except in a partial and
limited way, and to do this he must include, in his study of social facts,
the history of the theories about these facts, and also link his study of facts
of consciousness with their localization in history and their economic and
social infrastructure." (Lucien Goldmann, *Sciences humaines et philosophie*,
p. 18.)

57. "The introduction of the ideas of structure and system seems to be
the only means that science has found up to now to build a bridge between
two types of research which are too often separated: historical research and
theoretical analysis." (André Marchal, *Systèmes et structures économiques*,
p. 11.) It was none other than Marx who first succeeded in building this
bridge between history and economic analysis, by using historical categories
for analysis which made possible the introduction of the ideas of structure
and system referred to by André Marchal.

58. Similarly, in *Marxisme et philosophie* Karl Korsch is wrong when,
moved by the legitimate desire to re-establish the unity between theory
and practice in Marx's teaching and to defend its revolutionary significance
against the reformist epigones, he ends by questioning the objectively scientific character of Marx's economic analysis and sees nothing more in it
than "the theoretical expression of a revolutionary process" (p. 103). In

eries that he was able to realize what he himself regarded as the chief work of his life: *to give a scientific foundation to the socialist aspirations and struggles of the proletariat.* "Dialectical thought . . . makes it possible to understand the simultaneous existence of objectivity in knowledge of the social sciences and the political standpoint necessarily taken up in the social process by whoever is imbued with this objective knowledge." [59]

It is impossible to *dissociate* the sociologist from the revolutionary in Marx, the historian from the economist. But Marx was only able to be effectively—that is, scientifically—a sociologist, an historian, and above all a revolutionary because he was an economist, because he revolutionized economic science by discoveries whose genesis we have tried to follow step by step in this study. Once this work was accomplished, *Capital* was ready; all that remained was to write it.

---

order to be able to formulate his analysis of the class struggle under capitalism and of the advance toward the revolutionary overthrow of capital in a theoretically valid—that is, effective—way, Marx *had* first of all to master empirically all the data of the human sciences and to criticize them, transcending them scientifically. Marx himself defined his work this way too many times for it to be possible today to misrepresent its meaning or question its objective scientific value, independent of the "revolutionary passion" that animated his whole life and the revolutionary aim he constantly strove to attain.

59. Max Adler, *Marxistische Probleme*, p. 59.

Bibliography

Works by Marx and Engels

Marx, Karl. "Arbeitslohn." In *Kleine ökonomische Schriften*. Berlin: Dietz-Verlag, 1955.

————. *Briefe an Kugelmann*. Berlin: Dietz-Verlag, 1955.

————. *Capital: A Critique of Political Economy, Vol. I*. London: Lawrence & Wishart, 1970.

————. *Capital: A Critique of Political Economy, Vols. II and III*. Moscow: Progress Publishers, 1966, 1967.

————. *A Contribution to the Critique of Political Economy*. Chicago: Charles H. Kerr & Company, 1904.

————. *Economic and Philosophic Manuscripts of 1844*, edited by Dirk J. Struik. New York: International Publishers, 1964.

————. *Enthüllungen über den Kommunistenprozess zu Köln*. 4th ed. Edited by Franz Mehring. Berlin: Buchhandlung Vorwärts, 1914.

————. *Grundrisse der Kritik der politischen Ökonomie*. 2 vols. Berlin: Dietz-Verlag, 1953.

————. *The Poverty of Philosophy*. Introduction by Frederick Engels. New York: International Publishers, 1963.

————. *Pre-Capitalist Economic Formations*, edited by E. J. Hobsbawm. London: Lawrence & Wishart, 1964.

————. *Theorien uber den Mehrwert, Vol. III*. Berlin: Dietz-Verlag, 1956.

————. *Theories of Surplus Value, I and II*. Moscow: Progress Publishers, 1963 and 1968.

Engels, Frederick. *Herr Eugen Dühring's Revolution in Science (Anti-Dühring)*. New York: International Publishers, n.d.

————. "Karl Heinrich Marx." In *Handwörtebuch der Staatswissenschaften,* Vol. VI. 4th ed. Jena: Gustav Fischer-Verlag, 1925.

Marx, Karl, and Engels, Frederick. *Aus dem literarischen Nachlass von Karl Marx und Frederick Engels, 1841–1850*, edited by Franz Mehring. 3rd ed. Stuttgart: Dietz-Verlag, 1920.
————. *Ausgewählte Briefe.* Berlin: Dietz-Verlag, 1955.
————. *Briefe über "Das Kapital."* Berlin: Dietz-Verlag, 1954.
————. *Der Briefwechsel zwischen Friedrich Engels und Karl Marx 1844–1883*, edited by A. Bebel and Eduard Bernstein. Stuttgart: Dietz-Verlag, 1921.
————. *The German Ideology.* Moscow: Progress Publishers, 1964.
————. *Gesammelte Schriften 1852–1862*, edited by D. Ryazanov. Stuttgart: Dietz-Verlag, 1920.
————. *Historisch-kritische Gesamtausgabe (MEGA).* Frankfurt: Verlagsgesellschaft, 1927.
————. *The Holy Family, or Critique of Critical Critique.* Moscow: Foreign Languages Publishing House, 1956.
————. *Neue Rheinische Zeitung—Politisch-ökonomische Revue.* Facsimile edition.
————. *Selected Correspondence 1846–1895.* New York: International Publishers, 1942.
————. *Selected Works.* 3 vols. Moscow: Progress Publishers, 1969, 1970. This is the most complete currently available selection of the shorter works of Marx and Engels and includes the *Communist Manifesto; Class Struggles in France; Wages, Price and Profit; Wage Labor and Capital; Principles of Communism;* etc.
————. *Werke.* Berlin: Dietz-Verlag, 1961.

Other Works Consulted

Adhya, G. L. *Early Indian Economics.* Bombay: Asia Publishing House, 1966.
Adler, Max. *Marxistische Probleme.* 5th ed. Stuttgart: Dietz Nachfolger, 1922.
Agazzi, Emilio. "La formazione dell metodologia di Marx." *Rivista storica del socialismo*, September–December 1964.
Althusser, Louis. *For Marx.* New York: Pantheon, 1970.

—————. "L'objet du Capital." *Lire le Capital*, Vol. II. Paris: Maspero, 1966.

Andrieux, A., and Lignon, J. *L'Ouvrier d'aujourd'hui*. Paris: Rivière, 1960.

Arendt, Hannah. *The Human Condition*. Chicago: University of Chicago Press, 1958.

Aron, Raymond. *Dix-huit leçons sur la société industrielle*. Paris: Gallimard, 1962.

Avdijev [Avdiev], W. I. *Geschichte des Alten Orients*. Berlin: Volkseigner Verlag, 1953.

Axelos, Kostas. *Marx, penseur de la technique*. Paris: Editions de Minuit, 1961.

Baran, Paul A., and Sweezy, Paul M. *Monopoly Capital*. New York: Monthly Review Press, 1966.

Bendix, Reinhard. *Work and Authority in Industry*. New York: Harper and Row, 1956.

Bigo, R. P. *Humanisme et économie politique chez Karl Marx*. Paris: P.U.F., 1953.

Blackburn, Robin, and Cockburn, Alexander, eds. *The Incompatibles —Trade-Union Militancy and the Consensus*. Harmondsworth: Penguin, 1967.

Blauner, Robert. *Alienation and Freedom: The Factory-Worker and His Industry*. Chicago: University of Chicago Press, 1964.

Bloch-Laîné, François. *Pour une réforme de l'entreprise*. Paris: Editions du Seuil, 1963.

Böhm-Bawerk, Eugen von. *Karl Marx and the Close of His System*, edited by Paul M. Sweezy. New York: Augustus M. Kelley, 1949.

Boiteau, Pierre. "Les droits sur la terre dans la société malgache précoloniale." *La Pensée*, October 1964.

Bollhagen, Peter. *Soziologie und Geschichte*. Berlin: V.E.B. Deutscher Verlag der Wissenschaften, 1966.

Bottigelli, Emile. *Genèse du socialisme scientifique*. Paris: Editions Sociales, 1967.

—————. "Présentation." In Karl Marx, *Manuscrits de 1844*. Paris: Editions Sociales, 1962.

Buhr, Manfred. "Entfremdung—Philosophische Anthropologie—Marx-Kritik." *Deutsche Zeitschrift für Philosophie*, 14th year, no. 7 (1966). Berlin: V.E.B. Deutscher Verlag der Wissenschaften.

—————. "Entfremdung." In *Philosophisches Wörterbuch*, edited by Georg Klaus and Manfred Buhr. Leipzig: V.E.B. Verlag Enzyklopädie, 1964.

Calvez, R. P. Jean-Yves. *La Pensée de Karl Marx*. Paris: Editions du Seuil, 1956.

Chattopadhyaya, Debiprasad. *Lokayata: A Study in Ancient Indian Materialism*. New Delhi: People's Publishing House, 1959.

Chesneaux, Jean. "Le mode de production asiatique: quelques perspectives de recherche." *La Pensée*, April 1964.

Coates, Ken. "Wage Slaves." In *The Incompatibles—Trade-Union Militancy and the Consensus*, edited by Robin Blackburn and Alexander Cockburn. Harmondsworth: Penguin, 1967.

Cornu, Auguste. *Karl Marx, Die ökonomisch-philosophische Manuskripte*. Deutsche Akademie der Wissenschaften zu Berlin, Vorträge und Schriften, Vol. 57. Berlin, 1955.

————. *Karl Marx et Frédéric Engels*, Vol. I. Paris: P.U.F., 1955.

————. *Karl Marx, l'homme et l'oeuvre*. Paris: Librairie Félix Alcan, 1934.

————. *Karl Marx und Friedrich Engles: Leben und Werke*, Vol. II. Berlin: Aufbau-Verlag, 1962.

Dahrendorf, Rolf. *Class and Class Conflict in Industrial Society*. Rev. ed. Stanford: Stanford University Press, 1959.

Dawydow [Davidov], J. N. *Freiheit und Entfremdung*. Berlin: V.E.B. Deutscher Verlag der Wissenschaften, 1964.

De Man, Hendrik. "Der neue entdeckte Marx." *Der Kampf*, nos. 5 and 6 (1932), pp. 224–229 and 267–277.

Desai, A. R., ed. *Rural Sociology in India*. Bombay: The Indian Society of Agricultural Economics, 1959.

Dhuquois, Guy. *Le mode de production asiatique*. Roneoed manuscript.

Divitçioglu, Sencer. "The Asiatic Mode of Production and the Underdeveloped Countries." In *Recherches internationales à la lumière du marxisme*, May–June 1957.

Dutt, Romesh. *The Economic History of India*, Vol. I. New Delhi: The Publication Division of the Government of India, 1960.

Enzensberger, Hans Magnus. *Culture ou mise en condition*. Paris: Julliard, 1965.

Fallot, Jean. *Marx et le machinisme*. Paris: Editions Cujas, 1966.

Fanon, Frantz. *The Wretched of the Earth*. New York: Grove Press, 1965.

Feuersenger, M., ed. *Gibt es noch ein Proletariat?* Frankfurt: Europäische Verlagsanstalt, 1962.

Flam, Leopold. *Ethisch Socialisme*. Antwerp: Ontwikkeling, 1960.

Fleischer, Helmut. "Umrisse einer 'Philosophie des Menschen.'"

Hochschul-Informationen der Zentralstelle für Gesamtdeutsche Hochschufragen, no. 2 (1967).

Fourastié, Jean. *Le Grand Espoir du XXe Siécle*. Paris: P.U.F., 1952.

Friedan, Betty. *The Feminine Mystique*. New York: Dell Publishing, 1965.

Friedmann, G., and Naville, P., eds. *Traité de sociologie du travail*, Vol. I. Paris: Librairie Armand Colin, 1961.

Fromm, Erich. *Marx's Concept of Man*. New York: Frederick Ungar, 1966.

――――. *The Sane Society*. New York: Holt, Rinehart & Winston, 1955.

Garaudy, Roger. *Dieu est mort*. Paris: P.U.F., 1962.

Gehlen, Arnold. *Anthropologische Forschung*. Rowohlt Deutsche Enzyklopädie. Hamburg: Rowohlt-Verlag, 1961.

Goblot, Henri. "Dans l'ancien Iran: les techniques de l'eau et la grande histoire." *Annales ESC*, 18th year, no. 3 (May–June 1963).

Godelier, Maurice. "Bibliographie sommaire des écrits de Marx et d'Engels sur le mode de production asiatique." *La Pensée*, April 1964.

――――. "La notion de 'mode de production asiatique' et les schémas marxistes de l'évolution des sociétés." *Cahiers du Centre d'Etudes et de Recherches Marxistes*.

――――. *Rationalité et irrationalité en économie*. Paris: Maspero, 1966.

Goldmann, Lucien. *Sciences humaines et philosophie*. Paris: P.U.F., 1952.

――――. *Recherches dialectiques*. Paris: Gallimard, 1959.

Gramsci, Antonio. "Il Materialismo Storico e la Filosofia da Benedetto Croce." In *Quaderni del Carcere I*. Turin: Einaudi, 1964.

Grossmann, Henryk. "Die Aenderung des Aufbauplans des Marxschen Kapital und ihre Ursachen." *Archiv für die Geschichte des Sozialismus*, 1929.

Guérin, Daniel. *Anarchism*. New York and London: Monthly Review Press, 1969.

Habermas, Jürgen. *Theorie und Praxis*. Neuwied: Luchterhand Verlag, 1963.

Hansen, Alvin H., and Clemence, Richard V. *Readings in Business Cycles and National Income*. New York: W. W. Norton, 1953.

Harmatta, Jan. "La société des Huns à l'époque d'Attila." In *Recherches internationales à la lumière du marxisme*, May–June 1957.

Harrington, Michael. *The Other America: Poverty in the United States*. Baltimore: Penguin Books, 1962.

Hegel, G. W. F. *Aesthetik*. Berlin and Vienna: Aufbau-Verlag, 1965.

—————. *Die Wissenschaft der Logik*. Leipzig: Felix Meiner-Verlag, 1948.

—————. *Phenomenology of Mind*. New York: Humanities Press, 1964.

—————. *Philosophy of History, Section I, The Oriental World*. Chicago: Encyclopaedia Britannica, 1952.

—————. *Philosophy of Right*. Chicago: Encyclopedia Britannica, 1952.

Heise, Wolfgang. "Über die Entfremdung und ihre Überwindung." *Deutsche Zeitschrift für Philosophie*, no. 6 (1965).

Hillmann, Günther. "Zum Verständnis der Texte." In *Karl Marx, Texte zu Methode und Praxis, II, Pariser Manuskripte 1844*. Hamburg: Rowohlt-Verlag, 1966.

Hobsbawm, Eric. Introduction to Karl Marx, *Pre-Capitalist Economic Formations*. New York: International Publishers, 1965.

Hochfeld, Julian. *Studia o marksowskiej teorii spoleczenstwa*. Warsaw: Pantswowe Wydawnictwo Naukowa, 1963.

Hommes, Jakob. *Der technische Eros*. Freiburg, 1955.

Hook, Sidney. *From Hegel to Marx*. New York: The Humanities Press, 1950.

Horvat, Branko. *Toward a Theory of Planned Economy*. Belgrade: Yugoslav Institute of Research, 1964.

Hyppolite, Jean. *Studies on Marx and Hegel*. New York: Basic Books, 1969.

Ilenkov, Evald Vasilevich. *La dialettica dell'astratto e del concreto nel Capitale di Marx*. Milan: Feltrinelli, 1961.

Jahn, Wolfgang. "Der ökonomische Inhalt des Begriffs der Entfremdung der Arbeit in den Frühschriften von Karl Marx." *Wirtschaftswissenschaft*, no. 6 (1957).

James, Emile. *Histoire sommaire de la pensée économique*. 2nd rev. ed. Paris: Editions Montchrestien, 1959.

—————. Preface to Eliane Mossé, *Marx et le problème de la croissance dans une économie capitaliste*. Paris: Armand Colin, 1956.

Jankowska, N. B. "Extended Family Commune and Civil Self-Government in Arrapha in the 15th–14th Century b.c." In Russian; U.S.S.R. Academy of Sciences, *Ancient Mesopotamia: Socio-Economic History*. Moscow: Nauka Publishing House, 1969.

Kaegi, Paul. *Genesis des historischen Materialismus.* Zurich and Vienna: Europa-Verlag, 1965.

Klaus, Georg. *Kybernetik in philosophischer Sicht.* Berlin: Dietz-Verlag, 1965.

Klaus, Georg, and Buhr, Manfred, eds. *Philosophisches Wörterbuch.* Leipzig: V.E.B. Verlag Enzyklopädie, 1964.

Knight, Frank H. "Value and Price." In *Encyclopedia of Social Sciences,* Vol. 15. New York, 1935.

Kofler, Leo. *Marxistischer oder ethischer Sozialismus.* Bovenden: Verlag Sozialistische Politik, 1955.

———. *Geschichte und Dialektik.* Hamburg: Kogge-Verlag, 1955.

———. *Staat, Gesellschaft und Elite zwischen Humanismus und Nihilismus.* Ulm: Schotola-Verlag, 1960.

Korsch, Karl. *Karl Marx.* Frankfurt: Europäische Verlagsanstalt, 1967.

———. *Marxism and Philosophy.* New York: Monthly Review Press, 1971.

Kosambi, D. D. *An Introduction to the Study of Indian History.* Bombay: Popular Book Depot, 1956.

Kosic, Karel. *Die Dialektik des Konkreten.* Frankfurt: Suhrkamp Verlag, 1967.

Landshut, Siegfried, and Mayer, Gustav. Preface to Karl Marx, *Der historische Materialismus, die Frühschriften.* Leipzig: Verlag Alfred Kromer, 1932.

Lange, Oskar. "Marxian Economics and Modern Economic Theory." *Review of Economic Studies,* June 1935.

Lapin, N. I. *Der junge Marx im Spiegel der Literatur.* Berlin: Dietz-Verlag, 1965.

Lassalle, Ferdinand. *Nachgelassene Briefe und Schriften,* edited by Gustav Mayer. Leipzig: Deutsche Verlagsanstalt, 1922.

———. "Offenes Antwortschreiben an das Zentralkomitee zur Berufung eines Allgemeinen Deutschen Arbeiterkongresses zu Leipzig." In *Gesammelte Reden und Schriften,* Vol. III. Berlin: Paul Cassirer, 1919.

Leach, E. R. "Hydraulic Society in Ceylon." *Past and Present,* no. 15 (April 1959).

Leemans, Victor. *De jonge Marx en de Marxisten.* Brussels: Standaard-Boekhandel, 1962.

Lefebvre, Henri. *Critique de la Vie quotidienne.* Paris: Grasset, 1947.

———. *Critique de la Vie quotidienne.* 2nd ed., Vols. I and II. Paris: L'Arche Editeur, 1958 and 1961.

————. *Introduction à la modernité.* Paris: Editions de Minuit, 1962.

————. *Position: contre les technocrates.* Paris: Editions Gonthier, 1967.

Lenin, V. I. *Collected Works.* Moscow: Progress Publishers.

Leontief, Wassily. "The Significance of Marxian Economics for Present-Day Economic Theory." *American Economic Review,* Supplement (March 1938).

Levy, Reuben. *The Social Structure of Islam.* New York: Cambridge University Press, 1957.

Longo, Gino. *Il metodo dell'economia politica.* Rome: Editori Riuniti, 1965.

Löwith, Karl. *Von Hegel zu Nietzsche.* Stuttgart: W. Kohlhammer Verlag, 1950.

Lukacs, Georg. *Der junge Hegel.* Zurich and Vienna: Europa-Verlag, 1948.

————. *Geschichte und Klassenbewusstsein.* Berlin: Malik-Verlag, 1923.

Luxemburg, Rosa. *The Accumulation of Capital.* New York and London: Monthly Review Press, 1968.

Mandel, Ernest. *Marxist Economic Theory.* 2 vols. New York: Monthly Review Press, 1969.

Marchal, André. *Systèmes et structures économiques.* Paris: P.U.F., 1959.

Marchal, Jean. *Deux essais sur le marxisme.* Paris: Librairie de Médicis, 1955.

Marcuse, Herbert. "Les perspectives du socialisme dans la société industrielle développée." *Revue internationale du socialisme,* 2nd year, no. 8.

————. *Reason and Revolution, Hegel and the Rise of Social Theory.* 2nd ed. New York: The Humanities Press, 1954.

Mauke, Michael. "Thesen zur Klassentheorie von Marx." *Neue Kritik* (Frankfurt), February 1966.

Mayo, Elton. *The Human Problems of an Industrial Civilization.* New York: Viking Press, 1960.

Meek, Ronald L. *Studies in the Labor Theory of Value.* New York: International Publishers, 1956.

Mehring, Franz. Introduction and Notes to *Aus dem literarischen Nachlass von Karl Marx und Friedrich Engels 1841–1850,* edited by Franz Mehring. 3rd ed. Stuttgart: Dietz-Verlag, 1920.

————. *Karl Marx: The Story of His Life.* Ann Arbor: The University of Michigan Press, 1962.

Meillassoux, Claude. *Anthropologie économique des Gouro de Côte d'Ivoire.* Paris: Mouton, 1964.

Melman, Seymour. *Decision-Making and Productivity.* Oxford: Blackwell, 1958.

Melsen, A. G. M. Van. *Science and Technology.* Pittsburgh: Duquesne University Press, 1960.

Mészákos, Istvan. *Marx's Theory of Alienation.* London: Merlin Press, 1970.

Mills, C. Wright. *The Marxists.* New York: Dell Publishing, 1962.

Mitford, Jessica. *The American Way of Death.* New York: Fawcett, 1963.

Mo-jo, Kuo. "La société esclavagiste chinoise." In *Recherches internationales à la lumière du marxisme,* May–June 1957.

Morf, Otto. *Das Verhältnis von Wirtschaftstheorie und Wirtschaftsgeschichte bei Karl Marx.* Berne: A. Francke Verlag, 1951.

Morin, Edgar. *L'Esprit du Temps.* Paris: Grasset, 1962.

Mossé, Eliane. *Karl Marx et le problème de la croissance dans une économie capitaliste.* Paris: Armand Colin, 1956.

Naville, Pierre. *La Chine future.* Paris: Editions de Minuit, 1952.

————. *De l'aliénation à la jouissance.* Paris: Rivière, 1957. (Reissued 1967 by Editions Anthropos.)

Novack, George, ed. *Existentialism versus Marxism.* New York: Dell Publishing, 1966.

Oiserman, T. I. *Die Entfremdung als historische Kategorie.* Berlin: Dietz-Verlag, 1965.

Ossowski, Stanislaw. *Klassenstruktur im sozialen Bewusstsein.* Berlin: Luchterhand-Verlag, 1962.

Outline History of China, An. Peking: Foreign Languages Press, 1959.

Pajitnov, Leonid. "Les manuscrits économico-philosophiques de 1844." In "Le jeune Marx," *Recherches internationales à la lumière du marxisme,* no. 19 (1960).

Packard, Vance. *The Hidden Persuaders.* New York: Pocketbooks, 1958.

————. *The Pyramid Climbers.* New York: Fawcett, 1964.

Pappenheim, Fritz. *The Alienation of Modern Man.* New York and London: Monthly Review Press, 1959.

Pareto, Vilfredo. *Les Systèmes socialistes.* Paris: Marcel Giard, 1926.

Parsons, Talcott, and Smelser, Neil J. *Economy and Society: A Study*

in the Integration of Economic Theory and Sociological Theory.
Glencoe: The Free Press, 1956.

Pecirka, Jan. "Les discussions soviétiques sur le mode de production asiatique et sur la formation esclavagiste." In *Recherches internationales à la lumière du marxisme*, May–June 1957.

Perroux, François. "Aliénation et création collective." *Cahiers de l'Institut de Science Économique Appliquée*, June 1964.

————. Preface to Karl Marx, *Oeuvres—Economie I.* Bibliothèque de la Pléiade. Paris: NRF-Gallimard, 1963.

Pesić-Golubović, Zaga. "What Is the Meaning of Alienation?" *Praxis*, no. 5 (1966).

Petrović, Gajo. "Man as Economic Animal and Man as Praxis." *Inquiry*, vol. 6 (1963).

————. "Marx's Theory of Alienation." *Philosophy and Phenomenological Research.*

Plekhanov, George. *Fundamental Problems of Marxism.* New York: International Publishers, 1969.

————. *Introduction à l'histoire sociale de la Russie.* Paris: Bossard, 1926.

————. "La signification de Hegel." *Revue internationale*, April–June 1950.

Popitz, Heinrich. *Der entfremdete Mensch.* Basle: Verlag für Recht und Gesellschaft, 1953.

Popović, Milentije. "For the Re-Evaluation of Marx's Teaching on Production and Relations of Production." *Socialist Thought and Practice* (Yugoslavia), July–September 1965.

Rancière, Jacques. "La critique de l'économie politique des *Manuscrits de 1844* au *Capital.*" In *Lire le Capital*, Vol. I. Paris: Maspero, 1966.

Ricardo, David. *The Works and Correspondence of David Ricardo.* Edited by Piero Sraffa. New York: Cambridge University Press, 1951.

Robinson, Joan. *An Essay on Marxian Economics.* 2nd ed. New York: St. Martins, 1967.

————. "The Labor Theory of Value: A Discussion." *Science and Society*, 1954.

Rodinson, Maxime. *Islam et capitalisme.* Paris: Editions du Seuil, 1966.

————. "What Happened in History." *New Left Review*, January–February, 1966.

Rosdolsky, Roman. "Das 'Kapital im Allgemeinen' und die 'vielen Kapitalien.' " *Kyklos,* Vol. VI, no. 2 (1953).

———. "Der esoterische und der exoterische Marx." *Arbeit und Wirtschaft* (Vienna), November 1957 and January 1958.

———. "Ein neomarxistisches Lehrbuch der politischen Ökonomie." *Kyklos,* Vol. XVI, no. 4 (1963).

———. "Friedrich Engels und das Problem der 'geschichtslosen Völker.' " *Archiv für Sozialgeschichte.* Verlag für Literatur und Zeitgeschichte, Vol. 4. Hanover: 1964.

———. "Joan Robinsons Marx-Kritik." *Arbeit und Wirtschaft* (Vienna), June and July 1959.

———. *Zur Entstehungsgeschichte des Marxischen "Kapital."* 2 vols. Frankfurt: Europäische Verlagsanstalt, 1968.

Rosenberg, D. I. *Die Entwicklung der ökonomischen Lehre von Marx und Engels in den Vierziger Jahren des 19. Jahrhunderts.* Berlin: Dietz-Verlag, 1958.

Rubel, Maximilien. *Karl Marx, Pages choisies pour une éthique socialiste.* Paris: Rivière, 1948.

———. *Karl Marx: Essai de biographie intellectuelle.* Paris: Rivière, 1957.

———. Notes to Marx, *Oeuvres—Economie I.* Bibliothèque de la Pléiade. Paris: NRF-Gallimard, 1963.

Ruehle, Otto. *Karl Marx: His Life and Work.* London: 1939.

Ryazanov, D. Introduction and Notes to Marx and Engels, *Gesammelte Schriften 1852–1862.* Stuttgart: Dietz, 1917.

———. Introduction to Marx, "Ueber China und Indien," in *Unter dem Banner des Marxismus,* year I, no. 2 (1925).

———. Introduction to Marx and Engels, *Historisch-kritische Gesamtausgabe (MEGA),* Vols. I: 1 and II: 2. Frankfurt: Verlagsgesellschaft, 1927.

Schaff, Adam. *Marxism and the Human Individual.* New York: McGraw Hill, 1970.

Schmidt, Alfred. *Der Begriff der Natur in der Lehre von Marx.* Frankfurt: Europäische Verlagsanstalt, 1962.

Schumpeter, Joseph. *History of Economic Analysis.* New York: Oxford University Press, 1954.

Smith, Adam. *The Wealth of Nations.* New York: Random House/Modern Library, 1937.

Soule, George. *The Shape of Tomorrow.* New York: Signet Books, 1958.

Sraffa, Piero. Introduction to *The Works and Correspondence of*

David Ricardo, edited by Piero Sraffa. New York: Cambridge University Press, 1951.

—————. *Production of Commodities by Means of Commodities: Prelude to a Critique of Economic Theory*. Cambridge: Cambridge University Press, 1960.

Struve, V. "Comment Marx définissait les premières sociétés de classe." *Recherches internationales à la lumière du marxisme*, May–June 1957.

Supek, Rudi. "Dialectique de la pratique sociale." *Praxis*, no. 1 (1965).

Suret-Canale, Jean. "Les sociétés traditionnelles en Afrique tropicale et le concept de mode de production asiatique." *La Pensée*, October 1964.

Teilhac, Ernest. *L'Economie politique perdue et retrouvée*. Paris: Librairie Générale de Droit et de Jurisprudence, 1962.

Thier, Erich. *Das Menschenbild des jungen Marx*. Göttingen: Vandenbroeck und Ruprecht, 1957.

Togliatti, Palmiro. "De Hegel au marxisme." In "Le jeune Marx," *Recherches internationales à la lumière du marxisme*, no. 19 (1960).

Tökei, Ferenc. "La mode de production asiatique en Chine." *Recherches internationales à la lumière du marxisme*, May–June 1957.

Trotsky, Leon. *Die russische Revolution 1905*. 2nd ed. Berlin: VIVA-Verlag, 1923.

—————. *The Permanent Revolution* (with *Results and Prospects*). New York: Pathfinder Press, Inc., 1970.

Tuchscheerer, Walter. *Bevor "Das Kapital" entstand*. Berlin: Akademie-Verlag, 1968.

Tucker, Robert C. *Philosophy and Myth in Karl Marx*. Cambridge: Cambridge University Press, 1961.

Tugan-Baranovsky, Michael. *Studien zur Theorie und Geschichte der Handelskrisen in England*. Jena: Fischer-Verlag, 1901.

Varga, Eugene. *Essais sur l'économie politique du capitalisme*. Moscow: Progress Publishers, 1967.

Vidal-Naquet, Pierre. Foreword to Karl Wittfogel, *Le Despotisme oriental*. Paris: Editions de Minuit, 1964.

Volpe, Galvano Della. *Rousseau e Marx*. Rome: Editori Riuniti, 1964.

Vorlander, Karl. *Kant und Marx, Ein Beitrag zur Philosophie des Sozialismus*. Tübingen: J.C.B. Mohr, 1911.

Vranicki, Predrag. "Socialism and the Problem of Alienation." *Praxis*, no. 2–3 (1965).

————. "La signification actuelle de l'humanisme du jeune Marx." *Annali dell'Istituto Giangiacomo Feltrinelli*, 7th year, 1964–1965.

Weinstock, Heinrich. *Arbeit und Bildung*. Heidelberg, 1956.

Werner, Ernst. *Die Geburt einer Grossmacht, die Osmanen*. Berlin: Akademie-Verlag, 1966.

Wiener, Norbert. *The Human Use of Human Beings: Cybernetics and Society*. New York: Doubleday/Anchor, 1954.

Wittfogel, Karl A. *Oriental Despotism: A Comparative Study of Total Power*. New Haven: Yale University Press, 1957.

————. *Wirtschaft und Gesellschaft Chinas*. Leipzig: Verlag Hirschfeld, 1931.

Wygodski, Witali Solomonowitsch. *Die Geschichte einer grossen Entdeckung: Über die Entstehung des Werkes "Das Kapital" von Karl Marx*. Published in West Germany without publisher's name or date.

Ziherl, Boris. "On the Objective and Subjective Conditions of Dis-alienation Under Socialism." *Socialist Thought and Practice* (Yugoslavia), January–March 1965.

MONTHLY REVIEW

an independent socialist magazine
edited by Paul M. Sweezy and Harry Magdoff

Business Week: ". . . a brand of socialism that is thorough-going and tough-minded, drastic enough to provide the sharp break with the past that many left-wingers in the underdeveloped countries see as essential. At the same time they maintain a sturdy independence of both Moscow and Peking that appeals to neutralists. And their skill in manipulating the abstruse concepts of modern economics impresses would-be intellectuals. . . . Their analysis of the troubles of capitalism is just plausible enough to be disturbing."

Bertrand Russell: "Your journal has been of the greatest interest to me over a period of time. I am not a Marxist by any means as I have sought to show in critiques published in several books, but I recognize the power of much of your own analysis and where I disagree I find your journal valuable and of stimulating importance. I want to thank you for your work and to tell you of my appreciation of it."

The Wellesley Department of Economics: " . . . the leading Marxist intellectual (not Communist) economic journal published anywhere in the world, and is on our subscription list at the College library for good reasons."

Albert Einstein: "Clarity about the aims and problems of socialism is of greatest significance in our age of transition. . . . I consider the founding of this magazine to be an important public service." (In his article, "Why Socialism" in Vol. I, No. 1.)

DOMESTIC: $11 for one year, $20 for two years, $9 for one-year student subscription.
FOREIGN: $13 for one year, $23 for two years, $10 for one-year student subscription. (Subscription rates subject to change.)

62 West 14th Street, New York, New York 10011